Edited by Nick Pulford

Contributors

Richard Birch	Paul Kealy	Graeme Rodway
Marcus Buckland	Richard Lowther	Colin Russell
James Burn	Tim Mitchell	Brian Sheerin
David Carr	Kevin Morley	Alan Sweetman
Dave Edwards	Dave Orton	James Thomas
Nick Freedman	Bryan Pugh	Kitty Trice
Jack Haynes	Dave Randall	Sam Walker
David Jennings	Stuart Riley	Nick Watts

Designed by David Dew
Cover artwork by Jay Vincent
Inside artwork by David Cramphorn, Nigel Jones and Stefan Searle

Published in 2018 by Racing Post Books, Raceform Ltd, 27 Kingfisher Court, Hambridge Road, Newbury, RG14 5SJ
Copyright © Racing Post 2018

ISBN 978-1910497500

Printed by Henry Stones Ltd

WELCOME to the Racing Post Cheltenham Festival Guide 2018, now in its tenth year and firmly established as part of the build-up to the greatest four days in jump racing.

This 208-page guide is modelled as a 'Cheltenham preview night in book form' and once again the first half the book brings you the full range of opinion and insight from the unrivalled Racing Post team, including tipsters, Racing Post Ratings, Topspeed and the Raceform analysts, plus a bookmakers' Q&A on the big issues, trainer analysis, jockeys to watch and much more.

In the second half, Racing Post betting editor Paul Kealy provides his extensive race-by-race guide with forthright opinions and profiles of more than 100 of the top runners, along with key trends and race verdicts.

Looking back to 2009, the first year of publication, it is interesting to see how much the landscape has changed since then. That year Paul Nicholls was the dominant force, taking the leading trainer award for the fourth time in five years with Kauto Star leading the charge by becoming the first horse to regain the Gold Cup.

The depth in quality of the Nicholls team was remarkable and Master Minded took a second Queen Mother Champion Chase, while Big Buck's (a 6-1 shot, would you believe?) scored the first of his four World Hurdle wins.

Nicholls had five winners, followed on three by Nicky Henderson and Willie Mullins – but those two are now the champion trainers of Britain and Ireland and in recent years much stronger contenders than Nicholls at the top end.

Some things never change, however, with Ruby Walsh the leading rider for a fourth time with seven winners in 2009.

Along with Kauto Star, Master Minded and Big Buck's, other equine stars included Imperial Commander in the Ryanair Chase, Punjabi in the Champion Hurdle, Quevega winning the first of her six Mares' Hurdles, Go Native, Forpadydeplasterer, Mikael D'Haguenet and Wichita Lineman (and that amazing AP McCoy ride).

Mention of those names will conjure up images for a variety of reasons and therein lies one of the enduring attractions of the festival. It is a place where memories are made that last a lifetime.

We don't know yet who will become the stars of 2018 but it will be fun finding out. And the journey starts here.

Nick Pulford
Editor

VIEWS FROM THE SPECIALISTS

4

The Racing Post's top tipsters and form experts, along with the major bookmakers, pick their fancies and debate the big issues

RACE-BY-RACE GUIDE

110

In-depth form guide to the main contenders by Racing Post betting editor Paul Kealy, with all the key trends

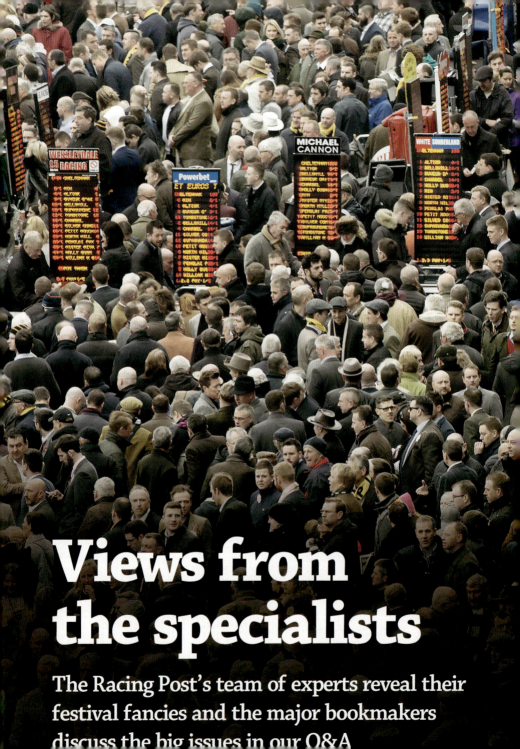

Views from the specialists

The Racing Post's team of experts reveal their festival fancies and the major bookmakers discuss the big issues in our Q&A

Tully East heading in the right direction

By Richard Birch

IT would be difficult to think of a more eyecatching Cheltenham trial this season than the one **Tully East** recorded at the Dublin Racing Festival in early February.

Impressive winner of the Close Brothers Novices' Handicap Chase last March, the Alan Fleming-trained eight-year-old is well set to bid for another festival victory in the Brown Advisory & Merriebelle Stable Plate after his third to Patricks Park in a 20-runner 2m1f Leopardstown handicap chase.

The form of Tully East's one-and-a-quarter-length defeat of Gold Present at the festival has been strongly boosted this season by the Nicky Henderson-trained runner-up, who won at Newbury and then put the prolific and highly progressive Frodon firmly in his place in an Ascot Listed event.

That is some of the best handicap form you can find in Britain – Frodon went on to run away with a Cheltenham Grade 3 on Trials Day – and Tully East simply must be backed at 8-1 to notch back-to-back festival successes.

Henderson's **Sugar Baron** leaps off the page as a standout wager at 16-1 for the Fulke Walwyn Kim Muir Handicap Chase.

Sixth to Domesday Book in the 3m2f amateur riders' event last year after being hampered at an early stage, Sugar Baron is just 2lb higher in the weights despite two excellent placed efforts at Cheltenham and Sandown this season.

The manner in which he powered up the Sandown hill to almost run down Benbens in first-time blinkers in December strongly suggests he is capable of winning a race of this nature.

It is no surprise Sugar Baron hasn't been seen since that fine effort as I would imagine connections believe him to be on a most attractive mark. Get on.

If Willie Mullins enjoys a successful week it is not hard to envisage his talented hurdler **Max Dynamite** going off at around 7-2 for the Randox Health County Handicap Hurdle, so be sure to take 8-1 as soon as you read this.

A 113-rated performer on the Flat who ran a blinder to finish third to Rekindling in the Melbourne Cup in November, Max Dynamite has clearly been laid out for Cheltenham ever since.

Although he failed to read the script when a heavily backed 7-2 favourite for the Galway Hurdle last summer, that defeat could prove a godsend in terms of Cheltenham as he will still be able to race off a mark in the low 140s.

Many others will have been carefully laid out for the County, but it is highly doubtful whether any rival possesses the sheer class and power of Max Dynamite, who can create a mighty explosion in the betting ring by landing what promises to develop into a huge gamble.

The Timico Cheltenham Gold Cup could see an epic battle up the hill between **Might Bite** and Native River.

I was firmly in the Native River camp last year and, even though he couldn't quite land some tasty bets, he emerged with his reputation enhanced. He looked in terrific shape when scoring at Newbury on his seasonal reappearance and has been trained with this one race in mind.

However, I can't help but think Might Bite will have too much class and speed for him at crucial stages of chasing's blue riband.

Although he didn't set the pulse racing in the King George over Christmas, there was never a moment when Might Bite didn't look like winning.

It's reasonable to assume he hasn't peaked just yet and, if that proves to be the case, he will prove devilishly difficult to beat. I'm sure you won't beat 7-2 on the day.

His stablemate **Santini** gets my punting juices flowing at 8-1 for the Albert Bartlett Novices' Hurdle.

The way he kept digging and responding to pressure up the Cheltenham hill when beating Black Op by three-quarters of a length in late January augurs well for his chance in this stamina test.

Don't forget that was only the second run of his career and he has abundant untapped potential. I'm really sweet on his chance.

Mengli Khan has twice blotted his copybook since I advised him for the Sky Bet Supreme Novices' Hurdle in December, but the opportunity to race on good ground for the first time this season could see him sharpen his act considerably.

I haven't given up and wouldn't put anyone off placing a few quid at 14-1.

The Unibet Champion Hurdle is booked for Buveur D'Air once again, but why not invest each-way at 12-1 on race stalwart **My Tent Or Yours**, who will be exceptionally hard to keep out of the first three.

Similarly, I expect the real **Politologue** to turn up in the Betway Queen Mother Champion Chase – he was never jumping or travelling with his customary fluency at Newbury – and, while it's a tall order to reverse the form with the brilliant Altior, he makes serious each-way appeal at 10-1 on ground that is far more likely to suit this slick-jumping strong traveller.

Santini: the one to be on
for the Albert Bartlett

Presenting the perfect case for RSA success

By David Jennings

THERE is always method to Pat Kelly's madness. Who else could campaign a leading contender for the RSA Chase by running him in a slog on soft ground around Fairyhouse over 3m5f against far more experienced rivals, return to hurdles at Gowran Park the following month and then take on a Gold Cup contender back over fences? It makes little sense to us mere mortals but who are we to question the actions of a trainer who has had two winners from just three runners at the Cheltenham Festival?

Presenting Percy is only a novice but is already rated 157 over fences, higher than the last six winners of the RSA. Might Bite (2017) went into the race with a mark of 154, Blaklion (2016) was rated 150, Don Poli (2015) 156, O'Faolains Boy (2014) 144, Lord Windermere (2013) 145 and even Bobs Worth (2012) was only 151 prior to his success in the race.

Last year's runaway Pertemps Handicap Hurdle winner has set a high standard over fences. His jumping is immaculate, he is a strong stayer and he has winning form on the course. Of all the favourites over the four days, he looks one of the better-value options.

Gordon Elliott has won the National Hunt Chase three times in the past seven runnings and **Jury Duty** could follow in the footsteps of Chicago Grey (2011), Cause Of Causes (2015) and Tiger Roll (2017).

There is no question Jury Duty has the class to win the race. He was rated 147 over hurdles, higher than the last three winners,

and is already a Grade 2 winner over fences, having seen off subsequent Grade 1 winner Shattered Love at Punchestown in November. That form was reversed at Leopardstown over Christmas but he lost little in defeat.

There is a theory out there that Jury Duty's stamina gave way in the closing stages of his latest outing in a Grade 3 over 3m at Naas, but he was left in front at the last when Mossback fell and history tells us that he idles badly when he is on his own for too long.

Jury Duty's rider – it could be Jamie Codd – will be trying to show his hand last of all. Those tactics could scoop the pot as Jury Duty is a natural jumper with plenty of experience who has the ability to get down and dirty when it matters. He ticks lots of boxes.

Don't Touch It has been my idea of a Grand Annual winner for the best part of two years and, while his recent form has left a lot to be desired, don't let that put you off him.

The son of Scorpion was a Grade 1 winner over hurdles and it was not just any Grade 1 he won either. He saw off Petit Mouchoir, Brain Power and Yorkhill in the Champion Novice Hurdle at Punchestown in 2016. That is strong form indeed.

He won a competitive handicap chase back at Punchestown last season off a mark of 144 and is only 5lb higher now. His form figures of 546U are not attractive but the last three of those were on soft ground. He needs better ground to be at his best and he wore cheekpieces when last successful at Punchestown, so expect them to be back on at Cheltenham.

Supasundae is now a short-priced favourite

for the Stayers' Hurdle on the back of his shock defeat of Faugheen over two miles in the Irish Champion Hurdle, but surely the forgotten horse of the race is **L'Ami Serge**.

He failed to avail of a more lenient chase mark in the Sky Bet Chase at Doncaster in January, but his Long Walk Hurdle second to Sam Spinner gives him outstanding claims of festival glory.

He was beaten less than three lengths by Sam Spinner at Ascot but the combination of a left-handed track and better ground could close that gap considerably at Cheltenham. Don't forget L'Ami Serge was agonisingly denied by just a neck in last year's County Hurdle off 152 and was third in the previous year's JLT Novices' Chase.

The Stayers' Hurdle is sure to be run to suit and expect Daryl Jacob, who gets on particularly well with him, to creep away and try to pounce after the last. He proved he stays this far when winning the French Champion Hurdle last June and has had only three runs since, so he should be reaching his peak. Thanks to Sam Spinner, he looks sure to get the frantic early pace he needs to help him settle.

Immaculate jumper: last season's Pertemps winner Presenting Percy is a rock-solid bet in the RSA Chase

Red definitely the one in wide-open Gold Cup

By Nick Watts

THE Cheltenham Gold Cup is one of the most open I can remember at this stage of the season and Might Bite is at the head of the market more because he has done the least wrong than because he has produced imperious performances on the track.

That might seem harsh on the King George winner, who was probably idling on the run to the line at Kempton, but that was still Double Shuffle chasing him home. Although the runner-up is a Kempton specialist, he was closer than you would like to see against a prospective Gold Cup winner.

With so many doubts swirling around the market leaders, this is a year to have a go at one who is a decent price and northern challenger **Definitly Red** fits the bill.

Brian Ellison's nine-year-old has always been a high-class performer but he has taken quite a leap forward in the last year or so with some great displays. He thrashed Wakanda

Gold Cup value: Definitly Red

and Blaklion in the Rowland Meyrick last season, did the same to The Last Samuri in the Grimthorpe, and on his last two starts has dished out similar beatings to some talented rivals.

Cloudy Dream was the victim at Aintree in December, beaten seven lengths, and then Definitly Red thumped American and Bristol De Mai in the Cotswold Chase on Cheltenham's Trials Day.

His efforts leave him only 2lb shy of Might Bite on official ratings, and if things get desperate up the run-in at Cheltenham I know which one I would rather be on.

The familiar line with a Gold Cup contender who has come out of handicaps is that he won't be good enough but the ratings show that to be a false argument with Definitly Red. He comes here in the form of his life, we know

he handles the track, he jumps soundly and he stays exceptionally well. What's not to like at 16-1?

The Stayers' Hurdle is just as open and offers the north a chance to take home another big prize, this time with Sam Spinner.

Jedd O'Keeffe's fast-improving six-year-old stays extremely well and, while Cheltenham is an unknown for him, there doesn't seem to be any good reason why he won't act there. He clearly handles a demanding, undulating track as he put in a great effort in the Silver Trophy at Chepstow on his seasonal debut.

The only thing not to like about him right now is his price, as there's not much room for his odds to contract any further and he might well be a drifter on the day.

Supasundae took over from Sam Spinner as favourite after his Irish Champion Hurdle victory but there is still a big question mark over whether he is a genuine stayer. The Irish Champion was over two miles and last season he won the Coral Cup over 2m5f, while he has been beaten both times he has been asked to go further, firstly by Yanworth at Aintree and then by Apple's Jade at Leopardstown.

My idea of the winner, if he goes for it, is **Yanworth**. Not everyone seems to like him but I don't know why. A record of 12 wins from 18 starts including two Grade 1s isn't bad and, while he can appear a bit lazy at times, that disguises the fact he has a massive engine.

He has gone chasing this season and won the Dipper last time out. Therefore he could easily go for the RSA Chase, but I would love to see him have a go at this race – he stays better than Supasundae, he has the class

and he has unfinished business over hurdles, having spent most of last season running over the wrong trip.

Sticking with the staying theme, there is an interesting one for the Pertemps Final in **Louis' Vac Pouch**. He hasn't been seen for a while, but last time he hit the racecourse he won a qualifier easily at Aintree over three miles in a race that has worked out very well – Beer Goggles was third and then went on to win at Newbury.

Although Louis' Vac Pouch has not been sighted since that November win, that might be no bad thing as the Philip Hobbs team has struggled for form in the last month or two. Hopefully Hobbs will snap out of it soon, in which case this unexposed six-year-old looks capable of a bold showing. Hobbs won the Pertemps with Fingal Bay in 2014 and was unlucky not to do it again two years later with If In Doubt.

William Henry can go well in the Coral Cup for the Nicky Henderson-Dai Walters combination that won with Whisper in 2014.

This eight-year-old has a huge amount of talent and has already shown he can win big handicaps by taking the Lanzarote last time out. The form is solid, with fourth-placed Topofthegame having since won a good handicap.

Good ground in the spring will suit William Henry perfectly and it would be no surprise to see him in a Graded race before the season is out. Henderson has other leading ante-post fancies in Jenkins and Diese Des Bieffes, but William Henry is the one I want to be siding with.

Stuart Riley on the horses who could be big stories of this year's festival

Altior

Through no fault of his own, Altior was in the news for negative reasons in November over the controversial timing of the disclosure that he needed a wind operation and would miss the Tingle Creek Chase, but Nicky Henderson's exciting chaser will make a much more positive impact at the festival if he confirms himself the true heir to Sprinter Sacre.

Like his erstwhile stablemate before him, Altior has followed a traditional path at the festival via the Supreme Novices' Hurdle (he won, Sprinter Sacre was third), the Arkle Chase (he won by six lengths, Sprinter Sacre by seven) and now the Queen Mother Champion Chase in his first senior season, having made a powerful statement with his return in the Game Spirit in February.

The Champion Chase is always one of the great spectacles of the festival and, with Min set to lead the opposition, Altior will have to produce something special to add his name to the illustrious roll of honour. If he does, it will confirm him as jump racing's biggest star.

Buveur D'Air

Repeat victories in the major championships are the stuff of legend and Altior's stablemate Buveur D'Air looks nailed on for a second Champion Hurdle that would take him into elite company.

The list of dual winners is just as impressive as the three-timers and a second Buveur D'Air victory – with the same speed and hurdling fluency he showed last year – might revive memories of the era when Bula (1971-72), Comedy Of Errors (1973 and 1975), Night Nurse (1976-77), Monksfield (1978-79) and Sea Pigeon (1980-81) ruled the scene.

With Buveur D'Air and Altior leading the charge – and Might Bite, Apple's Shakira, Top Notch and a host of promising novices also in

Big things ahead (clockwise from main): Altior, Buveur D'Air, Sizing John, Cause Of Causes and Samcro

dismantling of Djakadam by seven lengths in the John Durkan on his return in December are proof of what he can do at his best. If Jessica Harrington brings him back to winning form, it would be another triumph to savour for Cheltenham's first lady.

Cause Of Causes

Un De Sceaux would be chasing a fourth festival win but for bumping into a rejuvenated Sprinter Sacre in the 2016 Champion Chase, and instead it is fellow Irish raider Cause Of Causes who can make it a fab four.

The 2015 National Hunt Chase, 2016 Kim Muir and 2017 Cross Country winner may not be tackling the highest-profile races but a fourth win in JP McManus's green and gold silks would make him one of the biggest stories of this year's festival.

Samcro

Cause Of Causes' trainer Gordon Elliott has another potential headline-maker with Samcro, the hottest novice hurdler in Ireland or Britain.

The excitement surrounding Gigginstown's unbeaten six-year-old is unlike anything in recent seasons despite the conveyor belt of top-class novices from Ireland to Cheltenham. Samcro brings a bigger reputation into his first festival than Douvan, Vautour, Don Cossack or Yorkhill before him and by the time he is done the 2018 festival could be known as Samcro's first.

his team – Nicky Henderson could make a splash to rival his magnificent seven at the 2012 festival.

Sizing John

He is not the Gold Cup favourite but many eyes will be on him as the defending champion, and a return to winning form would see him emulate Golden Miller, Cottage Rake, Arkle, L'Escargot and Best Mate by going back-to-back in the big race.

His preparation has not gone anything like as swimmingly as last season and he has been given an extended break after a bitterly disappointing seventh, beaten 32 lengths, in the Leopardstown Christmas Chase.

But his run of Gold Cup wins last spring and his

'Might Bite deserves to be favourite but is worth taking on'

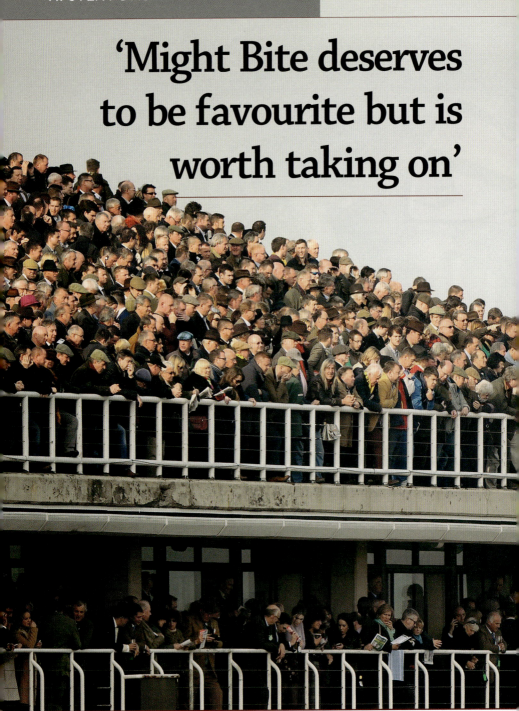

Who do you fancy for the Gold Cup?

Richard Birch It's not a vintage renewal, and for that reason alone there must be a significant chance Might Bite will simply outclass his rivals. I can't see how Native River can finish out of the first three, even if the ground doesn't come up soft.

Brian Sheerin Might Bite should be difficult to beat. He looked like he was idling in the King George and Double Shuffle was almost certainly flattered by how close he finished. But at the prices I like Road To Respect. He's improving and showed he can mix it with the big boys over staying trips when winning the Leopardstown Christmas Chase.

Graeme Rodway I don't like those at the head of the market. Might Bite is the most likely winner but is priced accordingly, Sizing John is coming off an abysmal run and Native River surely won't be quick enough unless the ground is bottomless. I've backed Minella Rocco, who finished ahead of Native River when second last year but is 20-1.

David Jennings Might Bite deserves to be favourite but is worth taking on given his quirks and the close proximity of some ordinary opponents in the King George. Our Duke is an out-and-out galloper who devoured a field of experienced handicappers in last year's Irish Grand National and still had enough class to win a Grade 2 over 2m4f at Gowran Park. He'll do for me.

Nick Watts I see no reason why Definitly Red can't get involved. He dismissed Cloudy Dream at Aintree just as easily as Native River did at Newbury recently and then hosed up in the Cotswold Chase. He's bang there on the ratings, he handles most types of ground, he stays very well, he jumps very well – what's not to like?

Can anything stop Buveur D'Air in the Champion Hurdle?

David Jennings No. He's electric over his hurdles and appears to be getting better. Faugheen looks a pale shadow of his former self and Melon ran very flat last time, so the two who interest me from a place point of view are last year's runner-up My Tent Or Yours and Mick Jazz.

Graeme Rodway No. Only a top-form Faugheen could stop him and his last two runs suggest that is unlikely. My Tent Or Yours could run well again but the bookmakers aren't taking any chances this year and 12-1 is short enough.

Richard Birch Buveur D'Air looks a class above the opposition, with Faugheen clearly

All eyes will be on the action at Prestbury Park

not the force of old. He could still be improving and rates as close to a certainty at Cheltenham as you will ever find. Race regular My Tent Or Yours provides a decent each-way bet.

Brian Sheerin The favourite hasn't beaten anything of note this season but has barely had to come out of second gear in doing so and it looks his race to lose. If Faugheen could come back to something like his best he'd be a big danger but it will take all of Willie Mullins' genius to reignite the spark in the 2015 winner.

Nick Watts I can't see anything stopping Buveur D'Air. Faugheen was beaten by a horse having a prep for the Stayers' Hurdle last time, so it's hard to see him winning. If you wanted a left-field one to finish in the frame, try John Constable – he doesn't have the best Cheltenham record but wasn't beaten far in the International and ran well behind Buveur D'Air last time.

What do you make of the Champion Chase?

Richard Birch Altior was simply stunning at Newbury. The way he breezed past Politologue must have been so disconcerting for connections of the runner-up, who is a Grade 1 winner still on the up. Altior will win and Politologue will finish second or third.

Brian Sheerin Politologue is a solid top-level performer but was made to look ordinary by Altior, who's one of the best, if not the best, in training right now. It's very hard to see him getting beat. Min was good at Leopardstown and is the best of the Irish but he'll struggle to beat Altior.

Nick Watts Altior's return at Newbury was everything you would want to see from him. He should win comfortably and, while Min is a good horse, Altior thrashed him in the Supreme and it might be the same story here.

Graeme Rodway If Altior turns up on his best form he'll win, but Min is a serious danger. They finished first and second, ahead of

Buveur D'Air in third, in a red-hot running of the Supreme Novices' Hurdle in 2016 and are likely to repeat those places in this race. It's hard to see Min reversing the form if Altior is at his best, but the Irish challenger has had a clear run and a full season under his belt this time and that might bring him closer to Altior.

David Jennings It would be very foolish to think Altior won't confirm his Supreme Novices' form over Min. The unknown quantity is obviously Douvan but even if he does return to something near his best, he might not beat Altior anyway. Special Tiara could nick a place at a nice price if the ground is good.

Who is your pick for an open-looking Stayers' Hurdle?

Nick Watts I really hope Yanworth goes for it. He showed at Aintree last season what he could do over a staying trip, beating Supasundae, and while he could go for the RSA I feel he has unfinished business over hurdles, having spent most of last season as a square peg in a round hole over two miles. He's a strong fancy for me if he goes.

Brian Sheerin I've been very impressed with Supasundae's progress this season and it's telling that connections are sticking to their guns and running him in this race. I've been a big fan of The Worlds End for a while now and have found out the hard way that he's a much better horse on nicer ground, which he proved last spring at Aintree. I think you'll see an improved performance from him on better ground at the festival and he's good value at 25-1.

Richard Birch I wouldn't be surprised if last year's third Unowhatimeanharry bounced back to his best. Clearly he has been below par this season but he has been freshened up and rates a fair each-way bet at around 14-1.

Graeme Rodway It's a near-impossible race to weigh up until we know who's going to run. Apple's Jade would be a big contender if she goes here but the Mares' Hurdle is probably

EXTRA PLACES
EVERY RACE, EVERY DAY

WITH  EACH WAY EDGE

GET AHEAD
AT CHELTENHAM 2018

a more likely target. If I had to play now I'd have an each-way bet on The Worlds End. He travelled well for a long way in the Cleeve before getting stuck in the mud and might improve on better ground.

David Jennings L'Ami Serge failed to exploit a low mark over fences in the Sky Bet Chase at Doncaster, but his Long Walk second to Sam Spinner was a cracking effort given that he's far more at home going left-handed. He has finished fourth in the Supreme, third in the JLT and second in the County Hurdle at the last three festivals and this could be his big chance to strike.

What do you fancy for the novice hurdles?

Graeme Rodway Samcro is the most exciting novice hurdler at the festival and it'll be disappointing if he doesn't win the Supreme or Ballymore, whichever connections choose to go for. I'm looking forward to seeing Santini in the Albert Bartlett. He reminds me a lot of a young Bobs Worth, who won this race for Nicky Henderson in 2011. I don't like On The Blind Side and will be opposing him if he lines up in the Ballymore.

Brian Sheerin The favourites for the

L'Ami Serge (red cap): could finally strike at the festival

betfair

FREE BET

UP TO £25 WITH
EVERY WINNER BACKED
AT 3/1 OR MORE
ON LIVE ITV RACES

GET AHEAD
AT CHELTENHAM 2018

respective races look very strong and I can't remember as much excitement surrounding a novice going to the festival as there is about Samcro. He's Ballymore bound, which suggests Getabird will avoid him and line out in the Supreme, while Cracking Smart has the right profile for the Albert Bartlett. I'd be keen to keep Willie Mullins' Duc Des Genievres on side wherever he goes and the stable's Laurina looks one of the bankers of the week in the mares' novice.

Richard Birch My Supreme hopes have been pinned on Mengli Khan for quite a while. I'm lukewarm about his chance now but haven't given up as I expect him to improve on good ground. Santini is a strong fancy for the Albert Bartlett – there is so much more to come from him – and Apple's Shakira looks the real deal in the Triumph.

***Mengli Khan:
expected to show
improvement on
better ground***

David Jennings Samcro has been stunning to date and it is hard to envisage any other scenario apart from him winning the Ballymore. Black Op could go well at a nice price in that, or would be very interesting if he went down the Albert Bartlett route. I get the impression Getabird might need soft ground to be at his best, so there could be an upset in the Supreme. Kalashnikov deserves respect but Paloma Blue looks a very big price. Apple's Shakira looks a worthy Triumph favourite.

Nick Watts Slate House might be interesting at a huge price for the Supreme – he's won twice at Cheltenham already and beat Tolworth winner Summerville Boy there in November. Samcro wins the Ballymore and Gowiththeflow could be a live one for the Albert Bartlett after a good win at Doncaster last time out. I'm not sure about Apple's Shakira in the Triumph and Sussex Ranger might be an interesting each-way alternative.

Which novice chasers stand out?

Richard Birch Footpad holds all the aces in the Arkle, while last year's Pertemps winner Presenting Percy boasts that all-important festival form and can score another Cheltenham success in the RSA.

Brian Sheerin Presenting Percy is my strongest fancy of the week in the RSA and I genuinely believe he's a Gold Cup horse in the making. In theory, he should be even better when he encounters nicer ground at the festival and I'm expecting a big performance. It's hard to get away from Footpad in the Arkle, while the JLT looks wide open.

Graeme Rodway Presenting Percy looks the most exciting staying novice this season. He's improving and will be hard to beat in either the National Hunt Chase or RSA. Saint Calvados might be able to upset favourite Footpad in the Arkle. The slick-jumping front-runner will make them all go if he handles better ground, and jockey Aidan Coleman reckons he will.

David Jennings Petit Mouchoir can give Footpad a much bigger scare than he did at Leopardstown and looks the each-way play in the Arkle. Modus was a 156-rated hurdler who has reached the same mark over fences. He's officially a better horse than JLT favourite Willoughby Court and looks overpriced at 14-1. The race looks sure to be run to suit. Presenting Percy is going to be a tough nut to crack in the RSA.

Nick Watts I don't like the price of Footpad in the Arkle even though I think he's the most likely winner. Willoughby Court was beaten last time but on winter ground, so he can bounce back in the JLT, while it wouldn't be a total shock to see Finian's Oscar run a big race, even though connections have had a few changes of heart with him through the season. If Yanworth goes for the RSA I'll be with him, and my alternative is Black Corton.

*Willoughby Court:
heads the market
for the JLT*

betfair EXCHANGE

A DECADE OF BEST ODDS

ON 94% OF CHELTENHAM HORSES SINCE 2008

GET AHEAD
AT CHELTENHAM 2018

Tickets

Except for the Friday of the festival, which is all ticket, badges and tickets can be bought at the entrances subject to availability, although savings can be made by booking in advance. To book tickets call 0344 579 3003 or buy online at cheltenham.thejockeyclub.co.uk.

Club is the most exclusive enclosure with the best viewing and refreshment facilities. A Club day badge allows access to all the facilities within Tattersalls. Tue-Thur day badges £80 in advance up to March 11, £90 on the day; Gold Cup day £110 in advance.

Tattersalls offers extensive grandstand views, a wide choice of betting and refreshment facilities, and access to all the bookmakers in the betting ring. There is also access to the Centaur, paddock and unsaddling enclosure, Hall of Fame and the trade stands in the tented village. Tue-Thur £55 in advance up to March 11, £60 on the day; Gold Cup day £75 in advance.

The Best Mate Enclosure, directly opposite the main stands, is the cheapest option, with betting, food and bars and entertainment. Tue-Thur £40 in advance up to March 11, £45 on the day; Gold Cup day £60 in advance.

Car parking at the course is £12 in advance (£20 on the day).

Preview evening

For early arrivals there is the chance to see a preview evening at the racecourse on Sunday, March 11 at 7pm. Jeremy Kyle is the host with guests John Francome, Ruby Walsh, Fergal O'Brien and Cornelius Lysaght. Admission is £6 and the event will be livestreamed by event sponsors OLBG.

Watch and listen

ITV will show the first five races live each day, starting at 1pm, with The Opening Show at 9.30am every morning on ITV4. Racing UK will show all 28 festival races live and there will be a live preview show from Cheltenham every morning until racing starts.

Festival Radio broadcasts within a five-mile radius of the course on 87.7FM, with traffic information, previews, interviews, news, commentaries and results. Radio earpieces are available to purchase on site from racecard kiosks, subject to availability

Amateur riders

Amateur riders now have to be better qualified to take part at the festival, with the

Fulke Walwyn Kim Muir Handicap Chase and the St James's Place Foxhunter Chase from this year restricted to those holding a category B permit. This brings those two races in line with the existing conditions for the National Hunt Chase, the other amateurs-only event.

Last year all those riding in the Kim Muir held a category B permit anyway, but four of the 23 riders in the Foxhunter were at the lower category A level and would have been barred from competing under the new rule.

Former Olympic cyclist Victoria Pendleton would not have been allowed to take part if the new rule had been in place in 2016, when she finished fifth in the Foxhunter under a category A permit.

Prize-money

Prize-money has been increased by seven per cent this year to a record £4,590,000 across the four days, with every day for the first time having over £1 million in prize-money.

Unibet has taken over from stable companion Stan James in backing the Champion Hurdle, while there are new sponsors with the Ballymore Novices' Hurdle (the 2m5f Grade 1 contest that opens Wednesday's card) and the Boodles Fred Winter Juvenile Handicap Hurdle, the sixth race on Wednesday. Previously the Fred Winter did not have a sponsor.

Presentations

Cheltenham has a new, larger presentation podium in the parade ring this season, constructed of steel and glass, with the aim of enabling a greater number of people to see the trophy presentations.

The winner's enclosure has also been enlarged to help ease capacity, particularly during the festival.

A quick guide to festival betting

In the shops Most betting shops open earlier during the festival, usually at 8.30-9am

Free bets Many bookmakers offer free bets for new customers during the festival, but remember to check the terms and conditions. For a great range of free bets, go to racingpost.com

Compare the odds Find the best odds on your selections from a range of bookmakers by using the odds comparison table at racingpost.com

Early prices Be quick if you want to take an advertised price on the morning of the race – most firms hold their prices for a maximum of 15 minutes and some offer no guarantee

Each-way Bookmakers often extend their place terms during the festival. In the big handicaps, it can pay to look for firms offering a quarter the odds for the first five places, or paying out on six places. The standard each-way terms are a quarter the odds for the first four places

Best odds Several firms offer 'best odds guaranteed', which means they will match the SP if you have taken an early price and your selection wins at bigger odds

Specials A vast range of special bets is available at the festival, including perennial favourites such as top trainer, top jockey and the number of Irish winners

'It's clear to see why Native River has been popular each-way'

Who do you fancy for the Gold Cup?

Bet365 **Pat Cooney** Native River, even on good ground, has solid claims, but more so if it's soft. He was only beaten a few lengths last year and has the proven stamina. Djakadam might be overpriced from an each-way angle.

Betbright **Gavin Geraghty** It could be argued that Might Bite should be a shorter price as he's the only leading contender who has had no hiccups this season. I couldn't put anyone off backing him and I would also take a stab at something at a big price, possibly the unexposed Bachasson.

Betfair **Niall O'Reilly** I fancy Road To Respect, while Might Bite is anything but a safe bet. For all I believe Sizing John has the ability to win it again, I wouldn't back him after his last run.

Betfred **Matt Hulmes** Native River ran well to be third off a busy campaign last season. He proved his jumping and staying qualities at Newbury and with a lighter campaign he can go two places better. I fancy Road To Respect will be thereabouts.

Betway **Alan Alger** I'm not sure Might Bite can ever be described as safe and we know how hard it is to win back-to-back Gold Cups, so Sizing John has it all to do. It's clear to see why Native River has been popular each-way. Of the up-and-comers, I like Road To Respect.

BoyleSports **Leon Blanche** Might Bite has all the credentials to go very close but he's short enough and I'd be willing to forgive the current champion Sizing John on his last run at Leopardstown. He'll go to Cheltenham fresh and that could make all the difference on the day. Edwulf was impressive in winning the Irish Gold Cup and at 25-1 he might just run into a place.

Coral **Andrew Lobo** It looks a decent renewal and Might Bite is pretty solid. Might Bite and Native River should make it a true test of stamina and I'd look for a big price each-way, possibly something like Total Recall if he runs, to pick up the pieces.

Ladbrokes **Matt Trounce** Might Bite looks opposable at the top of the market. His strength last year was breaking horses in the middle part of the race, but connections have said he'll be ridden with more restraint this time and that takes away his biggest weapon. Sizing John and Our Duke look alternatives if they turn up 100 per cent.

Paddy Power **Daniel Collins** After his shenanigans last year Might Bite is far from a safe bet, but he did the most to enhance his claims over Christmas. Sizing John still sets the standard if he bounces back.

Sky Bet **Richard Horner** Might Bite's antics up the run-in at Cheltenham will be a worry for his supporters. The up-and-comer is Road To Respect, who won at the festival last year and has shown he is up to Grade 1 level with a win in the Christmas Chase.

Sporting Index Charles Hitchings Might Bite still looks a fair price. I think he would be even shorter if it wasn't for his previous antics, yet he looks to have matured now. Sizing John could easily come back to form but it's not an ideal preparation.

William Hill Jamie McBride At current prices Might Bite and Sizing John look short enough. Road To Respect has done nothing wrong this season and, being proven at Cheltenham, looks to have solid claims.

188bet Jeff Parkes Native River is only eight and has shown significant improvement every season. His Newbury run was as good as anything he's previously done and he should improve further on that.

Can anything stop Buveur D'Air in the Champion Hurdle?

Bet365 Only a back-to-form Faugheen stands in his way but you've got to have doubts about Faugheen's current level of ability. A straight forecast of Buveur D'Air to beat My Tent Or Yours looks a reasonable assumption.

Betbright Buveur D'Air is in pole position but there's no value left in his price. Faugheen still has to rate as the main danger despite running probably more than a stone below his best at Leopardstown.

Betfair I can't see anything beating Buveur D'Air. Faugheen is the only one I give a small chance to if he comes on again for his run at Leopardstown.

Betfred With Faugheen looking a spent force, I can't see what else beats the reigning champion. The bet has to be My Tent Or Yours each-way or without the favourite.

Betway The each-way will be the play for many punters and I could see value in backing Verdana Blue if her connections go for the place prize-money here instead of the Mares' Hurdle.

Buveur D'Air: bookies find it hard to pick an alternative to the odds-on favourite

BoyleSports Buveur D'Air looks to have another Champion Hurdle crown at his mercy. If you're looking for a horse to be placed it has to be My Tent Or Yours.

Coral If it hadn't been for the fact that Faugheen was so short, you'd have been happy enough with his last run with a view to improving again at Cheltenham. He actually recorded a higher RPR than Buveur D'Air and he still has a chance.

Ladbrokes Buveur D'Air looks head and shoulders above the opposition and I'd prefer him even to an on-song Faugheen. I'd be looking for something at a big price to hit the frame and John Constable and Verdana Blue are the types to thrive back on faster ground in a strongly run race.

Paddy Power I would echo Nicky Henderson's concerns that Buveur D'Air hasn't had a real race this season, but he looks streets ahead of the opposition. Ch'Tibello is solid and has a place chance but lacks the class to win.

Sky Bet With the ground likely to be on the slow side of good on the first day, it's hard to see anything beating last year's champion. My Tent Or Yours without the favourite could be interesting. It wouldn't be a surprise if we had the same 1-2 as last year.

Sporting Index The main danger to Buveur D'Air would be a back-to-best Faugheen, but that seems unlikely. You can't go too far wrong with an each-way bet on My Tent Or Yours.

William Hill It looks a disappointing renewal and Buveur D'Air looks very difficult to beat. John Constable got as close to him at Sandown as anything of late and could be one to support each-way or in betting without the favourite.

188bet Race tactics are the main danger to Buveur D'Air. There is one speculative scenario where I can envisage Apple's Jade controlling the pace up front and Buveur never quite getting there. She may not run but Apple's Jade is as big as 18-1 NRNB, which has to be the each-way value.

What do you make of the Champion Chase?

Bet365 Altior has obvious claims but faces his toughest task so far against Min, who impressed last time, and also Politologue, who will improve for his recent run. Altior had to work hard to win last year's Arkle and there's no denying Min and Politologue are stronger rivals, so I'd rather lay him than back him at current prices.

Betbright Altior was really impressive on his comeback in the Game Spirit Chase. He should improve for the run as long as he avoids the dreaded bounce factor, as he looked to blow up before getting his second wind and winning comfortably.

Betfair I thought Altior was very impressive and he's hard to oppose, though whichever of Min or Douvan show up will definitely provide tougher opposition. It's set up to be a great race.

Betfred A fully fit Altior looks almost impossible to get beat, but the same was said of Douvan last year. He looked imperious at Newbury but I'd fancy Politologue to get closer to him when getting a lead. It wouldn't have suited him making it at Newbury and it played into Altior's hands. Politologue is cast iron to hit the places.

Betway Altior comfortably beat Politologue, who's still around the third favourite for this race. It's another championship race with an intriguing each-way picture. I'd plump for Forest Bihan to claim a place, as long as the ground isn't too soft.

BoyleSports Altior was very impressive at Newbury and is bound to come on a ton for the run. As a winner of a Supreme and an Arkle, he obviously acts around Cheltenham and that's a major plus. If Douvan were to turn up back to his best, he would definitely serve it up to him.

Coral Altior was impressive at Newbury and a repeat forecast of the 2016 Supreme looks on the cards with Min to follow him home.

Tough to beat: Altior is a popular choice for the Champion Chase

Ladbrokes Altior was impressive on his comeback at Newbury and if he progresses as expected from that he'll be very hard to beat.

Paddy Power We look to be getting the match we were cruelly denied in last year's Arkle. Altior will be hard to beat as long as Newbury didn't take too much out of him.

Sky Bet Altior looked very good at Newbury on ground he didn't relish and is going to be hard to beat. With Special Tiara sure to make it a good clip, that should suit Altior and he can get the better of Min, who looks the main danger.

Sporting Index Altior is top class and he was impressive in beating Politologue. As long as Altior doesn't bounce – and considering the easy manner of his victory the chance should be minimised – he'll be very hard to beat.

William Hill Altior was impressive on his reappearance and looks as though he will be tough to beat. Charbel and the reigning champion Special Tiara appeal most as each-way bets against him.

188bet An each-way punt on Politologue at around 10-1 wouldn't be a terrible bet. There are reasons to believe he'll be a lot better in March than on his last two runs at Kempton and Newbury. That said, Altior looks a good thing and your only real hope of getting him beat is the breathing op not working as well second time up.

Who is your pick for an open-looking Stayers' Hurdle?

Bet365 I don't see it as being that wide open as there are two dominant candidates in Supasundae and Sam Spinner. Both come here with a high level of recent form and backing both would give cover from a tactical view as Sam Spinner may make all and outstay his rivals and, if not, Supasundae has the class over shorter trips to win instead.

Betbright I have been really impressed with Sam Spinner, who can only be improving as he has just turned six. He put up the performance of the season in this division, where there is not a lot of depth.

Betfair I have my doubts about the favourite Supasundae over the trip and Sam Spinner is the most solid in the line-up. I get the feeling he could end up being the value bet on the day.

Betfred Victory for Sam Spinner would cap an incredible story while Supasundae has proved he has a quality blend of speed and stamina. I like the look of Bacardys each-way – he had excuses at last year's festival and has had an aborted chase campaign like a couple of Stayers' Hurdle winners.

Betway L'Ami Serge ticks all the boxes and I think it could be straightforward. Apple's Jade has been impressive but she's unlikely to end up here.

BoyleSports Supasundae appreciates good ground and therefore his run behind Apple's Jade at Christmas and his last run in the Irish Champion on slower ground than ideal must be taken seriously. He was an impressive winner of the Coral Cup and ran Yanworth mighty close last season at Aintree on good ground.

Coral I much prefer Supasundae to Sam Spinner – he has previous festival winning form and looks much more solid at a similar price.

Ladbrokes Originally I was against Sam Spinner but I feel he could drift out to a backable price. Supasundae looked good in Ireland last time, but if you took Faugheen out of that race and the racecard showed Mick Jazz in second, I don't think he'd be as short as he is. Yanworth beat Supasundae at Aintree and could come slightly under the radar if he reverts from chasing.

Paddy Power I can't get away from how well The Worlds End travelled in last year's Albert Bartlett and back on better ground I think he'll outrun his price. I would run Yanworth here and he could go off favourite if lining up.

Sky Bet It would be good to see Apple's Jade take her chance but that seems unlikely, so I'm keen for Warren Greatrex to run La Bague Au Roi here rather than the Mares' Hurdle and she looks fair value at 20-1.

Sporting Index This is fairly straightforward as Supasundae has every box ticked. He's a previous festival winner who has improved this season and has pace as well as stamina. His main rival looks to be Sam Spinner, whose rise up the ranks has been a joy to watch, but his front-running tactics may be harder to pull off in this ultra-competitive race.

William Hill I don't have a strong opinion other than Supasundae looks plenty short enough. Yanworth can go close if he's pointed this way and Wholestone could improve again on better ground.

188bet Of those most prominent in the market Sam Spinner would be my pick, though on better ground he may have to be a little more fluent at his hurdles than in the past. I'll be looking to back a true stayer each-way at a big price.

What do you fancy for the novice hurdles?

Bet365 Getabird was ultra-impressive last time on testing going and is likely to be even better on faster ground. Samcro will saunter round to win the Ballymore. Black Op was so tough in defeat last time and the Albert Bartlett trip will suit.

Betbright The standout novices have been Samcro, Getabird, Next Destination and On The Blind Side. At this stage my picks would be Getabird for the Supreme, Samcro for the Ballymore and Poetic Rhythm each-way for the Albert Bartlett.

Betfair If The Cap Fits (Supreme), Samcro (Ballymore), Santini (Albert Bartlett) and Farclas (Triumph). Samcro has to be the banker, while the other three represent some decent value at the prices, with Santini being the one I'm really keen on.

Betfred The whole novice hurdle scene revolves around Samcro as I'm sure many will

look to avoid him. I'm interested in wherever Willie Mullins sends Duc Des Genievres, who has caught the eye in his two runs in Grade 1s. I can't have Getabird at the prices considering his best form is over further and on soft.

Betway Kim Bailey's First Flow looks a great each-way bet for the Supreme. Getabird proved he can get the extra half-mile or so with his win over 2m4f on heavy in December and he might be a shout for the Ballymore. The Albert Bartlett can go to Kilbricken Storm, who won well over course and distance this season. The Triumph looks made for Apple's Shakira. Samcro isn't overrated but may well have been overhyped, so the market price on the day might end up too short.

BoyleSports Samcro looks to be in a different league to most novices around and will be a banker for many wherever he lines up. Without him, I'd go for Getabird in the Supreme and On The Blind Side in the Ballymore. Next Destination has done everything right for Willie Mullins and the step up to three miles in the Albert Bartlett will suit. Apple's Shakira has done most of her winning with cut in the ground and those who have backed her for the Triumph will be hoping for similar conditions. Mr Adjudicator was an impressive winner of our Triumph trial when he outbattled Farclas, who also has to come into consideration.

Coral Samcro looks a potential superstar but I'm not sure his last form amounted to much and a very different test awaits. Kalashnikov will warrant respect wherever he runs. If The Cap Fits' novice hurdle win at Kempton has worked out really well and he could be overpriced in the Supreme.

Ladbrokes Bar Samcro I'm not sure how strong the Irish novice hurdlers are, so I'll be looking for some value from the British horses. Kalashnikov was impressive in the Betfair Hurdle and should go close in the Supreme, while I was very taken by Black Op on Trials Day. He travelled all over the field and will hopefully relish an easier test in the Ballymore.

EQUESTRIAN SURFACES LTD

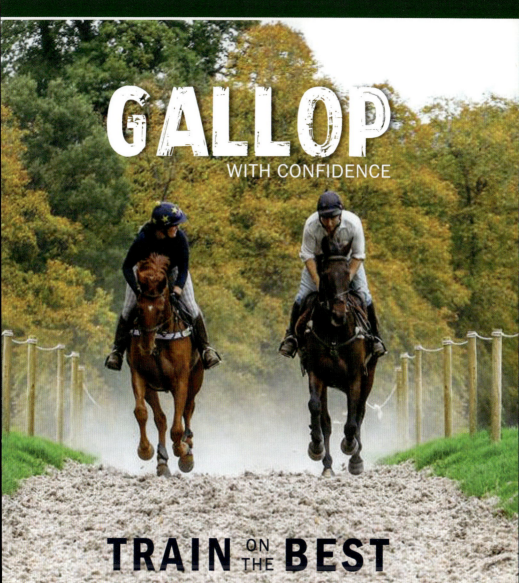

GALLOP
WITH CONFIDENCE

TRAIN ON THE **BEST**

Paddy Power Horses that look to be improving with each run and are of interest in their respective races include Paloma Blue, Black Op and Farclas, whilst Next Destination would be tough to beat in the Albert Bartlett. I've not been bowled over by Apple's Shakira, who could get tapped for toe on better ground.

Sky Bet If The Cap Fits would be my each-way selection in the Sky Bet Supreme as he has impressed in his three wins this season and will go there fresh after a break. Samcro is hard to oppose in the Ballymore after what he has done so far this season and Chef Des Obeaux is my pick in the Albert Bartlett.

Sporting Index It seems likely that Getabird and Samcro will start at deservedly short prices in the Supreme and the Ballymore. In the Albert Bartlett I'm very keen on Santini, whose form in beating stablemate Chef Des Obeaux was well advertised subsequently. I'd take on Apple's Shakira at the price with Redicean, who was decent on the Flat and should improve for better ground.

William Hill The Ballymore looks at the mercy of the impressive Samcro but the other short-priced favourites, Getabird and Apple's Shakira, look more beatable. Santini and Duc Des Genievres can run well in an open-looking Albert Bartlett.

188bet I'm sure Sharjah is a better horse on better ground and he may still come good in an open-looking Supreme. Three miles and goodish ground might prove ideal for Santini in the Albert Bartlett. Mr Adjudicator is the best juvenile I've seen this season and, while he'll only get better on decent ground, some of his Triumph rivals will lament the end of winter ground.

Which novice chasers stand out?

Bet365 Footpad saw off Petit Mouchoir well enough last time and that form is enough to win the Arkle. Modus is too talented to rule out in an open JLT. Presenting Percy would be banker material in the four-miler but is well up to winning this year's RSA.

Betbright I was really impressed with Petit Mouchoir's comeback against Footpad – after missing the first two, he ran really well and wasn't given a hard race. He had Footpad's measure over hurdles and at five times the price he's worth backing to do so in the Arkle. I would love to see Monalee go for the JLT. He's quite free-going and the faster pace of the JLT would really suit him and bring his slick jumping to the fore. The RSA looks tailor-made for Presenting Percy on spring ground. He's an impeccable jumper and will fly up the hill.

Betfair The Arkle is set up to be run at a ferocious pace, which points me tentatively towards Sceau Royal at the prices. Willoughby Court looks the solid option in the JLT and I really hope Yanworth shows up in the RSA as I think he has a class edge over the opposition.

Betfred Saint Calvados has impressed me with his quick jumping. He was foot-perfect at Warwick and could give Footpad something to think about in the Arkle. Willoughby Court rates as one of the bets of the meeting. His target is assured, he is a festival winner and he will improve from his Dipper third on much better ground.

Betway Footpad is a favourite who can be trusted in the Arkle having not put a foot wrong this season. Bigmartre looks a decent prospect each-way in the JLT – the step up in trip should suit as he got an extended two miles over hurdles. Black Corton is a strong fancy for the RSA Chase – he was so impressive at Cheltenham in October.

BoyleSports The Arkle is one of the best races of the festival in my opinion. Footpad has been sensational since his switch from hurdles to fences and I'm on at a nice price, so I won't desert him now. Yanworth has the ability and class to win the JLT and the same can be said of Al Boum Photo, who ran a cracker to finish second to Monalee last time out. Presenting Percy oozes class and I think he'll justify favouritism in the RSA.

Coral I was taken by Petit Mouchoir's most

recent run at Leopardstown off a long break and I think he can reverse placings with Footpad in the Arkle. Presenting Percy was most impressive in the Pertemps last year and he'll be hard to beat in the RSA.

Ladbrokes The Arkle looks the race of the festival if the top four in the market turn up. I'll take Saint Calvados to upset them all. He's been seriously impressive and connections think he'll handle quicker ground, so he'll do for me. Last year's festival winners, Willoughby Court and Presenting Percy, should take all the beating in the other novice chases.

Paddy Power We have some spectacular jumpers in the novice ranks this season with Footpad, Saint Calvados and Monalee all putting in superb rounds recently and they look the horses to focus on.

Sky Bet I'm a big fan of Footpad and he'll be hard to beat in the Arkle, but seeing him and Saint Calvados jumping those fences will be some spectacle. With better ground and a more attacking ride than in last year's Ballymore, I think we'll see a different Willoughby Court to the one beaten last time. Presenting Percy looks a class act who has course form and goes on any ground and he can take the RSA before going on to better things next year.

Sporting Index Footpad is the standout in the Arkle, but at the prices I'd rather be on Petit Mouchoir, who may well improve on his Leopardstown run. Willoughby Court should bounce back in the JLT on better ground, with Invitation Only the main danger. Monalee was second in the Albert Bartlett last year and has shown decent form chasing this season, so he looks the standout in the RSA.

William Hill The Arkle could be one of the races of the meeting and Saint Calvados is arguably still underrated in the betting. Presenting Percy looks the outstanding candidate for the RSA.

188bet Three of the front four in the Arkle betting would probably want to lead to show their optimum form and they can't all lead. Daryl Jacob will have Sceau Royal popping away out the back and could weave his way through for a place at least. Yanworth gets a bad rap but he can win a JLT. Presenting Percy looks a solid bet in the RSA.

What are the biggest losers in your book?

Bet365 We went non-runner no bet and best odds guaranteed on all festival races a lot earlier this year and have seen a much better spread of business in all the races. Like all bookmakers, we're always worried about the opening day and it's the same again this year with Footpad, Buveur D'Air and Apple's Jade all looking very punter friendly.

Betbright Apple's Shakira in the Triumph and Native River in the Gold Cup would be two

Bigmartre: each-way shot in the JLT

of the worst results but we're quite hopeful of getting both of them beat.

Betfair Might Bite is definitely the one we're most worried about at this stage. Apple's Shakira has also been very popular as we've been top price since her last run. An interesting one that we've built up a liability on is Vaniteux, who's into 14-1 for the Grand Annual from as big as 33-1.

Betfred Nothing is causing sleepless nights at present, but the liabilities are starting to mount up on the jollies. Footpad and Buveur D'Air start them off, Altior carries them through and punters have latched on to Might Bite as the final leg. If he wins the Gold Cup it will be a hefty payout.

Betway The biggest fear is the opening-day treble of Buveur D'Air, Apple's Jade and Footpad. Our biggest positions are Getabird (Supreme), Footpad (Arkle), Samcro (Ballymore), Willougby Court (JLT) and Might Bite (Gold Cup).

BoyleSports Samcro and Apple's Jade are by far our biggest losers. We have them in every type of bet and we'll be praying one of them gets beat.

Coral Faugheen in the Champion Hurdle and Samcro in the Ballymore have been well backed through the season and over fences Might Bite is shaping up to be a bad result in the Gold Cup.

Ladbrokes Our current biggest losers are Faugheen in the Champion Hurdle along with the Irish bankers, Footpad in the Arkle and Samcro in the Ballymore. We've been happy to be against Faugheen all season and I can't see that changing before the day.

Paddy Power A couple of Irish novice chasers, Footpad and Presenting Percy, are comfortably our worst results, so we were delighted when Saint Calvados and Monalee emerged as credible challengers. Might Bite wouldn't be pretty in the Gold Cup either.

Sky Bet Samcro (Ballymore), Faugheen (Champion Hurdle), Might Bite (Gold Cup)

and Getabird (Supreme) are the four worst results in our field books.

Sporting Index Come the day we'll have positions on a wide range of festival meeting markets, so it may not be a horse we're worried about, but it could be distances or winning favourites.

William Hill Getabird (Supreme), Samcro (Ballymore) and Apple's Shakira (Triumph) are our worst results. I'm particularly jealous of those clutching 16-1 vouchers for Samcro and we're likely to be behind the eight ball after the first race on Wednesday.

188bet We've laid Farclas in the Triumph to Pricewise punters, Getabird at fancy prices on the morning of his Punchestown success and Footpad for the Arkle back in November. All look great bets at the prices.

Who are the ones to watch from Ireland?

Bet365 The main Irish players are Apple's Jade, Footpad, Getabird, Laurina and Samcro. All five have clear chances, with Samcro the banker in the Ballymore.

Betbright Samcro, Getabird and Next Destination are leading the charge over hurdles and Footpad, Petit Mouchoir, Monalee and Presenting Percy are dominating the novice chase betting. At this stage the Irish bankers appear to be Samcro and Apple's Jade.

Betfair I can't wait to see Samcro again and Laurina looked a monster at Fairyhouse – she could end up being one of the bankers of the festival. Getabird has done nothing wrong but I can't help feeling he's very short in the market.

Betfred The Irish banker without a doubt is Samcro. He has done nothing wrong and his wins have appeared to be effortless. Keep an eye on Eagle Lion if he makes it to the Pertemps Final. Bleu Et Rouge has a big race in him too and could be County Hurdle or Coral Cup bound.

Betway I feel Samcro is overhyped rather than

TWO CHILDREN GO FREE WITH ADVANCE ADULT TICKETS

A CELEBRATION OF

GREAT
BRITISH
AGRICULTURE
ENTERTAINMENT
FOOD & DRINK

ROYAL
BATH & WEST
SHOW

WWW.BATHANDWEST.COM

30 MAY - 2 JUNE 2018

overrated. He's going to go off plenty short enough. Stay Humble has received plenty of whispers regarding the Champion Bumper.

BoyleSports Samcro, Footpad, Apple's Jade, Cause Of Causes, Laurina and Un De Sceaux will all be very popular. Apple's Jade is looking unbeatable in the Mares' Hurdle.

Coral Of the shorties I'd rather bet Laurina in the Mares' Novices' Hurdle – she really impressed me last time at Fairyhouse and I'd expect her to be very hard to beat. Getabird was impressive last time but that form hasn't much substance in the context of his Supreme price and for much of the season he was due to be targeting longer trips. He looks opposable to me.

Ladbrokes The Irish pick up the mares' races at every festival and Apple's Jade and Laurina look strong favourites this year. I'll be looking to get Getabird beat in the opener as I think he's flattered by getting an easy lead last time. He's yet to run on fast ground or go left-handed under rules.

Paddy Power Apart from Samcro, who could be an all-time great, I was really impressed with Monalee in the Flogas Chase and he'll be very tough to beat in the RSA. Getabird has done nothing wrong but at this stage is looking like being shorter than his superstar stablemates, Vautour and Douvan, were in the Supreme.

Sky Bet Tully East, Mall Dini and Burning Ambition would be the three at bigger prices I'd be keen on. The two bankers are Samcro and Apple's Jade – if neither of those two oblige, the amount of euros staying over this side of the water will be colossal.

Sporting Index Samcro will have the mantle of Irish banker this year. At the prices Supasundae is my main Irish fancy. I would be loath to suggest any Irish horse is overrated but Footpad seems short enough in the betting.

William Hill Away from the obvious headline acts, Duc Des Genievres and Dounikos can go close if pointed towards the Albert Bartlett

and National Hunt Chase respectively. Bon Papa may be of interest in a handicap.

188bet There's loads more to come from Off You Go and he'll be popular in whatever handicap he goes in. Both Blackbow and Rhinestone look well set for the Bumper and Farclas and Mr Adjudicator are to be feared in the Triumph.

Give us a value bet for the festival

Bet365 Daryl Jacob for top jockey at around 16-1 looks interesting. We'll give him Footpad in the Arkle, then maybe We Have A Dream in the Triumph, plus several other good rides in the Simon Munir and Isaac Souede green colours.

Betbright I'd be very interested in The Storyteller if he turns up for the Ultima Handicap Chase on the first day. He's crying out for three miles, he's on a nice handicap mark and can be backed at 16-1 NRNB.

Betfair Act Of Valour ran a big race against We Have a Dream at Musselburgh and he could be interesting in the Fred Winter if given a mark in the low 130s. He's a general 20-1 shot with most firms.

Betfred Sugar Baron ran an eyecatcher in last year's Kim Muir when staying on for sixth place. He ran a close second at the November meeting and, off a similar layoff and just a 2lb higher mark, he's worth following for the same race.

Betway L'Ami Serge in the Stayers' Hurdle.

BoyleSports Hollowgraphic to win the Champion Bumper.

Coral Barney Dwan was an excellent second in the Pertemps Hurdle last season and has been brought along steadily over fences. He could get in one of the staying handicap chases off a fair mark for the excellent Fergal O'Brien stable.

Ladbrokes Black Op is a massive each-way runner against Samcro at 16-1 in the Ballymore. He should relish better conditions and The New One took this race five years

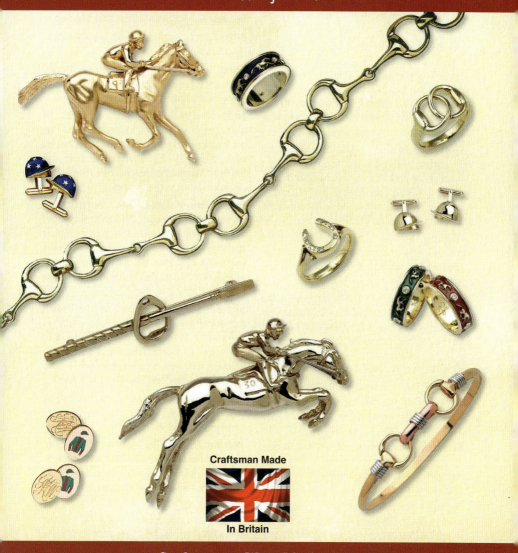

ago after being outstayed in the same race as Black Op.

Paddy Power King's Socks came with a lofty reputation and had a lovely spin round at Kempton on his first run. He has obviously had issues since arriving in England but a mark of 140 and 20-1 could both seriously underestimate his ability for connections who have a good record in the Brown Advisory Plate.

Sky Bet Nube Negra at 16-1 in the Fred Winter. He ran well against Apple's Shakira before hammering a poor field at Doncaster. He looks to be on a fair mark, has course experience and a big-field handicap will suit him. He should go well for Dan Skelton, who is a very good target trainer.

Sporting Index At 14-1 Virak in the Foxhunter looks a bit of value. He had been contesting highly competitive handicaps trying to take on the likes of Bristol De Mai and lost his way, but he may have had his confidence restored at this level.

William Hill The Champion Hurdle could cut up badly and backing John Constable each-way at around 50-1 might not be the worst idea.

188bet You can bet Hell's Kitchen in the Close Brothers' Novices' Handicap Chase at 12-1 currently, but he'll be less than half that on the day and I think he'll win.

What's your best festival bet?

Bet365 Tully East in Thursday's Brown Advisory Plate appeals. He won at the festival last year and it looks as though all is going to plan with him after a rock-solid run last time.

Betbright Sam Spinner in the Stayers' Hurdle. He's improving with every run and has only just turned six, so it's quite likely he should improve again come March.

Betfair Road To Respect has the most solid credentials in the Gold Cup. He has festival form from last year, loves good ground and is an improving seven-year-old yet to reach his full potential, coming off a career-best effort in the Christmas Chase.

Betfred Willoughby Court in the JLT. We'll see a different horse on better ground than we did on New Year's Day, when he still ran with plenty of credit. With festival victory already on his CV and opposition potentially thin on the ground, he looks a solid option.

Betway Black Corton in the RSA Chase.

BoyleSports Ireland to have more winners than Britain.

Coral Laurina in the Trull House Mares' Novices' Hurdle. She wouldn't look out of place in the Supreme.

Ladbrokes Willoughby Court in the JLT. All four previous festival winners to run in this have gone on to win again and I think he can make it five. He had excuses last time and his front-running style suits this course and distance down to the ground.

Paddy Power Voix Du Reve looks to have been campaigned with Cheltenham in mind and will only be a couple of pounds higher than for his luckless run in the Fred Winter two years ago. He'll be carrying my money in whichever handicap Willie Mullins thinks suits him best.

Sky Bet Tully East at 10-1 for the Brown Advisory Plate. It looks like he's been trained for this race and, with the trip and likely better ground sure to suit, he should go close to winning here again after his impressive victory in the Close Brothers Handicap last year.

Sporting Index Waiting Patiently each-way in the Ryanair. He deserves to be a shorter price as he keeps on improving.

William Hill The Arkle will cut up to four or five serious contenders and I think there's too much daylight between the prices of Footpad and Saint Calvados, so the latter is a solid each-way bet.

188bet Mr Adjudicator looks a bet in the Triumph at around 8-1. He jumps, he stays and he quickens.

DISCOVER

Shared Racehorse Ownership

Search for your perfect ownership experience at
inthepaddock.co.uk

Stuart Riley on the horses who excel at Cheltenham

When it comes to course form at the Cheltenham Festival, no horse has more of it than **Cause Of Causes**.

He has run at every festival since 2013, although seventh place in that year's Supreme Novices' Hurdle, beaten 28 lengths by Champagne Fever, did not suggest this was a three-time festival winner in waiting. But he has been transformed over fences.

The following year Gordon Elliott felt he was so well treated as a novice chaser he ran in the Kim Muir, where a mistake at the last cost him dear and he finished second to Spring Loaded. It was to be his last defeat at the festival.

In 2015 he teamed up with Jamie Codd and landed the National Hunt Chase before coming from a mile back to right wrongs and win the Kim Muir by 12 lengths in 2016. Last season it was another distance – and even different fences in the Cross Country Chase – but it did not matter as he romped home nine lengths clear.

He is not the only Elliott-

trained multiple festival winner under consideration for this year's renewal, with 2014 Triumph Hurdle and last year's National Hunt Chase winner **Tiger Roll** – he finished 13th in Cole Harden's World Hurdle in between – given a spin around the unique cross-country course at the December meeting.

The trainer's **Apple's Jade** could join their ranks

to defend the Mares' Hurdle crown she won last year. She was also somehow only second to Ivanovich Gorbatov in the 2016 Triumph Hurdle.

Her half-sister, the Nicky Henderson-trained **Apple's Shakira**, had not seen a racecourse at the time of last year's festival, so this will be her first, but she has already proved her liking for the track with three wins from three visits by a combined

Cause Of Causes (main) and Apple's Jade (left) won at the festival last year while Black Corton (above) has scored twice at the track this season

Altior, winner of the 2016 Supreme and last year's Arkle Chase, and **Un De Sceaux** – second to Sprinter Sacre in the 2016 Champion Chase in his otherwise blemish-free festival attendance that includes victories in the 2015 Arkle and last year's Ryanair – have enviable records at the festival and will be hard to beat again.

Also worth noting are a couple of last year's winners who come into the 2018 edition with stronger form claims than they possessed then – and now with course form to boot.

Presenting Percy sauntered to success in the Pertemps Handicap Hurdle last year and has since won twice over fences before reverting to hurdles to win a Grade 2. Still improving over hurdles and fences, he is well fancied to maintain his 100 per cent course record.

Coral Cup winner **Supasundae** has gone from strength to strength since that success. He finished second to Yanworth in a Grade 1 at Aintree in April and chased home Apple's Jade and Nichols Canyon on his seasonal debut in the Hatton's Grace before finding Apple's Jade half a length too good in the Christmas Hurdle. He has since got the better of Faugheen over a mile shorter in the Irish Champion Hurdle and comes into this year's festival in riotously good form.

28 and a half lengths. The Paul Nicholls-trained **Black Corton** (two from two, by a combined 14 lengths) and Dan Skelton's **North Hill Harvey** (two from two, 18 and a quarter lengths) are the other horses to have visited the track on multiple occasions this season and maintained a 100 per cent winning record.

Everything may have gone wrong this season for last year's Triumph Hurdle hero **Defi Du Seuil**, but he is four from four at Cheltenham. Another who could show better form at this track is **Unowhatimeanharry**, whose third place in last year's Stayers' Hurdle was his first defeat in five visits. He won the 2016 Albert Bartlett Novices' Hurdle at the festival and also landed the 2017 Cleeve Hurdle at Cheltenham.

River back in the flow and ready for victory surge

By Sam Walker

GOLD CUP The Gold Cup normally goes to a horse with proven stamina but last year was an exception, with the first six home covered by less than ten lengths.

Therefore it could pay to side with the stamina horse Native River (174) this time round, especially on the back of a gentler campaign and with a stunning return to action at Newbury in the bag.

Native River *(above)* finished third last year but things might have been different if Richard Johnson had set a stronger gallop. The champion jockey probably couldn't believe his luck ambling along at his own pace but the resulting bunch finish and slow overall time meant there was an emphasis on speed over stamina, which may not have suited his mount.

In the end the prize fell to Sizing John, who arrived with Grade 1 form over two miles, and not Native River, who had just won a Welsh National under top weight.

Might Bite (173) tops the market but the distance is a slight question mark for him as he's never been tested over this trip and has always looked at his most vulnerable in the closing stages.

Throw in the fact that his weary legs could be looking to veer off towards the safety of the unsaddling area, just as he did when almost throwing away the RSA Chase last year, and

there's a chance he could run out of steam when they get to the hill.

That said, if he stays and runs straight he's still got a leading chance.

Sizing John (173) had excuses after being beaten into seventh at Leopardstown in December, when he was found to be "clinically abnormal". That run was just 18 days after his successful return to action and it may have come too soon.

The question is whether he will be suited to a different type of Gold Cup if the emphasis is placed on stamina this year.

Definitly Red (172) is interesting as he stays really well. He doesn't always travel like the best horse in the race but is always strong at the finish.

Killultagh Vic (168) might be the one to take out of the Irish Gold Cup. He has been sparingly raced over the past few seasons but is clearly talented and might well have won at Leopardstown last time if he hadn't fallen at the last.

At big odds Double Shuffle (170) makes some appeal, as he was battling back against Might Bite in the King George VI Chase over 3m in December.

CHAMPION HURDLE Buveur D'Air (171) can become the first double winner since Hurricane Fly after bagging three wins from three starts this season.

He hasn't had much to beat and has

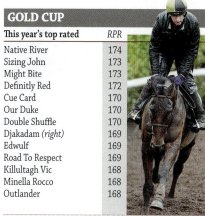

GOLD CUP	
This year's top rated	RPR
Native River	174
Sizing John	173
Might Bite	173
Definitly Red	172
Cue Card	170
Our Duke	170
Double Shuffle	170
Djakadam (right)	169
Edwulf	169
Road To Respect	169
Killultagh Vic	168
Minella Rocco	168
Outlander	168

How the past ten winners rated		
Year Winner	Win RPR	Pre-race RPR
2017 Sizing John	171	168
2016 Don Cossack	182	181
2015 Coneygree	178	168
2014 Lord Windermere	170	157
2013 Bobs Worth	181	174
2012 Synchronised	173	171
2011 Long Run	181	181
2010 Imperial Commander	182	177
2009 Kauto Star	185	184
2008 Denman	184	183
10yr winning average RPR: 178		

CHAMPION HURDLE	
This year's top rated	RPR
Buveur D'Air	171
Faugheen	171
My Tent Or Yours (right)	165
Wicklow Brave	165
Apple's Jade*	164
Melon	160
Ch'Tibello	158
Mick Jazz	158
Verdana Blue*	157
John Constable	156
Call Me Lord	155
*Includes 7lb mares' allowance	

How the past ten winners rated		
Year Winner	Win RPR	Pre-race RPR
2017 Buveur D'Air	170	159
2016 Annie Power	162	164
2015 Faugheen	170	169
2014 Jezki	173	167
2013 Hurricane Fly	173	173
2012 Rock On Ruby	171	166
2011 Hurricane Fly	171	169
2010 Binocular	172	172
2009 Punjabi	165	164
2008 Katchit	165	162
10yr winning average RPR: 169		

returned a best RPR of just 160 in recent months but there has been nothing to suggest he has lost his edge from last season and if he runs to his best he should be too good for any other two-miler in training.

Faugheen ran to 171 when demolishing the field on his return to action at Punchestown in November but he has been very disappointing since, being pulled up behind Mick Jazz in December and then getting outbattled by Supasundae in February.

The chances of him bouncing back to 171 are not good and, with Buveur D'Air lying in wait, connections might be tempted to tackle a softer option, perhaps by stepping him up in trip.

The fact that veteran My Tent Or Yours (165) is near the top of the RPR list highlights the lack of depth and new blood in the two-mile division, even if he is a three-time runner-up.

Ch'Tibello (158) has been knocking on the door for the last couple of seasons. He's unlikely to beat the favourite but there's a chance he can improve enough to hit the frame at a big price.

Yorkhill still ranks as a potential spoiler despite a dismal display in the Dublin Chase last time. He has never looked a natural chaser and a return to hurdles looks the obvious move after twice underlining his incompetence over fences. There is a chance he has lost the plot completely, but there's so much talent there he might just pull off an upset back in this more suitable sphere.

CHAMPION CHASE Altior (177) was one of the best chasers in training last season

CHAMPION CHASE

This year's top rated	RPR
Douvan	178
Altior	177
Fox Norton	174
Min	174
Un De Sceaux	174
Top Notch	171
Politologue	170
Special Tiara (right)	170
God's Own	167
Ar Mad	166
Charbel	166

How the past ten winners rated

Year Winner	Win RPR	Pre-race RPR
2017 Special Tiara	170	170
2016 Sprinter Sacre	176	173
2015 Dodging Bullets	169	173
2014 Sire De Grugy	173	174
2013 Sprinter Sacre	190	178
2012 Finian's Rainbow	175	167
2011 Sizing Europe	176	166
2010 Big Zeb	172	171
2009 Master Minded	169	186
2008 Master Minded	186	168

10yr winning average RPR: 176

STAYERS' HURDLE

This year's top rated	RPR
Faugheen	171
Supasundae	165
The New One	165
Unowhatimeanharry	165
Yanworth (right)	165
Apple's Jade*	164
Diakali	164
Lil Rockerfeller	164
Sam Spinner	164
L'Ami Serge	161
La Bague Au Roi*	160

*Includes 7lb mares' allowance

How the past ten winners rated

Year Winner	Win RPR	Pre-race RPR
2017 Nichols Canyon	164	166
2016 Thistlecrack	178	172
2015 Cole Harden	168	158
2014 More Of That	172	161
2013 Solwhit	166	165
2012 Big Buck's	170	175
2011 Big Buck's	162	176
2010 Big Buck's	174	176
2009 Big Buck's	176	166
2008 Inglis Drever	174	170

10yr winning average RPR: 170

despite being a novice and there was always a chance he would improve again this time round.

He missed much of this season with a breathing problem but came back with a bang at Newbury in February to sweep aside the in-form Politologue (170).

There were just three runners but Politologue made it a test for the returning champ and Altior passed it with flying colours, scoring by a cosy four lengths.

Altior is clearly the one to beat if he can build on that, although Min (174) ranks a clear number two after his runaway success in a Grade 2 at Leopardstown.

Altior and Min finished first and second in the Supreme Novices' Hurdle two years ago and they were set for a big rematch in last year's Arkle before Min was forced to miss the festival after picking up a knock.

This time it is Altior who has had the interrupted preparation, which could see Min threaten his old adversary.

Doctor Phoenix has been in great form since joining Gordon Elliott, improving his peak RPR from 145 to 161.

He already ranks high enough to finish third in a typical Champion Chase and (at a big price) there's a chance the improvement hasn't stopped yet.

STAYERS' HURDLE If there's a horse in the line-up capable of matching the ten-year average for this race (170) it is probably Penhill, who was the leading staying novice last season.

He had a peak RPR of 155 last season and will definitely need to take a big step up but that is entirely possible and nothing else in the race currently rates higher than 165.

CHELTENHAM FESTIVAL AT THE OX

CELEBRATE THE BIGGEST DATE IN CHELTENHAM'S CALENDAR WITH OUR CHAMPION'S BRUNCH, BREAKFAST COCKTAILS AND FESTIVAL DINNER! BOOK YOUR TABLE AT THEOXCHELTENHAM.COM

BRUNCH - 9:00AM - 1:00PM
DINNER - 5:00PM - 10:30PM

10 CAMBRAY PLACE
CHELTENHAM, GL50 1JS
01242 234 779
THEOXCHELTENHAM.COM

TUESDAY, 13TH MARCH
TO FRIDAY, 16TH MARCH

Penhill has had his sights trained firmly on this race and considering the dominance and stamina he showed to land the Albert Bartlett last year he could be the bet to improve markedly and upset the odds.

The current favourite is Supasundae, who got the better of Faugheen in the Irish Champion Hurdle. That was a great effort over the minimum trip, especially considering some of his best efforts have come over 3m.

He was progressive last spring, winning the Coral Cup over 2m5f and then finishing second to Yanworth in the Liverpool Hurdle over 3m, and has continued in the same vein this season, improving his RPR to 165. Back at Cheltenham and up in trip, there is a chance he will improve again to a new high.

Unowhatimeanharry (165) finished third last year and a place may be the best hope again after defeats behind Beer Goggles and Sam Spinner (164).

RYANAIR CHASE Un De Sceaux (174) won the race last year and arrives in top form on the back of easy wins at Cork and Ascot.

He has had the odd hiccup in his career but on the whole he has been very reliable with 20 wins under rules. He sets a decent standard but he is not miles clear of the rest.

Top Notch (171) was second to Yorkhill in the JLT Novices' Chase last year and has improved this season. His win over Double Shuffle and Frodon at Ascot has worked out particularly well and he shouldn't need to improve much from there to get involved.

NOVICE CHASES Footpad (168) sets a high standard in the Arkle Chase after a perfect three-from-three start to his chasing career.

The ten-year average RPR for winners of the Arkle stands at 167 but Footpad has already earned a mark higher than that after his cosy victory over Petit Mouchoir (161) in the Irish Arkle.

He jumped and travelled well that day and there is no reason to think he can't run a similar race at Cheltenham.

Saint Calvados (168) leads the British charge after three easy wins. He has never faced more than three rivals over fences and better ground will be an unknown but he could not have been more emphatic in his first efforts over fences.

The average RPR for a third placer in the Arkle stands at 155 and Capitaine (156) looks interesting to hit the frame at a big price.

RYANAIR CHASE	
This year's top rated	*RPR*
Fox Norton	174
Min	174
Un De Sceaux	174
Waiting Patiently	174
Frodon	173
Djakadam	171
Top Notch	171
Cue Card	170
Balko Des Flos	168
Outlander	168
Coney Island	167
God's Own	167
10yr winning average RPR: 171	

Top Notch: could put up a big effort

VINTAGE – Tradition Meets high-tech

The VINTAGE outer fabric is woven exclusively for Blaser Outfis and is visually reminiscent of the traditional loden fabric of days gone by. Combined with high tech materials, the VINTAGE line stands out due to its attractive styles, comfortable cuts and ultimate functionality.

For more information on Blaser Outfis please go to **www.blaser.de/outfits**

Blaser

ARKLE CHASE	
This year's top rated	*RPR*
Footpad	168
Saint Calvados	168
Sceau Royal	166
Brain Power	162
Cyrname	162
Petit Mouchoir	161
North Hill Harvey	158
Capitaine	156
Modus	156
Big Martre	154
Invitation Only	154
10yr winning average RPR: 167	

RSA CHASE	
This year's top rated	*RPR*
Mia's Storm*	162
Terrefort	162
Ballyoptic	161
Black Corton	161
Finian's Oscar	160
Presenting Percy	160
Elegant Escape	158
Shattered Love*	158
Jury Duty	157
Rathvinden	157
Willoughby Court	157
Includes 7lb mares' allowance	
10yr winning average RPR: 163	

Monalee (156) doesn't top the RPR list but he could be the one to beat in the RSA Chase.

He was a top staying novice hurdler last season, finishing second in the Albert Bartlett at the festival, and he was a most impressive winner on his debut over fences, earning an RPR of 155.

He fell when sent off a short-priced favourite for a Grade 1 at Leopardstown in December but put to rest any jumping concerns with a beautiful round to land a 2m5f Grade 1 at the same track in February.

There was a bunch finish to that race and Monalee registered an RPR of 156, which wouldn't be good enough to win a typical RSA (ten-year average RPR 163), but he is entitled to improve for a step up in trip.

Once you factor in her mares' allowance, Mia's Storm (162) comes out near the top of the ratings. She needs good ground, so it was no surprise to see her flounder before falling behind Black Corton (161) at Kempton. She could hit the frame at a nice price.

Last year's Pertemps Final winner Presenting Percy (160) tops the market after running away with the Porterstown Handicap Chase under top weight, but his price is short enough for such a competitive race.

NOVICE HURDLES Samcro (154) went odds-on for the Ballymore Novices' Hurdle after his impressive Grade 1 victory at Leopardstown in February.

That may have been the point at which the hype overtook the evidence, as he didn't need to improve on his best form to win, posting an RPR of 152, yet people immediately started talking about him as a Champion Hurdle candidate.

Samcro: very talented but hype overtook the evidence last time

SUPREME

This year's top rated	RPR
Samcro	154
Getabird	152
Next Destination	152
Mengli Khan	150
Summerville Boy	150
First Flow	147
Sharjah	147
Dame Rose*	146
Duc Des Genievres	146
If The Cap Fits	145
Real Steel	145
Early Doors	144
Trainwreck	144
Western Ryder	144

10yr winning average RPR: 157

BALLYMORE

This year's top rated	RPR
Samcro	154
Cracking Smart	153
Next Destination	152
Getabird	152
On The Blind Side	152
Summerville Boy	150
Poetic Rhythm	149
Vinndication	149
Mr Whipped	148
Red River	148
Fabulous Saga	147
Sharjah	147
Duc Des Genievres	146

10yr winning average RPR: 155

TRIUMPH

This year's top rated	RPR
Apple's Shakira*	144
Stormy Ireland*	143
Mr Adjudicator	142
Farclas	141
Espoir D'Allen	140
We Have A Dream	138
Mitchouka	136
Gumball	135
Sussex Ranger	135
Pesk Ebrel	132

10yr winning average RPR: 151

*Includes 7lb mares' allowance

He is obviously very talented but connections are eager to put a lid on the hype, especially as at the moment he may not even be the best novice hurdler in Ireland.

There aren't many Irish novices with the potential to be better than Samcro, but Supreme Novices' Hurdle favourite Getabird (152) is certainly a live contender.

Willie Mullins's six-year-old was a top-notch bumper horse last season and has racked up two easy victories this season, most recently beating Grade 1 winner Mengli Khan (150) by nine lengths.

Mullins and owner Rich Ricci have a great record in the Supreme, with three winners and a second from their last four runners, and the super-slick jumping Getabird showed at Punchestown in January must give them a great chance of adding another win in the festival curtain-raiser.

The biggest dangers could be Kalashnikov (153), who impressed when winning the Betfair Hurdle, and Summerville Boy (150), who got the better of Kalashnikov in the Tolworth.

On The Blind Side (152) leads the British charge in the Ballymore. He looked really impressive when winning at Sandown and has a course-and-distance success to his name, so he will have fans among those looking to get Samcro beaten.

Apple's Shakira (144) looks the one to beat in the Triumph Hurdle after cosy wins in three separate Cheltenham trials.

She is unbeaten in four career starts, has never come close to defeat, and with course form in the book it's hard to see her not running a good race.

She has a bit to find to match the ten-year average RPR for Triumph winners (151), but that's standard for the race as the last ten winners improved on their peak ratings by an average of 10lb on the day.

Willie Mullins has two interesting contenders with Mr Adjudicator (142), who won the Spring Juvenile at Leopardstown, and Stormy Ireland (143), who scored by 58 lengths on her first start in Ireland after being bought from France.

Either of those could step forward again and give the favourite a race, as could a few others including We Have A Dream (138), Sao (129) and Redicean (128).

Cracking Smart (153) is another who could rival Getabird and Samcro for leading Irish novice honours this season.

He was caught out for speed over 2m4f in Ireland on his last two starts, staying on late to finish second behind Next Destination (152) in small-field contests where his stamina did not come into play.

He is set to contest the Albert Bartlett over 3m, which should be more his cup of tea and could see him gain revenge on Next Destination.

Kim Bailey's improving Red River (148) could prove best of the Brits after getting the better of Mr Whipped (148) over 3m at Musselburgh last time.

Racing's Leading International Media Rights Company

+44 1666 822 769   racing@hbamedia.tv   www.hbamedia.tv

A Henry Birtles Associates Company

Festival ace Respect on the road to golden glory

By Dave Edwards

GOLD CUP Eight of the last ten Gold Cup winners had achieved a pre-race Topspeed rating above 150 and in the race itself a rating of at least 157 has been needed for victory on eight occasions. With a career-best of just 139, leading fancy Might Bite is a glaring omission from the accompanying tables and has plenty to prove on this timepiece.

The ante-post favourite is worth taking on with Road To Respect (above). Several above him in the rankings have questions to answer but his performance on the clock when winning the Plate handicap chase at last year's festival stacked up pretty well. He underlined his progress with a determined success in the Leopardstown Christmas Chase and several potential Gold Cup rivals, including last year's winner Sizing John, were well held. Admirably tough and consistent, he will be suited by the trip and, although he only just scrapes into the list, he looks a major player.

Sizing John was clearly below par last time and should not be written off. Native River, third last year, looked as good as ever on his recent Newbury return and goes to the festival much fresher this time.

CHAMPION HURDLE Only the brave or foolish would take on last year's winner Buveur D'Air. Nicky Henderson's highly polished performer earned a Topspeed of 160 with his imperious victory 12 months ago and that figure has been bettered just twice in the past decade. His three wins this season have been in moderately paced events and merely confirmed that he is in a league of his own.

Worthwhile opposition is thin on the ground and it would be no surprise to see My Tent Or Yours finish runner-up for the fourth time even at the age of 11. He has a Cheltenham timeline far superior to most and looks as good as ever this season.

Faugheen earned a Topspeed of 132 when successful in 2015 – making him the lowest-rated winner in the last ten years – and his recent lacklustre efforts suggest he has a mountain to climb to regain the hurdling crown. On the clock, the others look out of their depth.

CHAMPION CHASE The average winning Topspeed rating in the past decade is almost 160, with at least 153 needed to land the race on eight occasions, and just a couple of previous winners lined up with a pre-race figure below 154.

Last season's Arkle winner Altior is difficult to oppose. Five from five over hurdles and a magnificent seven out of seven over fences, Nicky Henderson's spring-heeled favourite cruised home on his recent reappearance at Newbury and looks a cut above his potential rivals.

Doubts remain over the participation of

GOLD CUP

Topspeed figures	Career best	Season best
Djakadam	163	104
Cue Card	161	154
Sizing John	158	112
Sub Lieutenant	157	101
Valseur Lido	157	125
Minella Rocco	155	130
Native River	154	136
The Last Samuri	154	151
Blaklion	153	153
Road To Respect	150	141
Saphir Du Rheu	150	97

How the past ten winners rated

Year Winner	Win TS	Pre-race TS
2017 Sizing John	158	146
2016 Don Cossack	167	165
2015 Coneygree	169	152
2014 Lord Windermere	144	123
2013 Bobs Worth	144	164
2012 Synchronised	164	151
2011 Long Run	157	163
2010 Imperial Commander	180	173
2009 Kauto Star	172	176
2008 Denman	178	157

CHAMPION HURDLE

Topspeed figures	Career best	Season best
Buveur D'Air	160	114
My Tent Or Yours	159	123
Faugheen	152	139
Wicklow Brave	147	-
Min	145	138
Apple's Jade*	142	97
Melon	142	130
Elgin**	140	106
Identity Thief	140	99
Pingshou	139	-
Verdana Blue*	139	139

*Includes 7lb mares' allowance
**Needs to be supplemented

How the past ten winners rated

Year Winner	Win TS	Pre-race TS
2017 Buveur D'Air	160	143
2016 Annie Power	154	139
2015 Faugheen	132	141
2014 Jezki	160	151
2013 Hurricane Fly	135	161
2012 Rock On Ruby	167	160
2011 Hurricane Fly	149	153
2010 Binocular	163	158
2009 Punjabi	155	160
2008 Katchit	157	157

Altior cruises home in last year's Arkle and he's hard to oppose in the Champion Chase this time

last year's beaten favourite Douvan, who has not been sighted since, but even at his best he would struggle against Altior. Min, who romped home at Leopardstown recently, looks the main stumbling block and should at least make a race of it.

Special Tiara and Fox Norton were separated by a whisker 12 months ago but both have something to prove and are likely to be vying for minor honours this time.

STAYERS' HURDLE This race does not always develop into a stamina test and only four of the last ten winners broke the 150 mark, with Nichols Canyon last year and Solwhit in 2013 being high-class two-milers who used their finishing speed to devastating effect. A pre-race best of at least 154 has been achieved by four winners but the average is 146 and that puts plenty in the mix, although leading hopeful Sam Spinner with a career-best 124 is well short of that yardstick.

The New One has won six of his 14 starts at Cheltenham and, although his best speed figures have been earned at around 2m, he won the Neptune (2m5f) here in 2013. If the race unfolds in its customary fashion, he could have too many guns for his rivals.

RYANAIR CHASE The figures prove that this race has evolved into a true championship test, with each of the last ten winners needing to go above 150 to prevail and only three having a pre-race best below that level.

Plenty are in contention on the figures but Un De Sceaux was scintillating 12 months ago and it will take an exceptional performance to lower his colours. Apart from the odd mistake, he jumped with aplomb in last year's race and once in front his pace and exuberance had his rivals toiling. He has won both starts this season with the minimum of fuss and is a worthy favourite.

Last year's runner-up Sub Lieutenant and Fox Norton, who claimed the scalp of Un De Sceaux over 2m at Punchestown in April, could make the frame.

CHAMPION CHASE

Topspeed figures	Career best	Season best
Douvan	159	-
Un De Sceaux	158	145
Special Tiara	156	138
Altior	154	146
Fox Norton	153	148
Min	152	152
God's Own	150	130
Ar Mad	148	132
The Game Changer	146	122
Top Gamble	146	115
Top Notch	143	143
Politologue	141	141

How the past ten winners rated

Year	Winner	Win TS	Pre-race TS
2017	Special Tiara	154	156
2016	Sprinter Sacre	159	165
2015	Dodging Bullets	144	159
2014	Sire De Grugy	152	158
2013	Sprinter Sacre	153	165
2012	Finian's Rainbow	159	154
2011	Sizing Europe	146	166
2010	Big Zeb	168	159
2009	Master Minded	161	185
2008	Master Minded	185	143

The New One could be the one for Stayers' glory, while Un De Sceaux (right) will be tough to beat in the Ryanair

STAYERS' HURDLE

Topspeed figures	Career best	Season best
The New One	156	150
Faugheen	152	139
Yanworth	145	-
Lil Rockerfeller	144	108
Diakali	144	-
L'Ami Serge	143	122
Apple's Jade*	142	97
The Worlds End	141	115
Unowhatimeanharry	141	125
Penhill	138	-
Old Guard	138	131

*Includes 7lb mares' allowance

How the past ten winners rated

Year Winner	Win TS	Pre-race TS
2017 Nichols Canyon	145	156
2016 Thistlecrack	158	133
2015 Cole Harden	151	135
2014 More Of That	135	118
2013 Solwhit	31	167
2012 Big Buck's	161	154
2011 Big Buck's	119	147
2010 Big Buck's	139	147
2009 Big Buck's	131	147
2008 Inglis Drever	175	162

RYANAIR CHASE

Topspeed figures	Career best	Season best
Djakadam	163	104
Cue Card	161	154
Douvan	159	-
Un De Sceaux	158	145
Sub Lieutenant	157	101
Valseur Lido	157	125
Waiting Patiently	157	157
Fox Norton	153	148
Min	152	152
Aso	151	104
God's Own	150	130
Ar Mad	148	132

How the past ten winners rated

Year Winner	Win TS	Pre-race TS
2017 Un De Sceaux	158	155
2016 Vautour	163	150
2015 Uxizandre	163	130
2014 Dynaste	160	127
2013 Cue Card	151	156
2012 Riverside Theatre	162	160
2011 Albertas Run	157	152
2010 Albertas Run	152	148
2009 Imperial Commander	159	160
2008 Our Vic	158	162

David Carr and Dave Randall assess five of last year's winners

Buveur D'Air

Hurdling was plan B last season but it's the only thing on the agenda this term and 2017-18 could hardly have gone much better for the reigning champion, who is on a winning run of nine races over hurdles and fences.

Buveur D'Air went chasing last winter, winning two out of two over fences, yet the decision to switch back in mid-season was richly rewarded as he won his warm-up race at Sandown and then gave Nicky Henderson a record sixth Champion Hurdle triumph at Cheltenham before following up in Grade 1 company at Aintree.

Things have been much more straightforward this term in the Fighting Fifth Hurdle, Christmas Hurdle and Contenders Hurdle – he was long odds-on for each race and not unduly troubled in any of them.

The accidental hurdler is now red-hot favourite to become the first horse to win back-to-back Champions since Hardy Eustace in 2004 and 2005.

Sizing John

Last year it was his stamina that punters had to take

on trust, this time it's his wellbeing.

Sizing John had never raced beyond 2m4f prior to landing the 3m Irish Gold Cup and the 3m2½f Cheltenham Gold Cup last season.

He looked the one to beat again when making a successful return in the John Durkan Chase at Punchestown in December, only to run a stinker in the Leopardstown Christmas Chase.

Jessica Harrington feels that race may have come too soon and has kept him fresh for March, so there will be no more clues as to whether he's in the shape to become the first to retain the Gold Cup crown since Best Mate.

Un De Sceaux

Un De Sceaux will be favourite for the Ryanair Chase once again, that goes without saying.

He has topped the betting in 23 of his 24 races since joining Willie Mullins. The only exception was when he was unable to gain revenge on his Champion Chase conqueror Sprinter Sacre at Sandown in 2016.

The free-running, bold-jumping ten-year-old has rewarded his backers on 18 of those 23 occasions, notably when winning the Ryanair with authority last season.

And few who have seen Un De Sceaux bolt up at Cork

Back for more: Un De Sceaux (left) and Road To Respect

and victory in the Grade 1 Leopardstown Christmas Chase, when he wore a hood for the first time and recorded a career-high RPR of 169.

Having skipped the Dublin Racing Festival, he will arrive fresh with significant each-way claims for the Gold Cup, with a Ryanair entry in reserve if conditions are softer.

Presenting Percy
Patrick Kelly's second consecutive Pertemps Handicap Hurdle winner was even more impressive than the first, Mall Dini in 2016, as he scored by almost four lengths off a mark of 146 that gave him near top weight of 11st 11lb. He was then well beaten in a Grade 1 novice hurdle at Punchestown but has resumed his upward progress this season.

Having won at Galway and finished third at Punchestown in his first two chases, the son of Sir Percy hacked up off 145 in a handicap chase over 3m5f, readily won the Grade 2 Galmoy Hurdle and then finished second to Irish Grand National winner Our Duke in the Red Mills Chase.

He is a leading RSA Chase candidate, with the longer National Hunt Chase as a back-up option.

and Ascot in his two runs this term would bet heavily against him doing the same again.

Road To Respect
Road To Respect hasn't looked back since joining Noel Meade from Eoin Griffin at the beginning of last season and his first campaign culminated in festival success as a novice in the 2m5f Stable Plate before a first Grade 1 win in the Ryanair Gold Cup against a wayward Yorkhill.

This season he has moved into the top rank of chasers in Ireland, following a reappearance Grade 3 win with a close second in the Champion Chase at Down Royal

Our Duke can ensure coveted crown stays with Harrington

Racing Post analysts Richard Lowther and Dave Orton assess the big winter action

GOLD CUP The King George VI Chase is not always the best of Gold Cup trials, with Long Run in 2011 the last horse to win both races in the same season, but this term's King George winner Might Bite deservedly heads the Timico Cheltenham Gold Cup market.

A one-length defeat of Double Shuffle at Kempton needs improving upon, but it doesn't tell the whole story as he was doing little in front. While there's no doubting his class, Might Bite has twice hung badly to his right up the Cheltenham hill, almost throwing away the RSA Chase last year, and there must be a real chance he'll do it again. The Gold Cup will test his stamina to the full too.

Colin Tizzard purposely kept Native River fresh for a spring campaign and the chestnut made a pleasing return in the Denman Chase at Newbury, a race he won en route to third spot in last year's Gold Cup. He had only two opponents this time but RPRs have him not far off his best and he looks set for a big run at Cheltenham, although a slight doubt is that he has yet to win in four visits to the track.

Last year's winner Sizing John got his season off to a bright start in the John Durkan Memorial at Punchestown, jumping flawlessly after an early mistake, but his reputation then took a dent as he could finish only seventh in the Leopardstown Christmas Chase. He obviously wasn't himself that day – it's the only time he has ever finished out of the first three over jumps – and Jessica Harrington believes the race came too soon for him. He has something to prove now.

Harrington has another gunning for Gold Cup glory in Our Duke, a brilliant winner of last Easter's Irish Grand National. His return to the track at Down Royal proved a write-off and he underwent minor back surgery before returning in the Irish Gold Cup at Leopardstown in February, where he would have finished closer had he not blundered at the second-last. Two weeks later he was back on top form in winning the Red Mills Chase at Gowran Park by a length from leading novice chaser Presenting Percy. He isn't always the tidiest of jumpers, but the stamina demands of the race will suit him.

Another who has to allay concerns over his jumping is Killultagh Vic, who was in front when falling foul of Leopardstown's final fence in the Gold Cup. He won a Punchestown hurdle in December after nearly two years off the track and Cheltenham will be just his fourth run over fences. The Leopardstown run confirms he needs to make only minor improvement to trouble the best.

Killultagh Vic's fall left Outlander in front, but he was run down by Edwulf close home. The winner nearly died at last year's festival but made a miraculous recovery and is clearly made of stern stuff. He stays very well but the Leopardstown form is questionable.

The Irish Gold Cup third, Djakadam, has figured large in the last three Gold Cups, but he has won only once over 3m-plus and has not been at his best this term.

You need to go back to 1993 to find the last northern-trained Gold Cup winner, but Definitly Red is a genuine candidate. Brian Ellison's nine-year-old toughed it out in testing ground to land the Cotswold Chase in January, proving his effectiveness at Cheltenham, and he won't fail through any stamina shortage. He's fully effective in a quagmire but his trainer thinks he'll be better on good ground.

Road To Respect beat several Gold Cup entries in the Leopardstown Christmas Chase and will go to Cheltenham a fresh horse. He'll appreciate drying conditions, having won the Plate on good ground at last year's festival, and is young enough to improve further.

Verdict Might Bite looks vulnerable and Jessica Harrington can win it again, but this time with Our Duke. Native River can chase him home *(Richard Lowther)*

Our Duke (left) battles with Presenting Percy before winning the Grade 2 Red Mills Chase at Gowran Park

Vital statistics

Races with the 'festival factor'

BetVictor Gold Cup

Cheltenham, November 18, 2017, 2m4½f, soft

1 **Splash Of Ginge** 9 10-6 T Bellamy 25-1
2 **Starchitect** 6 11-2 T Scudamore 10-1
3 **Le Prezien** 6 11-8 B Geraghty 6-1
4 **Ballyalton** 10 11-1 T O'Brien 8-1
Trainer: Nigel Twiston-Davies
Distances: nk, 2½l, 3¾l; 17 ran

Festival pointer This has been one of the better races for finding a festival winner and, while none has emerged in the past three years, five of last year's first seven would have rewarded each-way backers with top-four finishes at the festival. Four of the first five Ryanair winners came out of this race (and the other was a former winner of this race) but it has not had the same influence in recent years

🐎*Three festival winners have come out of this race in the past ten years*

Betfair Chase

Haydock, November 25, 2017, 3m1½f, heavy

1 **Bristol De Mai** 6 11-7 D Jacob 11-10f
2 **Cue Card** 11 11-7 H Cobden 2-1
3 **Outlander** 9 11-7 J Kennedy 5-1
Trainer: Nigel Twiston-Davies
Distances: 57l, 9l; 6 ran

Festival pointer Betfair Chase winners to run in the Gold Cup had finishing positions of 012P3PPF7FF (only Kauto Star in 2006-07 has won both in the same season)

🐎*Three festival winners in the past ten years*

Races with the 'festival factor'

Unibet Fighting Fifth Hurdle

Newcastle, December 2, 2017, 2m½f, soft

1 **Buveur D'Air** 6 11-7 B Geraghty 1-6f

2 **Irving** 9 11-7 S Bowen 9-2

3 **Flying Tiger** 4 11-7 T Scudamore 9-1

Trainer: Nicky Henderson

Distances: 3½l, 1l; 5 ran

Festival pointer The key British trial for the Champion Hurdle in recent years, featuring the winners of 2008, 2009 and 2010, the runner-up in 2011, 2012, 2014 and 2015 and the third in 2013 and 2017 (their respective finishing positions in the Fighting Fifth were 31511113F). Apple's Jade, runner-up last season, went on to win the Mares' Hurdle. Only Punjabi (2008-09) has done the Fighting Fifth-Champion double in the past 20 years

🐎 *Four festival winners in the past ten years*

Ladbrokes Trophy Chase

Newbury, December 2, 2017, 3m2f, good to soft

1 **Total Recall** 8 10-8 P Townend 9-2f

2 **Whisper** 9 11-8 D Russell 8-1

3 **Regal Encore** 9 10-11 R McLernon 66-1

4 **Braqueur D'Or** 6 10-0 H Cobden 33-1

Trainer: Willie Mullins

Distances: nk, 9l, 3¾l; 20 ran

Festival pointer Five of the past six runnings of this often informative race have featured a subsequent festival winner, most recently Un Temps Pour Tout (tenth here, won Ultima Handicap Chase). The 2014 Gold Cup winner Lord Windermere had finished eighth here that season; before that Denman (2007-08) and Bobs Worth (2012-13) completed the Hennessy-Gold Cup double and the 2011, 2012 and 2015 Gold Cup runners-up came from this race

🐎 *Seven festival winners in the past ten years*

My Tent Or Yours: looks set to finish second to stablemate Buveur D'Air at best

CHAMPION HURDLE Genuine candidates for the hurdling crown are in short supply. Current champ Buveur D'Air has cemented his place at the head of the betting, with the next two in the market, Faugheen and My Tent Or Yours, aged ten and 11 respectively. Only Hatton's Grace and Sea Pigeon have won the race aged in double figures.

Buveur D'Air hasn't been seriously tested in three starts this season, beginning with an easy win in the Fighting Fifth at Newcastle. Another Grade 1 success followed in Kempton's Christmas Hurdle, where The New One gave him most to do, before he easily accounted for two rivals in the Contenders Hurdle at Sandown. Nicky Henderson's main problem will be getting enough work into this burly individual, who rates a worthy odds-on chance to become the 15th horse to win the race more than once.

The 2015 champion Faugheen had been sidelined for 22 months before the Morgiana Hurdle at Punchestown in November, where a 16-length victory showed that much of his old ability was intact. Hopes were high for Faugheen in the Ryanair Hurdle at Leopardstown's Christmas meeting, but he was pulled up two from home and quickly dismounted. Fears that was the last we'd seen of him proved unfounded and he was more like his old self in the Irish Champion Hurdle in February. It was still disappointing that he was outspeeded by Supasundae, who is earmarked for the Stayers' Hurdle, and it may well be that Faugheen needs further than 2m these days.

Carrying JP McManus's first colours in last season's Champion Hurdle, My Tent Or Yours finished four and a half lengths behind Buveur D'Air, the third time he had finished runner-up in the big one. He has appeared just once this

Vital statistics

Races with the 'festival factor'

Betfair Tingle Creek Chase

Sandown, December 9, 2017, 1m7½f, good to soft

1 **Politologue** 6 11-7 H Cobden 7-2

2 **Fox Norton** 7 11-7 R Power 8-13f

3 **Ar Mad** 7 11-7 Josh Moore 8-1

Trainer: Paul Nicholls

Distances: ½l, 5l; 6 ran

Festival pointer The key guide to the Champion Chase. Seven of the 19 to try have won both races since the Tingle Creek became a Grade 1 and the Champion Chase winner had run in the Tingle Creek in 11 of the past 17 years. Last season's winner Un De Sceaux went on to land the Ryanair Chase

🐎*Six festival winners in the past ten years*

Caspian Caviar Gold Cup

Cheltenham, December 16, 2017, 2m5f, soft

1 **Guitar Pete** 7 10-2 R Day 9-1

2 **Clan Des Obeaux** 5 11-12 H Cobden 3-1f

3 **King's Odyssey** 8 10-11 A Wedge 9-1

4 **Ballyalton** 10 11-0 T O'Brien 15-2

Trainer: Nicky Richards

Distances: 2¾l, 5l, 1¾l; 10 ran

Festival pointer None of the festival scorers to come out of this race in the past ten years had won here, with the latest example being 2015 fifth Darna, who went on to land the Brown Advisory & Merriebelle Stable Plate. The first three Ryanair Chase winners ran in this race (form figures of 2B3) but none has since and nowadays it is more likely to be a guide to the handicap chases

🐎*Three festival winners in the past ten years*

Vital statistics

Races with the 'festival factor'

Unibet International Hurdle

Cheltenham, December 16, 2017, 2m1f, soft

1 **My Tent Or Yours** 10 11-0 B Geraghty 5-1

2 **The New One** 9 11-6 S Twiston-Davies 5-2

3 **Melon** 5 11-6 David Mullins 7-4f

Trainer: Nicky Henderson

Distances: 1¼l, 1l; 7 ran

Festival pointer Rooster Booster (2002-03) is the only winner of this race to land the Champion Hurdle since Comedy Of Errors (1974-75) and it has been a poor guide recently, with Katchit the only runner to have gone on to festival success in the past decade. In the past 20 years, two who were beaten here went on to take the Champion Hurdle crown and four of the last eight winners to line up in the Champion finished in the first three

🐎*One festival winner in the past ten years*

32Red King George VI Chase

Kempton, December 26, 2017, 3m, soft

1 **Might Bite** 8 11-10 N de Boinville 6-4f

2 **Double Shuffle** 7 11-10 A Heskin 50-1

3 **Tea For Two** 8 11-10 L Kelly 20-1

Trainer: Nicky Henderson

Distances: 1l, 2l; 8 ran

Festival pointer Seven of the last ten festivals have featured at least one winner who had run here. Desert Orchid (1988-89) was the last to complete the King George/Gold Cup double until 2002-2003, since when the double has been done by five of the 11 to try. Since Desert Orchid, 25 festival winners have come out of this race (in the Gold Cup, Champion Chase or Ryanair Chase)

🐎*Ten festival winners in the past ten years*

season, landing the International Hurdle over the New course at Cheltenham in December. He battled on grittily to see off old foe The New One and has been kept fresh since for another bite at the Champion Hurdle cherry. It's hard to see him proving good enough at this stage of his career but he may well run into a place again.

In the International the eye was drawn to how well Melon travelled, but Faugheen's stablemate found less than his two battle-hardened rivals up the final hill. A hood was enlisted when he next appeared, in the Irish Champion, but although he settled well enough the response under pressure was sorely lacking and he finished only fifth.

Verdict It could be a repeat of last year as it's very hard to look past Buveur D'Air and My Tent Or Yours may have to settle for second again *(Richard Lowther)*

Vital statistics

Races with the 'festival factor'

Unibet Christmas Hurdle

Kempton, December 26, 2017, 2m, soft

1 **Buveur D'Air** 6 11-7 B Geraghty 2-11f
2 **The New One** 9 11-7 S Twiston-Davies 5-1
3 **Mohaayed** 5 11-7 H Skelton 20-1

Trainer: Nicky Henderson

Distances: 2¼l, 3¾l; 4 ran

Festival pointer Faugheen in 2014-15 is the only one to have completed the Christmas/ Champion Hurdle double since Kribensis (1989-90). Four beaten horses in the past 16 runnings have landed the Champion (the most recent was 2011 runner-up Rock On Ruby)

🏇Four festival winners in the past ten years

Leopardstown Christmas Chase

Leopardstown, December 28, 2017, 3m, yielding

1 **Road To Respect** 6 11-10 S Flanagan 8-1
2 **Balko Des Flos** 6 11-10 D O'Regan 66-1
3 **Outlander** 9 11-10 R Blackmore 16-1

Trainer: Noel Meade

Distances: 1¼l, 2¼l; 12 ran

Festival pointer Four of the past 12 runnings have featured that season's Gold Cup winner. Two were British raiders who won here (Denman and Synchronised) while the two Irish-trained Gold Cup winners to come out of this race were both beaten here (War Of Attrition was runner-up and Lord Windermere was seventh)

🏇Three festival winners in the past ten years

Vital statistics

Races with the 'festival factor'

Galliardhomes.com Cleeve Hurdle

Cheltenham, January 27, 2018, 3m, heavy

1 **Agrapart** 7 11-6 L Kelly 9-1
2 **Wholestone** 7 11-6 D Jacob 9-2
3 **Colin's Sister** 7 10-13 P Brennan 10-1

Trainer: Nick Williams

Distances: 3l, 8l; 9 ran

Festival pointer Principally a World Hurdle trial (four of the past ten winners did the double, most recently Thistlecrack in 2016) but has been used as a successful prep for a variety of races – the Champion Hurdle, National Hunt Chase and Ultima Handicap Chase (four times in the past eight years, most recently with Un Temps Pour Tout last year)

🏇Nine festival winners in the past ten years

BHP Insurance Irish Champion Hurdle

Leopardstown, February 3, 2018, 2m, soft

1 **Supasundae** 8 11-10 R Power 8-1
2 **Faugheen** 10 11-10 P Townend 9-10f
3 **Mick Jazz** 7 11-10 D Russell 8-1

Trainer: Jessica Harrington

Distances: 2¼l, 4¾l; 8 ran

Festival pointer The most important hurdle race in Ireland before the festival, with eight of the 12 Irish-trained winners in the past 19 runnings of the Champion Hurdle having run here (six won). Nichols Canyon fell at the last in 2017 before moving up in trip to land the Stayers' Hurdle

🏇Four festival winners in the past ten years

CHAMPION CHASE and RYANAIR CHASE

A Champion Chase picture that looked rather cloudy at the beginning of February became a lot clearer once Altior had returned to the track. Last year's Racing Post Arkle hero was forced to miss his intended comeback in the Tingle Creek due to a wind issue and needed minor surgery on his larynx. He, and his supporters, could breathe easier when he toyed with Politologue in the Game Spirit at Newbury. A four-length victory downplays his superiority and he'll be even more effective on the likely better ground.

Second favourite for the Champion Chase is Min, who won a three-runner race at Gowran Park before beating Simply Ned half a length in the Grade 1 Paddy's Rewards Club Chase at Leopardstown over Christmas, although the placings were reversed by the stewards. The pair locked horns again over the same track and trip in the Dublin Chase in February, Min winning by 12 lengths in a quick time. The only time he hasn't been first past the post for Willie Mullins was in the 2016 Supreme Novices' Hurdle, where Altior proved seven lengths his superior.

Third in the Dublin Chase was Special Tiara, a regular in the top two-mile events for five seasons and winner of the big one last year. This exuberant jumper will run his heart out again, with spring ground sure to suit him, but will surely find a couple too good.

Politologue cashed in on the absence of Altior and Douvan to take the Tingle Creek, holding off Fox Norton up the final hill. The grey added the Desert Orchid Chase at Kempton, helped by the fall of Special Tiara before the race had heated up, but Altior cantered all over him at Newbury. Some cut in the ground would help Politologue at Cheltenham.

Fox Norton had to miss the Game Spirit after picking up a foot infection. An experiment with three miles in the King George failed to pay off, but he had shown smart form in winning the Shloer Chase at Cheltenham's November meeting before making Politologue sweat at Sandown.

Eight of the 21 horses holding a Champion Chase entry at the time of writing, including Fox Norton, also have the option of the Ryanair Chase a day later.

These include Un De Sceaux, who flew home in the 2017 Ryanair and is two from two this term. A routine win at Cork was followed by a more meaningful performance in Ascot's Clarence House Chase, in which his closest pursuer, Brain Power, fell at the second-last. Un De Sceaux has stuck to two miles since last season's festival but the plan is for him to defend his Ryanair crown. This remarkable horse has finished out of the first two just once in 24 completed starts.

A win for Waiting Patiently would be hugely popular following the death of trainer Malcolm Jefferson, whose daughter Ruth has taken over at Newstead Cottage Stables. The seven-year-old is unbeaten in six chases and he was impressive at Kempton in January and when landing his first Grade 1 win in the Ascot Chase. He'll face an even sterner test if he is given the green light for the Ryanair but the likely decent gallop would benefit him.

One who seems sure to go the Ryanair route is Top Notch, who won his first two starts over fences this season before finishing fourth in the Ascot Chase. Despite worthy efforts at the last three festivals, he doesn't have a Cheltenham win on his CV.

Ryanair chief Michael O'Leary would love to win his own race and his number one candidate looks to be Balko Des Flos. The

Galway Plate winner was below that level on his next two starts before posting a career best in the Leopardstown Christmas Chase, where he split fellow Gigginstown runners Road To Respect and Outlander. That came over three miles, but he'll be just as happy back in trip and a quicker surface will be right up his street.

Verdict Altior is unbeaten in a dozen races over obstacles and can make it lucky 13 in the Champion Chase. Balko Des Flos can topple Un De Sceaux in the Ryanair Chase *(Richard Lowther)*

STAYERS' HURDLE After taking the scalp of Faugheen in the Irish Champion Hurdle back down to 2m at Leopardstown in February, Supasundae was unsurprisingly promoted to the top of the ante-post market for the Sun Bets Stayers' Hurdle. That win was preceded by a narrow defeat to Apple's Jade at the same venue in December over 3m in the Grade 1 Christmas Hurdle and there's no doubt Jessica Harrington's eight-year-old is a big player as he bids to add to his 2017 Coral Cup success.

However, he has yet to win over this far and would be vulnerable if owners Gigginstown Stud sanctioned Apple's Jade's participation, rather than the easier option of defending the OLGB Mares' Hurdle, with her 7lb sex allowance a big advantage. Gordon Elliott's mare made it 3-3 for the season at Christmas despite substitute rider Davy Russell, by his

Supasundae bags the Irish Champion Hurdle and shoots to Stayers' Hurdle favouritism

own admission, leaving her challenge late in the piece. She's better than the bare result, has top festival form and would prove hard to stop if taking her chance.

The Irish challenge is clearly strong again this season, with last year's Albert Bartlett winner Penhill a potential fly in the ointment for Willie Mullins. Despite being absent since his defeat at last year's Punchestown festival, he has been solid in the ante-post betting and remains unexposed as a stayer. Victory would be a big ask, but his novice form is hard to knock.

The British contingent is headed by Sam Spinner, who took his form to the next level when making all in the Grade 1 Long Walk Hurdle at Ascot in December. He has been a real success story for trainer Jedd O'Keeffe, who has deliberately kept him fresh since, and he is still only a six-year-old, which makes further improvement likely. The doubt about him is a lack of Cheltenham form and the strong likelihood of being taken on for the lead, but reverting to quicker ground wouldn't pose too much of an issue.

The Ascot form is solid, with decent benchmark Unowhatimeanharry ten lengths away in third, although the runner-up L'Ami Serge has decent claims of gaining revenge. This highly talented performer subsequently finished a close third in the Sky Bet Handicap Chase at Doncaster and is fully proven around Cheltenham. He should get the strong pace he craves and makes definite each-way appeal if he reverts to hurdles, as seems likely.

The same owners have the consistent Wholestone, who readily took the Relkeel at Cheltenham on New Year's Day before failing to confirm that form with runner-up Agrapart back up to 3m in the Cleeve Hurdle on Trials Day next time out. The winner didn't even hold a Stayers' entry on account of the likely better going in March, while the issue with Wholestone, as was evident behind Penhill at last year's festival, is that 3m stretches his stamina to the limit.

Yanworth would be respected if Alan King

abandons chasing for a return to hurdles. He saw off Supasundae at Aintree's Grand National meeting last year but it remains to be seen whether he is quite the same force.

Verdict If allowed to take her chance, Apple's Jade would be a confident selection to see off old rival Supasundae again. In her absence Jessica Harrington's runner should take some beating, although L'Ami Serge is a viable each-way alternative (Dave Orton)

NOVICE CHASES The Racing Post Arkle has gone the way of an odds-on favourite in five of the past six seasons and the ante-post betting has been dominated by Footpad since he embarked on a novice chase campaign with a bloodless win at Navan in November. A step up to the Grade 1 Racing Post Novice Chase saw a mightily impressive display at Leopardstown's Christmas meeting and he bagged a hat-trick with a clear-cut success in the Irish Arkle back there in February. In beating Petit Mouchoir by five lengths there, with old rival Any Second Now way back in third, he took his chase form near the level shown by Willie Mullins' previous top-class Arkle winners Un De Sceaux and Douvan. A fine jumper, he acts on spring ground and is considered by many to be an Irish banker of the festival.

Petit Mouchoir's second in the Irish Arkle was his first outing since easily beating a decent benchmark on his chasing debut at Punchestown in October and there are sound reasons to think he can get closer in March. Last season he beat Footpad in the Irish Champion Hurdle and also had him one place behind when chasing home Buveur D'Air in the big one at the festival. He is entitled to improve for the run, and added experience, so he could make things interesting if ridden more positively again. He was happiest when dominating as a hurdler.

In the same ownership as Footpad, Alan King's Sceau Royal has come into his own as a novice chaser this term. Since being touched off by North Hill Harvey at Cheltenham's

GALLERY

LONDON

Country Excellence in London

October meeting, the compact six-year-old hasn't looked back and became Britain's leading candidate when taking the Henry VIII at Sandown in December, turning around that October form by 11 lengths. A subsequent win in the Grade 2 Lightning at Doncaster ensures he heads there high on confidence.

However, Sceau Royal was usurped as the top home challenger when Saint Calvados served up a treat in the Grade 2 Kingmaker at Warwick in February, making it 3-3 since joining Harry Whittington for a chasing career. The ex-French five-year-old came through handicaps prior to that, but at a high-class level, and his Warwick form is equal to that of Footpad. If he can mix it on quicker going he'll be the one they all have to catch.

The RSA needed some time to take shape but last year's Pertemps Final winner Presenting Percy set the ante-post market alight, following up an easy 3m5f handicap win over fences when successfully reverting to hurdles in the Grade 2 Galmoy at Gowran in January and then finishing second to Gold Cup candidate Our Duke in the Grade 2 Red Mills Chase, also at Gowran. Patrick Kelly's seven-year-old bounces off spring ground and ticks plenty of boxes.

The British challenge is headed by Paul Nicholls' Black Corton, who has been an amazing improver given that he kicked off over fences last summer. His Grade 1 win at Kempton on Boxing Day has been franked and he's 2-2 at Cheltenham.

Yanworth entered the equation when taking the Grade 2 Dipper at Cheltenham on New Year's Day. That form leaves him with plenty to find with the leading hopes, though, and if he stays over fences it's likely he'll go for the JLT instead.

Original RSA ante-post favourite Monalee gamely landed a red-hot Grade 1 Flogas Novice Chase at Leopardstown in February. That came off the back of a crunching fall there at the Christmas meeting and he did well to hold off the closers dropped back to 2m5f. Trainer Henry de Bromhead was quick

Vital statistics

Races with the 'festival factor'

Coral Hurdle

Leopardstown, February 3, 2018, 2m, soft

1 **Off You Go** 5 9-10 M Enright 6-1
2 **Deal D'Estruval** 5 10-0 K Walsh 9-1
3 **Grand Partner** 10 10-2 B Cooper 33-1
4 **Makitorix** 5 10-1 B Hayes 25-1

Trainer: Charles Byrnes

Distances: 1¼l, 2½l, 1¼l; 28 ran

Festival pointer Five of the nine Irish-trained County Hurdle winners in the past 15 years had run in this race (only Final Approach, in 2011, won both) – two of the other three ran in the Betfair Hurdle at Newbury. Xenophon followed up victory here by taking the Coral Cup in 2003

🐎 *Four festival winners in the past ten years*

Deloitte Novice Hurdle

Leopardstown, February 4, 2018, 2m, soft

1 **Samcro** 6 11-10 J Kennedy 4-6f
2 **Duc Des Genievres** 5 11-9 N Fehily 9-1
3 **Paloma Blue** 6 11-10 D Russell 16-1

Trainer: Gordon Elliott

Distances: 5½l, 3¾l; 11 ran

Festival pointer This race – reduced in distance this year to 2m – produced a festival winner each year from 2002 to 2004 and after a long gap enjoyed a resurgence with Champagne Fever, Vautour (both won here) and Windsor Park (second) scoring at the festivals of 2013, 2014 and 2015. While most winners over the old 2m2f trip since 2000 dropped back to land the Supreme, Windsor Park was a runner-up who stepped up to win the Ballymore over 2m5f (as did the top-class Istabraq and Danoli in the 1990s)

🐎 *Three festival winners in the past ten years*

to nominate the RSA as the target for last year's Albert Bartlett runner-up and reverting to a sounder surface should suit.

Monalee would also have solid claims if switched to the JLT, although the placed horses from the Flogas, the Mullins-trained pair Al Boum Photo and Invitation Only, would have chances of revenge.

The former is relatively unexposed and

THE REAL WOOD FURNITURE Co

We have been making beautiful furniture from British oak, burr oak, ash, elm and walnut since 1989, and have built a nationwide reputation for design, quality and customer service.

"Have nothing in your house that you do not know to be useful or believe to be beautiful..." William Morris

did some strong work at the finish that day, whereas Invitation Only showed a neat turn of foot having charted a wide course throughout. His clear-cut Grade 3 win at Punchestown in January rates sound form.

Although beaten by Yanworth in the Dipper, last year's Neptune (now Ballymore) winner Willoughby Court still held his position as ante-post favourite leader for the JLT. That was on the back of his convincing win over his old rival in the Grade 2 Ladbrokes Novice Chase in December, with a return to more aggressive tactics on quicker going expected to suit. The fact that trainer Ben Pauling went through a lean spell in January is another factor that points to a better showing.

Nicky Henderson saddled Top Notch to finish second in last year's JLT behind Yorkhill and, in the same ownership, his French recruit Terrefort came into consideration with a brave win over Cyrname in the Grade

1 Scilly Isles at Sandown in February. He's a superb jumper but he seems right at home on deep ground.

Verdict Saint Calvados is a value alternative to Footpad in what should be a fast and furious Arkle. Presenting Percy holds all the aces in the RSA and rates a solid favourite, while Invitation Only ought to make a bold bid to hand Willie Mullins a fifth JLT since its inception in 2011 *(Dave Orton)*

NOVICE HURDLES It took an age for the Supreme Novices' Hurdle market to come alive, but a worthy favourite emerged when Getabird hosed up in the Grade 2 Moscow Flyer Novice Hurdle at Punchestown in January. That made it 4-4 since he went under rules, he jumps particularly well and, being an

*Invitation Only should prove
a force in the JLT Chase*

SPORTING AGENCY
Experiences to last a lifetime in unforgettable locations

SHOOTING SCHOOL
Tuition for all ages and abilities with our professional instructors

AIR RIFLE RANGE
Nine covered lanes for practice, competition or a family day out

CORPORATE HOSPITALITY
Build relationships with clients or reward hard-working teams

GUN ROOM
Over 1000 quality new and used guns in stock at any one time

COUNTRY CLOTHING
Country clothing from top brands such as Harkila, Seeland & Schoffel

📞 01242 870391

IAN COLEY
GUNSHOP • SHOOTING SCHOOL
SPORTING AGENCY • COUNTRY CLOTHING

✉ info@iancoley.co.uk
🌐 www.iancoley.co.uk

Ian Coley Sporting Ltd | Nr. Andoversford | Cheltenham | Gloucestershire | GL54 4AX

Vital statistics

Races with the 'festival factor'

Flogas Novice Chase

Leopardstown, February 4, 2018, 2m5f, soft

1 **Monalee** 7 11-10 N Fehily 11-4jf

2 **Al Boum Photo** 6 11-10 David Mullins 9-1

3 **Invitation Only** 7 11-10 P Townend 7-2

Trainer: Henry de Bromhead

Distances: ¾l, hd; 11 ran

Festival pointer This has emerged as an excellent guide in recent years, with four of the last nine RSA Chase winners having run here (two won, one was second and the other was third), as well as an Arkle winner who finished second here and then dropped back in trip

🐎*Five festival winners in the past ten years*

Unibet Irish Gold Cup

Leopardstown, February 4, 2018, 3m, soft

1 **Edwulf** 9 11-10 D O'Connor 33-1

2 **Outlander** 10 11-10 J Kennedy 6-1

3 **Djakadam** 9 11-10 Patrick Mullins 13-2

Trainer: Joseph O'Brien

Distances: nk, 10l; 10 ran

Festival pointer Last year Sizing John became only the third winner since the race's inception in 1987 to land the Gold Cup in the same year, joining Jodami (1993) and Imperial Call (1996). Lord Windermere won the Gold Cup in 2014 after finishing sixth of seven here, while five more have placed in the Gold Cup in the past decade after running in this race (Minella Rocco unseated early last year before finishing runner-up to Sizing John at Cheltenham)

🐎*Two festival winners in the past ten years*

Vital statistics

Races with the 'festival factor'

Betfair Hurdle

Newbury, February 10, 2018, 2m½f, soft

1 **Kalashnikov** 5 11-5 J Quinlan 8-1cf

2 **Bleu Et Rouge** 7 11-10 B Geraghty 10-1

3 **Spiritofthegames** 6 11-0 B Andrews 20-1

4 **Coeur Blimey** 7 10-7 L Gardner 14-1

Trainer: Amy Murphy

Distances: 4½l, 8l, 9l; 24 ran

Festival pointer One abandonment means there have been only nine runnings of this valuable handicap hurdle in the past decade. The race is a good pointer, although Wicklow Brave (11th in 2015 before landing the County Hurdle at 25-1) is the only winner to emerge since 2010. However, also-rans from the last seven editions have gone on to take five seconds and five thirds at the festival

🐎*Two festival winners in the past ten years*

Betfair Ascot Chase

Ascot, February 17, 2018, 2m5f, soft

1 **Waiting Patiently** 7 11-7 B Hughes 2-1f

2 **Cue Card** 12 11-7 P Brennan 9-1

3 **Frodon** 6 11-7 B Frost 9-1

Trainer: Ruth Jefferson

Distances: 2¾l, 15l; 7 ran

Festival pointer A good guide to the Ryanair Chase, with four winners having prepped here (two of the last six Ryanair winners took this race first). In the past nine years, first-three finishers from this race have finished 25181316472P7 in the Ryanair.

🐎*Three festival winners in the past ten years*

Irish point winner, ought to relish the famous climb for home. Willie Mullins used the Moscow Flyer as a prep for previous winners Vautour and Douvan in the past decade.

Getabird won by nine lengths from the Gordon Elliott-trained Mengli Khan, who was the top Irish two-mile novice prior to that humbling defeat, having won the Grade 1 Royal Bond at Fairyhouse in November. That rival is a little better than the bare form, but it's hard to see placings being reversed.

The home challenge is spearheaded by Betfair Hurdle winner Kalashnikov, whose sole defeat came when runner-up to Summerville Boy in the Grade 1 Tolworth in January. The going was too taxing for him that day and, while it was sodden when he won Newbury's showpiece handicap in February, connections firmly expect he'll improve for quicker ground. He's a big player with an official rating of 154, although he's more exposed than the other market leaders.

NOW OPEN

STRATTON COURT
CIRENCESTER

Retire to our
Luxurious & Cotswold Apartments
Nursing Home

FREE*
SERVICE CHARGE
FOR THE FIRST YEAR
RRP: £7,000
TERMS & CONDITIONS APPLY

LUXURIOUS RETIREMENT APARTMENTS

Stratton Court offers an exclusive neighbourhood of 31 stunning apartments and luxury care facilities in the most beautiful environment. It boasts a collection of lifestyle collections that may well exceed expectations, including our fabulous Relaxation & Wellness Suite and Kensington Bar & Café.

Our prices range from **£337,000 - £650,000*** for a 1 or 2 bedroom apartment
*Annual Service Charges and Deferred (Event) fees apply.

NURSING HOME & UNIQUE COUPLE CARE SUITES

OPENING
OFFER:
£950*pp/pw
ONLY 10
SPACES LEFT
TERMS & CONDITIONS APPLY

Our Nursing Home has 61 boutique-style en-suite bedrooms, offering Residential, Residential Dementia, Nursing and Respite Care in the most elegant surroundings bordered by beautifully-landscaped gardens. You can rest assured that every last detail has been considered for the ultimate in comfort and care for our Residents. For individuals or couples wishing a larger space, our care suites offer that little extra sense of comfort:

Ideal for couples where one or both have care needs • 24hr Care on site • Dementia friendly • Generous lounge & dining area within the suite • Fully fitted kitchen • Unlimited tea, coffee and snacks throughout the day • Breakfast, lunch and dinner prepared by our award winning chefs • Secluded and secure sensory garden • Choice of relaxing lounges and dining areas throughout the Nursing Home • Cinema • Mayfair Café & Bar Mayfair Restaurant.

Prices - Nursing beds: **£1,350 - £1,650*** Couple Care Suites: **£2,000** pw/pa*
*Subject to Terms & Conditions.

VISIT OUR
OTHER SITES
ONLINE
auracareliving.com

CONTACT US TODAY

01285 283 132
enquiries@auracareliving.com
auracareliving.com

Knight Frank
Luxury Care Home Awards
AWARD WINNING

AURA
CARE LIVING

Stratton Court Village, Stratton, Cirencester, Gloucestershire, GL7 2NB

Harry Fry's If The Cap Fits also enters calculations. He made it 3-3 over hurdles in Kempton's opening novice hurdle on Boxing Day, the same prep used for Altior prior to his Supreme win in 2016. His level of form means he's got to step up plenty, although the six-year-old is a raw talent and the best of him has surely still to be seen.

If Samcro headed for the Supreme, the race would change complexion completely. Gordon Elliott's unbeaten six-year-old has shown rare brilliance since embarking over hurdles and a commanding win in Grade 3 company at Navan in November was followed by a romp in the Grade 1 Deloitte Hurdle at Leopardstown in February. That's a leading Supreme trial and he's clearly quick, although the vibes are that the Ballymore will be his preferred festival option.

The only potential chinks in his armour are a likely switch to quicker ground and his ability to cope with Cheltenham. It would be a shock if he didn't overcome both obstacles, however.

The main opposition to Samcro on form in the Ballymore is On The Blind Side, a highly progressive ex-Irish point winner who lines up bidding to make it 4-4 over hurdles for champion trainer Nicky Henderson. His Grade 2 course win in November is rock-solid form and he defied a penalty with ease when winning at the same level in the Winter Novices' Hurdle in December, usually a decent pointer for the Ballymore. He ought to have a big say, although a run since the turn of the year would have been preferred.

Willie Mullins' leading Ballymore contender is Next Destination, who made the frame in the Champion Bumper last year and is unbeaten over hurdles. He slammed Elliott's Listed winner Cracking Smart in the Grade 2 Navan Novice Hurdle in December before readily beating the same rival despite a steady gallop in the Grade 1 Lawlor's of Naas Novice Hurdle the following month. He has collateral form with Samcro and would represent each-way value if going for this race over the Albert Bartlett, as seems likely. Mullins also has Deloitte runner-up Duc Des Genievres, who seems sure to relish the extra distance in the Ballymore.

A decent crop of juveniles are set to contest the Triumph Hurdle and Nicky Henderson's Apple's Shakira, who has impressed in winning three times at Cheltenham since coming over from France, has been a clear ante-post favourite for much of the winter.

She has taken a similar path to last year's winner Defi Du Seuil, also owned by JP McManus, and showed a willing attitude in the Grade 2 Triumph trial in January. She has to prove herself on the expected quicker going, although she's a sister to 2016 runner-up Apple's Jade and connections expect those conditions would suit her ideally.

Henderson also has We Have A Dream, a rapid improver since switching from France, who gamely saw off Gary Moore's Sussex Ranger in the Grade 1 Finale at Chepstow in January when the mud was flying, a race also won by Defi Du Seuil last term. Some spring ground would be ideal and there's lots to like, although he's not so certain to appreciate the testing finish of the Triumph.

The top Irish contender is the Mullins-trained Mr Adjudicator, who burst bubbles when recording a decent time figure in the Grade 1 Spring Novice Hurdle at Leopardstown in February. Main rival Espoir D'Allen flopped, but that's a key trial and arguably the best juvenile form on offer.

Mullins also has unexposed filly Stormy Ireland, who looked special in winning a maiden by 58 lengths on her Irish debut in December. A lack of experience would be a negative if she made it to the Triumph, however.

Verdict Much revolves around Samcro, but assuming he heads for the Ballymore then he should win that and leave the Supreme at the mercy of Getabird. Apple's Shakira has to prove she's as effective on quicker going and good-ground Flat winner Mr Adjudicator makes plenty of appeal against her in the Triumph *(Dave Orton)*

RACING POST MEMBERS' CLUB

REPLAY THE FESTIVAL

WITH MEMBERS' CLUB ULTIMATE

Subscribe to Members' Club Ultimate
and you can watch unlimited video
replays of every race from the
Cheltenham Festival

RACING POST.com/membersclub

James Thomas of Racing Post Bloodstock looks for some clues

Saddle up

The name Saddler Maker may not have meant much to fans of jumps pedigrees just a couple of years ago but the late son of Sadler's Wells has since made quite an impression. He is the sire of Mares' Hurdle heroine Apple's Jade, who is likely to go back to defend her crown this year, and the supporting cast give this lesser-known stallion a genuine chance of scooping the leading sire crown at this year's festival. He could be represented by Triumph Hurdle favourite Apple's Shakira (below) – a sister to Apple's Jade and many people's idea of a festival banker – the smart novice chaser Dinaria Des Obeaux and the progressive Chef Des Obeaux (Albert Bartlett Novices' Hurdle), to name but a few.

Not just the daddy

It is always worth paying close attention to the bottom line of a horse's pedigree. Presenting,

Leading festival sires in past five years			
Stallion	Sire	Stud	Winners
Robin Des Champs	Garde Royale	Glenview	7
King's Theatre	Sadler's Wells	*Dead*	6
Kayf Tara	Sadler's Wells	Overbury	5
Milan	Sadler's Wells	Grange	5
Beneficial	Top Ville	*Dead*	4
Oscar	Sadler's Wells	*Retired*	4
Westerner	Danehill Castle	Hyde	4
Authorized	Montjeu	Haras du Logis	3
Dynaformer	Roberto	*Dead*	3
High Chaparral	Sadler's Wells	*Dead*	3
Poliglote	Sadler's Wells	Haras d'Etreham	3
Shantou	Alleged	Burgage	3
Shirocco	Monsun	Glenview	3
Voix Du Nord	Valanour	*Dead*	3

who has sired festival winners such as Denman, War Of Attrition and Yorkhill, has also emerged as a broodmare sire of growing importance in recent years. Festival fancies such as Might Bite, Presenting Percy and Rathvinden are all out of his daughters and other contenders with a Presenting-sired dam are worthy of attention.

Derby form guide

Four stallions who won the Derby during their racing career supplied winners at last year's festival. Authorized claimed leading sire honours courtesy of two winners, Nichols Canyon and Tiger Roll, while Galileo (Supasundae), High Chaparral (Altior) and Sir Percy (Presenting Percy) also got on the scoresheet with one winner each. Those Epsom heroes all look to have chances of bagging more Cheltenham glory this year and another with live contenders is Motivator, the sire of JLT Novices' Chase contender Modus and exciting juvenile filly Stormy Ireland.

Frankel's Solo

Cheltenham might be the epicentre of jump racing but the progeny of sires more regularly associated with the Flat can be expected to make their presence felt. Last year stallions such as Street Cry – the sire of Flat wonder mares Winx and Zenyatta – Galileo, High Chaparral and Orpen all supplied winners. Frankel might even pop up on the winners' list this year, with Dan Skelton's unbeaten Solo Saxophone a likely candidate for one of the juvenile contests.

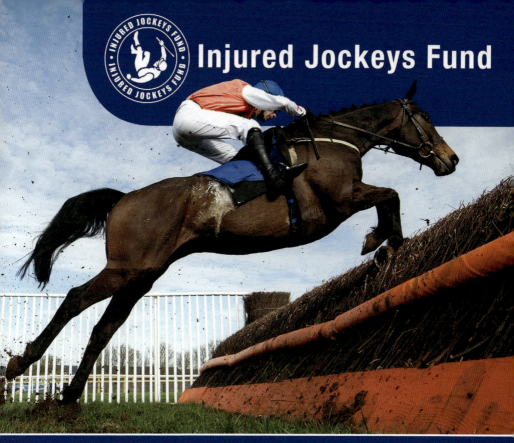

Samcro adds stardust to another strong cast

By Alan Sweetman

A RECORD tally of 19 Irish-trained winners at the 2017 festival has set the bar closer to the level of the pole vault than the high jump. Mind you, we said much the same 12 months ago after a 15-winner haul in 2016 and then even greater heights were reached.

Right now the balance of power in jump racing is tilted strongly toward the Irish side, chiefly on account of the mighty operations run by Willie Mullins and Gordon Elliott, who had six festival winners apiece last year in their battle for supremacy. They are backed up by a quartet comprising Henry de Bromhead, Jessica Harrington, Noel Meade and new kid on the block Joseph O'Brien, who all have live chances this year.

This group will provide the vast majority of serious Irish contenders for the festival's Grade 1 races. As was the case in 2017, Irish influence is likely to extend to the handicap arena, with leading owners Gigginstown and JP McManus holding a wide range of options.

The depth of talent in the main Irish yards makes the handicaps much more difficult for the home team to defend than in the past.

The Irish season came alive at the inaugural Dublin Racing Festival. At least four of the winners – brilliant novice hurdler Samcro, Queen Mother Champion Chase candidate Min, Arkle hopeful Footpad and bold-jumping novice chaser Monalee – put down significant markers. In addition, Harrington's 2017 Coral Cup winner Supasundae, warming up for the Stayers' Hurdle, showed he is in fine shape with a surprise Irish Champion Hurdle victory. The Mullins-trained Grade 2 bumper winners Blackbow and Relegate emerged as attractive Champion Bumper challengers and a recent recruit to the stable, Patricks Park, put himself in line for a handicap chase bid at the festival. The JP McManus-owned, Charles Byrnes-trained Off You Go entered the Coral Cup picture.

Only three races into his hurdling career,

Samcro has already acquired the aura of a champion and will travel under a heavy burden of expectation for a date with destiny, most probably in the Ballymore Novices' Hurdle. For the Irish contingent, it will be the shock of the meeting if he is defeated.

Not all the omens at the Dublin Racing Festival were favourable, as the fixture delivered multiple blows to Irish prospects of winning the Champion Hurdle and failed to produce any enhancement of Cheltenham Gold Cup hopes, already dented by the fact that defending champion Sizing John has been under a cloud since his seasonal debut.

Following an abject display at Christmas, the 2015 Champion Hurdle winner Faugheen needed a big performance to put himself firmly back in the picture. His second place behind Supasundae suggests he is not the horse he was. Melon's tame fifth in the same race and a poor showing from the enigmatic Yorkhill in the Coral Dublin Chase

Supasundae beats Faugheen in the Irish Champion Hurdle

also represented significant reverses for the Mullins team.

Edwulf's 33-1 win in the Irish Gold Cup was heartwarming, but it takes a leap of the imagination to see him as a Cheltenham Gold Cup winner. Killultagh Vic looked set for victory until falling at the last, but that was not the ideal note on which to head for Cheltenham. Runner-up Outlander has failed to prosper on previous visits and will not be travelling. Djakadam, fourth to Sizing John in last year's Gold Cup and runner-up in the two previous

Min: set to lead Irish challenge to Altior in the Champion Chase

Moorcroft
Racehorse Welfare Centre

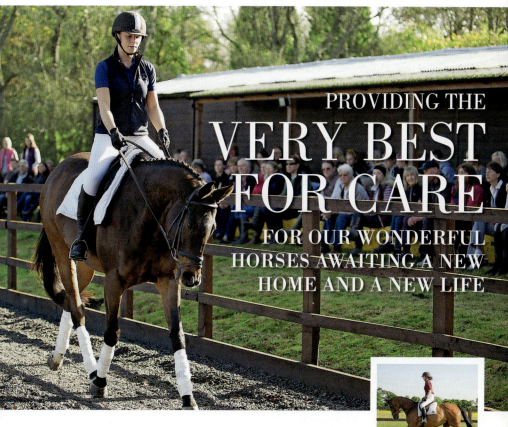

PROVIDING THE
VERY BEST
FOR CARE
FOR OUR WONDERFUL
HORSES AWAITING A NEW
HOME AND A NEW LIFE

This centre in the south of England was set up to ensure that retired racehorses whatever age, can be re-trained to find another career in life. Much care and attention is given to each individual horse and when fully retrained new homes are found. The centre retains ownership for life and visits these horses every year to ensure that all is well.

This charity depends on generous donations from horse lovers. Many horses need a time for rehabilitation due to injury etc and start to enjoy an easier life after their racing careers. Visits by appointment are welcomed. Please ring Mary Frances, Manager, on 07929 666408 for more information or to arrange a visit.

Huntingrove Stud, Slinfold, West Sussex. RH13 0RB

Tel: 07929 666408 | Email: moorcroftracehorse@gmail.com | www.moorcroftracehorse.org.uk

editions, is struggling to retrieve peak form. Last season's Irish Grand National winner Our Duke did not advance his claims there, losing his chance with a mistake at the second-last, but came right back into the reckoning when he bounced back to win the Red Mills Chase at Gowran Park a fortnight later.

In contrast, the Noel Meade-trained seven-year-old Road To Respect has enjoyed a solid preparation. His trainer, who has had more than his fair share of Cheltenham heartaches over the decades, enjoyed a first festival success over fences last season with the Gigginstown gelding, who now provides the veteran trainer with a realistic chance of a first victory in one of the showpiece races.

Assuming Douvan does not defy the odds by making it back in time, Min will lead the challenge to Altior, his conqueror in the 2016 Supreme Novices' Hurdle, in the Queen Mother Champion Chase. His Leopardstown victims included last season's long-priced Champion Chase winner, Special Tiara, making a rare Irish appearance.

Better ground at Cheltenham would suit Henry de Bromhead's 11-year-old, but history is against him as Moscow Flyer is the only horse of that age to have won the race in the past 40 years.

Back-to-back success for Un De Sceaux is much easier to envisage. In winning Ascot's Clarence House for the third consecutive year, he looked as good as ever and well primed to repeat last year's Ryanair Chase victory.

Last year's Pertemps Final winner Presenting Percy also returns with bright prospects. Having finished second to Our Duke in the Red Mills Chase following a comfortable victory in the 3m5f Porterstown Handicap Chase at Fairyhouse (and with a Grade 2 hurdles success in between), Pat Kelly's seven-year-old would set a high standard in the RSA Chase, for which last season's Albert Bartlett second Monalee is also a strong contender.

Samcro's participation in the Ballymore would leave the Mullins-trained Getabird, emphatic winner of a 2m Grade 2 event at Punchestown in January, as the pick of the Irish contingent for the Supreme Novices', with stablemate Duc Des Genievres also in the mix following his Deloitte second.

Next Destination, last season's Champion Bumper fourth and unbeaten in three runs over hurdles, can bypass a clash with Samcro in favour of the Albert Bartlett to face a crucial rematch with the Elliott-trained Cracking Smart, whom he beat in a 2m4f Grade 1 race at Naas in January.

The Mullins-trained pair Stormy Ireland and Mr Adjudicator will do well to threaten Apple's Shakira in the Triumph, for which the Gavin Cromwell-trained Espoir D'Allen had been the main Irish fancy until a Leopardstown flop.

The mares' races at the meeting should provide the statutory Irish winners. Apple's Jade, a serious Champion Hurdle candidate if Gigginstown felt so inclined, looks a near certainty to repeat last year's win in the senior race. Mullins is two from two in the junior event and can collect with Laurina, who has impressed in winning both starts since her arrival from France.

Elliott and event specialist Enda Bolger have a range of options for the Cross Country Chase. The pair supplied the first four in last year's edition, led home by Elliott's Cause Of Causes. Bolger's leading hopes Auvergnat and Josies Orders, the promoted 2016 winner, completed preparations satisfactorily by fighting out a tight finish on a Punchestown card that also featured a good Foxhunter trial for up-and-coming hunter chaser Burning Ambition, who has progressed through the point-to-point ranks in the care of little-known trainer Pierce Power. He made a race of it with the Bolger-trained Gilgamboa, a good yardstick but ineligible for Cheltenham.

Foxrock, the former Ted Walsh-trained staying chaser, is another strong Irish contender for the Foxhunter. He is now with Alan Fleming, whose Tully East, a novice handicap chase winner at last year's festival, is being aimed at the 2m5f Brown Advisory Plate with good prospects.

The Racing Post's regional correspondents pick their big-race fancies

Definitly bet on northern revival

Lambourn James Burn

Nicky Henderson has a strong hand in the Unibet Champion Hurdle and Betway Queen Mother Champion Chase with Buveur D'Air and Altior, but **Might Bite** represents more value than the odds-on pair in the Timico Cheltenham Gold Cup.

The King George VI Chase hero has his quirks but also a turbo-charged engine and he should be hard to beat, especially as he seems more straightforward this term.

One-time Henderson protege Harry Whittington has enjoyed a fine season, which **Saint Calvados** can cap in style in the Racing Post Arkle. Unbeaten in three runs since joining Whittington, the French import is an impressive sort held in the highest regard by the trainer.

Warren Greatrex thinks plenty of **La Bague Au Roi**, who has relished stepping up to 3m this season and looks a player if the trainer aims her at the Sun Bets Stayers' Hurdle – a race he won with Cole Harden three years ago.

Versatile with regard to ground, she has a touch of class and is more than capable of making the frame at a tasty price.

West Country Tim Mitchell

Native River will be fresher than most for the Timico Cheltenham Gold Cup and, with doubts surrounding many of the runners in an open year, he can improve on his gallant third 12 months ago. He made an encouraging reappearance at Newbury, again showing an admirable attitude to outstay and outjump his two rivals.

Movewiththetimes is still progressing over fences and, on decent ground, the JP McManus-owned gelding could run a big race in the Close Brothers Novices' Handicap Chase.

Elegant Escape booked his ticket to the festival with a commanding display at Exeter and can make his presence felt in the RSA Chase, which connections are slightly favouring at present. However, the National Hunt Chase has not been ruled out and that might be the easier option, with the step up to 4m sure to suit.

Vaniteux has kept decent company this season but has not had his ideal conditions. The switch back to handicaps off a competitive mark and on better ground could see him bounce back to form in the Grand Annual.

Ireland Brian Sheerin

Presenting Percy has charted an unusual path towards the RSA Chase but his trainer Pat Kelly has always been more comfortable taking the road less travelled.

Rather than going down the traditional Grade 1 route, Presenting Percy landed the Porterstown Handicap Chase at Fairyhouse in December before winning the Grade 2 Galmoy Hurdle at Gowran Park in January and then going back over fences to finish runner-up to Our Duke in the Red Mills Chase.

Already a Cheltenham winner in last year's Pertemps Handicap Hurdle, he sets a high standard in the RSA and is a fair price at anything above 3-1. He is one of the strongest Irish fancies of the week.

The Albert Bartlett Novices' Hurdle is not for the faint hearted and, while Gordon Elliott has had leading fancies No More Heroes and Death Duty beaten in the past two renewals, he can gain compensation of sorts with **Cracking Smart**.

The Gigginstown-owned gelding has looked really good over distances a little shy of his best for most of the season and he should relish the stamina-sapping Albert Bartlett trip. He doesn't have an overly sexy profile but he ticks all the boxes for what you need to win this race.

The North Colin Russell

Having endured three barren festival years, there is growing confidence that there will be at least one winner from the north this time. Several yards are in good form and the region could field three contenders with solid credentials for the major championship races.

They are headed in the Timico Cheltenham Gold Cup by **Definitly Red**, who has always been held in high regard by trainer Brian Ellison. Although the nine-year-old went for the Grand National last season, which didn't work out after he met interference,

Ellison has long considered him to be more of a Gold Cup horse.

Having put up a career best with a fine staying performance to win the Cotswold Chase on Trials Day, Definitly Red looks very much a leading contender. He is no one-paced mudlark either, as his trainer has always maintained good ground will bring out the best in him.

The other Malton-trained festival candidate is **Waiting Patiently**, who is under serious consideration for the Ryanair Chase. Unbeaten in six runs over fences, he was impressive in the Ascot Chase and it would be an emotional success for the late Malcolm Jefferson's daughter Ruth if he triumphs at the festival.

This year's other northern hope is **Sam Spinner**. Trained in Middleham by Jedd O'Keeffe, he is a progressive young staying hurdler who was pretty impressive when winning the Long Walk Hurdle at Ascot in December and looks the one to beat in the Sun Bets Stayers' Hurdle.

Definitly Red: big player in the Gold Cup

Watch for wind ops

The most recent winner at the Cheltenham Festival was Rock The World, who took the final race of the 2017 meeting – the Grand Annual Chase – at 10-1 for Jessica Harrington.

There was one important detail missing on the racecard for that contest, however, and that was the fact that Rock The World had undergone corrective surgery on his wind in the five months he had spent off the course before returning for the Grand Annual.

That point was not lost on winning rider Robbie Power after Rock The World produced the best run of his career to that point on Racing Post Ratings to score by a length and three-quarters.

"Full marks to Jessie because he ran terrible here in October," Power said. "He had a wind operation afterwards and hadn't run since, so it was a fantastic training performance."

Punters looking at the racecard were in the dark about that significant operation, but that won't be the case any longer as this season it became mandatory in Britain for wind surgery to be notified by trainers and included on racecards.

On racecards in the Racing Post, look for a small w to the left of a runner's age and weight *(as shown above)*. That signifies a runner is having its first run since a wind

operation and this will be the first Cheltenham Festival where that information has been available.

Although Ireland has not followed Britain by introducing this rule, Irish runners at Cheltenham having their first outing since a wind

op must also be notified by trainers.

How punters use this information is up to them, but at least they have the option to build it into calculations. And if it happens to be a Harrington-trained runner, it might be worth a close look.

Rock The World: last season's 10-1 Grand Annual winner showed the benefit of a wind op

and/or of the winning variety, but a couple of Irish fancies will have to overcome their lack of that vital commodity.

Total Recall's only previous run in Britain was at Newbury in December, albeit winning the Ladbrokes Trophy, while last year's Irish Grand National winner Our Duke has never left home shores.

The last Gold Cup winner without course experience was Imperial Call in 1996 and the only other in the past 25 years was Jodami in 1993.

Shortie alert

Favourite backers at short prices are on shaky ground in the handicaps – the last winner at 5-1 or lower was Fingal Bay (9-2) *(below)* in the 2014 Pertemps Handicap Hurdle (with 21 losers in that category since then).

In the past decade, handicap favourites at 5-1 or lower have an overall record of seven wins from 61 runs (11%) for a level-stakes loss of -25.17pts.

Grade 1 favourites tend to be more reliable but punters should tread carefully in the Champion Bumper, which often has an overbet favourite and has been won by just four market leaders in 25 runnings (16%, -7.5pt).

One-race horse

Altior's pre-Christmas wind operation means he arrives at this year's festival with just one run under his belt and, while he was undeniably impressive in the Game Spirit Chase, his interrupted campaign has raised the difficulty level in his bid to win the Queen Mother Champion Chase.

You have to go back to Flagship Uberalles in 2002 to find the last Champion Chase winner with only one previous run that season. The average number of pre-festival runs since then is 3.5, although an encouraging aspect for Altior is that some of the best winners – such as Master Minded in 2009 and Sprinter Sacre for both his victories (2013 and 2016) – were lightly raced, with two previous runs apiece that season.

Golden first-timers

The principal contenders for the Cheltenham Gold Cup have plenty of course experience, often at the festival

Strong all round but big profits in handicap hurdles

WILLIE MULLINS

Favourites have a high strike-rate, particularly in Grade 1s

County and Martin Pipe handicap hurdles have proved profitable

Eleven of his 13 chase winners were in novice races

Mullins had a rare old tussle for the leading trainer award last year and was narrowly denied a fifth successive title by his big Irish rival Gordon Elliott, who claimed victory by virtue of one more second place after they finished tied on six winners.

That was the third year in a row that Mullins had exceeded five winners (he had a record eight in 2015 and seven in 2016). Nicky Henderson (seven in 2012) and now Elliott are the only other trainers to have had more than five at a single meeting.

Mullins now has 54 winners going back to Tourist Attraction's Supreme Novices' Hurdle success in 1995 and is just four behind Henderson, the festival's winningmost trainer on 58 (amassed over a decade longer than Mullins).

Usually Mullins relies on a big opening day to get him off and running, but last year was different as he had blanks on the first two days before roaring back with four winners on the Thursday and two more on the Friday. Despite that strong finish, the Gold Cup continued to elude him and the best he managed last year was Djakadam's fourth place.

The market tells its story. At the past five festivals, Mullins has had a total of 42 favourites and 20 (48%) have won, perhaps surprisingly producing a profit in three of the years (+8.72pts overall). Only ten of his 30 winners in that period did not start favourite (and four of those were second favourite).

Traditionally the stable's main strength in Grade 1 races has been over hurdles, particularly over 2m, but Mullins has won seven Grade 1 chases in the past three years (having not done so since 2009).

He has had seven handicap hurdle winners since 2010 (five at double-figure odds), the latest coming last year with his remarkable feat in bringing back Arctic Fire from a 14-month absence to win the County Hurdle under top weight at 20-1. Excluding the Fred Winter Juvenile Handicap Hurdle, which he has never won, his strike-rate in that period is 7-59 (+46.5pts) and the key targets have been the County Hurdle (4-21, +58pts) and Martin Pipe Conditional Jockeys' Hurdle (3-14, +12.5pts).

Of his eight Champion Bumper winners, six were five-year-olds who had won their sole outing prior to arriving at Cheltenham.

Hot favourites carry promise of sizzling festival

NICKY HENDERSON

Proiftable record with Grade 1 favourites

Never one to discount in handicaps at rewarding odds

The master of Seven Barrows is the most successful trainer at the festival with 58 winners and among his many highlights was a magnificent seven in 2012, a then record but since eclipsed by Willie Mullins' eight winners in 2015.

It is not far-fetched to imagine Henderson threatening the record again this year as he has two of the hottest favourites in Buveur D'Air for the Champion Hurdle and Altior for the Champion Chase, plus Might Bite leading the Gold Cup market. Those stable stars provided his three winners last year, but this time he appears to have plenty of ammunition in support.

Seven Barrows has a strong team of novices, with his highly regarded hurdlers including Triumph favourite Apple's Shakira, On The Blind Side (Ballymore) and Santini (Albert Bartlett) and the chasers headed by Terrefort (JLT or RSA) and Brain Power (Arkle). There are other Grade 1 chances among the seniors with Top Notch in the Ryanair Chase and L'Ami Serge in the Stayers' Hurdle, while William Henry (Coral Cup) is just one who could make a strong showing in the handicaps.

Second-season hurdlers like William Henry are always worth noting, along with the booking of claiming jockeys – four of Henderson's seven handicap winners since 2009 have had the benefit of a weight allowance.

The quality that runs though his string means the market doesn't always provide an accurate guide and longer-priced runners in handicaps are always worth a look, especially if they are lightly raced. Call The Cops at 9-1 in the 2015 Pertemps Final was the only one of the trainer's 11 handicap winners since 2005 to have been returned shorter than 12-1.

It is also worth noting that eight of those 11 handicap winners since 2005 came over trips of at least 2m4f.

Among Henderson's favourite races is the Triumph Hurdle, in which he holds the record with six wins. In the past decade, when his most fancied runner has been under 10-1, their finishing positions have been 1136616 for a level-stakes profit of 9.5pts. That is a good pointer for favourite backers with Apple's Shakira.

Overall he has an excellent record of delivering with the hot ones in Grade 1 races. In the past decade he has sent out 21 favourites in that category and 11 have won, returning a level-stakes profit of 10.89pts. That also bodes well for his biggest fancies this year.

Decent chasing team offers hope of better showing

PAUL NICHOLLS

13 of his last 16 festival winners have been over hurdles

Seven of his last nine successes were achieved in handicaps

Does well with young, unexposed horses in handicaps

The ten-time British champion was leading trainer at the festival five times in six years between 2004 and 2009 but has not had that accolade since then, with the flood of winners having slowed to a trickle.

Last year he had only one winner, Pacha Du Polder in the Foxhunter, which mirrored his showing in 2013 and 2014 and was a drop back from the three winners he enjoyed in 2015 and 2016. With just one second place (also in the Foxhunter, with Wonderful Charm) and one third, he had little strength in depth last year.

The change in status is reflected in his type of winners. Whereas he used to dominate the Grade 1 races, seven of his nine winners in the past five years have been in handicaps. Since the end of the Big Buck's four-timer in the Stayers' Hurdle in 2012, Nicholls' only Grade 1 winner at the festival has been Dodging Bullets in the 2015 Queen Mother Champion Chase.

That race may provide his best chance at the top level this time with Politologue, who like Dodging Bullets has won the Tingle Creek en route to the festival but perhaps not been given the credit he deserves. The grey was put in his place by Altior at Newbury last time and faces a tough task to reverse the form, but the Nicky Henderson-trained favourite (Sprinter Sacre) blew out in Dodging Bullets' year and Politologue merits a shot at the title.

Overall the chasing team is stronger this year, with Cyrname, Modus and Black Corton among a decent crop of novices, and Nicholls is likely to have handicap options as well as some hope of Grade 1 success. Frodon, who has gone from a mark of 152 to 164 this season, is set for a shot at the Ryanair Chase over the same course and distance of his impressive handicap win on Trials Day. Nicholls also has Pacha Du Polder and Wonderful Charm lined up for the Foxhunter again.

The key to finding a Nicholls handicap winner at the festival, especially over hurdles, is to identify a young, lightly raced type yet to be exposed to the handicapper. Eight of his ten handicap hurdle winners were aged four or five, and nine of his 14 handicap winners overall have carried between 10st 10lb and 11st 1lb (the only two above that weight were in the Martin Pipe).

It is worth noting that Nicholls has won the County on four occasions and the Grand Annual Chase three times – both are over 2m, and that is another factor to take into account.

Last year's leader has staying power just like his horses

GORDON ELLIOTT

Look out for single representatives

Be wary of favourites

Emphasis on stamina, especially in chases

Elliott was leading trainer at the festival for the first time last year, becoming the only one apart from Howard Johnson in 2005 to break the monopoly of Willie Mullins, Nicky Henderson and Paul Nicholls at the last 14 festivals. Unlike Johnson, Elliott is here to stay and the big three has now become the big four.

With six winners last year – beating Mullins on countback of second places – Elliott's total has risen to 14, accumulated at just seven festivals after his breakthrough double in 2011 with Chicago Grey in the National Hunt Chase and Carlito Brigante in the Coral Cup.

He already has a Cheltenham Gold Cup on the list with Don Cossack in 2016 – one of five Grade 1 wins among the 14 – and that highlights a key strength with staying chasers. All six chase wins have come at distances in excess of 3m, in the National Hunt Chase (three times), the Gold Cup, the Fulke Walwyn Kim Muir Handicap Chase and the Cross Country. Three of the six were provided by the remarkable Cause Of Causes, who is set to bid for a fourth in the Cross Country he won last year.

Some of Elliott's seven successes over hurdles also emphasise the stable's accent on stamina, with two wins in the Coral Cup and last year's victories with Apple's Jade (Mares' Hurdle) and Champagne Classic (Martin Pipe Conditional Jockeys' Handicap Hurdle) coming at distances of 2m4f-plus.

The market is not that good at identifying Elliott's winning chances, with only two of his ten festival favourites having been successful (for a slight loss overall), but the trainer's selection process is clearly working well as 12 of his 14 winners came in races where he had only one representative.

If punters had restricted themselves to backing Elliott runners when he had only one representative at last year's festival, they would have had four winners from 11 bets for a level-stakes profit of 44.5pts. All runners when he had more than one representative showed figures of 2-17 for a small 1pt profit.

Backing single representatives in 2016 would also have yielded a good profit (9.75pts) against a loss of 7pts when he had more than one runner.

The only two winners who raced against stablemates were both last year – Cause Of Causes in the Cross Country (stablemate Bless The Wings second) and Champagne Classic in the Martin Pipe (stablemates third and 12th).

Look for handicap chase fancies
David Pipe

Pipe has failed to register at only two festivals since landing the 2007 Fred Winter Juvenile Handicap Hurdle with Gaspara in his first season. He has a long way to go to match his father Martin's total of 34 festival winners but Un Temps Pour Tout's second consecutive Ultima Handicap Chase victory last year took his overall tally to 15, of which 11 have been in chases. Handicaps are the main route, as he has won the Ultima, Kim Muir and Stable Plate on three occasions apiece. Watch the market closely: from 25 runners priced at 12-1 or below in those three handicap chases, he has had seven winners (28%, +38.83pts), two seconds and a third.

This has been a poor season by the high standards of the Pipe stable, with the number of runners and winners well down, but there is still enough quality to pose a threat.

Vaniteux, third in the 2014 Supreme and a faller when in second behind Douvan in the 2016 Arkle, joined the stable from Nicky Henderson this season and could drop into handicap company for the Grand Annual. In the three handicap chases he has targeted so successfully, Pipe has chances with What A Moment (Kim Muir), Ramses De Teillee (Ultima – though it seems unlikely Un Temps Pour Tout will be there) and King's Socks (Plate).

Eleven of his 15 festival victories have come over fences
Note his fancied runners in staying handicap chases

Strong team in the hunt again
Colin Tizzard

Expectations were high for Tizzard last year but the festival was the one arena where he fell short in an otherwise spectacular season. King George winner Thistlecrack and leading novice hurdler Finian's Oscar failed to make the meeting at the 11th hour, while Fox Norton lost out narrowly in the Champion Chase and Native River finished third in the Gold Cup, with Cue Card falling in that race for the second consecutive year.

Despite those disappointments, and the fact that three of his five festival winners have been big prices (40-1 twice and 28-1), Tizzard's fancied runners generally show up well. He has had only ten runners priced under 10-1 at the past six festivals and they finished 201521F23F.

Tizzard has not reached the heights of last season but he is still fifth in the trainers' table and will have a strong team again. Fox Norton merits great respect in the Ryanair or Champion Chase, particularly on soft over the shorter trip, Native River is prominent again in the Gold Cup betting after his belated return with an impressive win in the Denman Chase, while Cue Card could drop back to the Ryanair (which he won in 2013) if he doesn't go for Gold.

Elegant Escape, seventh in last year's Albert Bartlett Novices' Hurdle, can be expected to go well in the 4m National Hunt Chase after a bright novice campaign. Finian's Oscar once again faces a race against time to make the meeting, having reportedly had wind surgery before his planned return to fences in the JLT or RSA Chase.

Tizzard's strength in depth with staying chasers should mean he becomes more of a force in handicaps, and two who could go well are Sizing Tennessee and Robinsfirth.

Fancied runners usually perform well
But don't rule out a surprise. Three of his five festival winners were returned at huge prices

Staying chasers offer best hope

Jonjo O'Neill

O'Neill is a consistent trainer of winners at the festival and his total of 26 winners puts him in clear fourth place behind Nicky Henderson, Willie Mullins and Paul Nicholls. He has had only three blanks at the meeting since the turn of the century, but perhaps the power of his Jackdaws Castle stable is waning as two of those have been in the past three years.

His last winner was Minella Rocco in the 2016 National Hunt Chase, his sixth success in that race. His first five came in 12 runnings from 1995 to 2007 but the recent changes in the race conditions (which made it a higher-class contest) appeared to have taken away his edge until Minella Rocco's victory.

It is worth taking note of his fancied runners and staying races are clearly where O'Neill does best, with 21 of his 26 festival victories coming in races over 3m or further, and he also has a good record in the Pertemps Final (four wins) and the Ultima Handicap Chase (three wins).

Minella Rocco was his most significant performer in 2017, running on well for second in the Gold Cup, and the strong stayer has an each-way shout again.

Go Conquer is one of the better handicap chase prospects for the yard, having shown up well before fading into fifth in the Ultima Handicap Chase last year.

Excellent record in races over 3m-plus
Ten of his 12 winners in the past decade came over fences
Don't ignore the stable second string – two of his recent handicap winners beat a better-fancied stablemate

Fresh target for The New One

Nigel Twiston-Davies

Twiston-Davies's festival record comes in fits and starts. He had two winners in 2009, three in 2010 (including the Gold Cup with Imperial Commander), two in 2013 and two again in 2016, but he drew a blank in 2017 and in the other four years in that period.

His two most recent winners in 2016 both came in Grade 1 races – the RSA Chase with Blaklion and the Champion Bumper with Ballyandy – and his overall total stands at 17.

Blaklion could return as a Gold Cup outsider, having moved above stablemate Bristol De Mai in the reckoning since being beaten half a length by the grey in the Charlie Hall Chase in November.

The 2013 Neptune (now Ballymore) winner The New One will be back again with claims if he stays the longer trip in his new target, the Stayers' Hurdle. Wholestone, second in the Cleeve Hurdle here in January and third in the Albert Bartlett in 2017, also has each-way claims in the Stayers' Hurdle.

Good Boy Bobby in the Champion Bumper, having won his first two starts at Chepstow and finished third in a Listed contest, is another contender to note.

It is notable that Twiston-Davies did well with fancied runners at the past two festivals. Nine were priced at under 10-1 and they finished 411224F63.

Novice chasers and fancied runners are a traditional strength
The New One is the yard's only festival winner over hurdles since 2008

Handicap hurdlers worth a look
Philip Hobbs

The Somerset trainer got back on the scoresheet last year, after a couple of blank festivals, courtesy of long-time Triumph Hurdle favourite Defi Du Seuil. Hobbs had not had a Triumph runner for five years but has a good record in the Grade 1 contest for juvenile hurdlers, having previously won with Made In Japan in 2004 and Detroit City in 2006. The stable regularly delivers with fancied runners like Defi Du Seuil – five of the last six winners were sent off no bigger than 6-1 – and can also turn up rewarding each-way odds in handicap hurdles.

Hobbs's 19 festival wins have come in 14 different races but four of the last seven were gained over fences. Several of his early festival winners came in handicap hurdles (two wins in both the County and the Coral Cup) but he has had only one in that sphere since 2004. His runners in big handicaps always merit respect, however, and last year Verni finished second in the Martin Pipe at 25-1 and Ozzie The Oscar (50-1) was third in the County. In 2016 Hobbs had the third in the Pertemps Final and the third and fourth in the County Hurdle.

Louis' Vac Pouch could have a good shout in the Pertemps Final, having won a qualifier at Aintree in November.

Cheltenian won the Champion Bumper for the yard in 2011 and Crooks Peak is an interesting prospect this year, having followed up a debut success at Newton Abbot with victory over the Cheltenham course and distance on unhelpfully soft ground in November.

Watch the market closely
Each-way prospects in big handicap hurdles

Arkle shot with Sceau Royal
Alan King

King had a golden period with 11 festival winners from 2004 to 2009 but has scored only in singles since then (in 2011, 2013, 2014 and 2015) to take his score to 15. He remains a competitive force, with 14 runners finishing in the first four at the past four festivals in addition to his two winners, including four placed horses last year.

Most of King's chase wins at the festival have been with novices, not only in Grade 1s and the National Hunt Chase but also in handicaps, but his squad is expected to be much lighter on numbers this time. Last season's Champion Hurdle sixth Sceau Royal is a prominent Arkle hope, having won four of his five starts over fences, including a Grade 1 at Sandown in December. Yanworth was seen as one of the British bankers for the Neptune in 2016, only to finish second, and proved a disappointing Champion Hurdle favourite in 2017. He could remain over fences for the JLT or RSA or revert to last year's original target over hurdles in the Stayers'.

King has a good record with juveniles and won the Triumph Hurdle with Penzance (2005) and Katchit (2007). This year he has Redicean, unbeaten in two starts, towards the head of the Triumph betting. In the past 11 years eight of his 37 runners (22%) in the Triumph and Fred Winter made the first three.

More select squad headed by Sceau Royal in the Arkle
Strong juvenile record points to Redicean in the Triumph

Gloucester Cleaning Solutions

Freephone: 0800 170 1441

www.gloscleansolutions.co.uk

Select approach pays dividends

Jessica Harrington

Harrington now stands alone as the winningmost female trainer in festival history after last year's treble took her total to 11, three ahead of Jenny Pitman.

Her record is outstanding as she has never sent a team of more than eight runners in 21 festivals, yet has achieved much more than most of her rival trainers.

Sizing John's victory in the 2017 Gold Cup at Harrington's first attempt means she has won three of the four monuments of the festival, following Moscow Flyer's Champion Chase triumphs in 2003 and 2005 and Jezki's 2014 Champion Hurdle, and she has a great chance of completing the set this year with Supasundae, who became ante-post favourite for the Stayers' Hurdle after winning the Irish Champion Hurdle.

Harrington's select approach and winning habit mean her followers would be in profit if they had backed every festival runner (11-75, +21.75pts), although like her they would have had to sit through several blank festivals to reap the rewards in the long term.

One thing punters can rely on is that Harrington doesn't have festival runners for the sake of it. As well as her 11 winners, she has had 12 others in the first four, which means 31 per cent of her runners have made the first four.

Her record with fancied runners is also worth noting, with nine of her 11 winners priced at 10-1 or below. Punters who restricted their bets to Harrington runners in that price bracket would have had nine winners from 32 (28%) for a level-stakes profit of 30.75pts.

It is also worth noting that nine of the other 12 who made the first four were also 10-1 or lower, which emphasises it is the fancied runners that should be the main focus. That bodes well for Supasundae and makes Sizing John and Our Duke look a serious two-pronged challenge in the Gold Cup.

Excellent record with runners at 10-1 or lower
Eight of her 11 wins have been at around 2m

Three more to note at right price

Henry de Bromhead has had four festival wins, including two in the Champion Chase with Sizing Europe (2011) and Special Tiara last year. Although Special Tiara was 11-1, De Bromhead usually does best with runners at 10-1 or lower – his other three winners were in that category, plus four seconds and three thirds, from 16 runners in the past decade (3-16, +9.5pts).

Dan Skelton has had only one festival winner (Superb Story at 8-1 in the 2016 County Hurdle) but his record is sure to improve and perhaps handicap success is more likely for now. Superb Story is one of just four handicap runners he has had under 10-1 and one of the others was third at 7-1.

Harry Fry, who oversaw Rock On Ruby's prep for his 2012 Champion Hurdle win when assistant to Paul Nicholls, went close to a first festival success with Neon Wolf in the Neptune last year. He has a number of live hopes again and his turn looks near – his festival runners at 10-1 or lower have finished 28837234 with two of them beaten no more than half a length.

Russell a go-to rider with high profit margin

Ruby Walsh

The most successful jockey in festival history has his best record, not surprisingly, with Ireland's champion trainer Willie Mullins (25-122 rides). In Grade 1 races since 2015, Mullins is 16-106 overall, with Walsh aboard for all but three of those wins. Over the past three festivals, Walsh has ridden in 40 Grade 1s at the festival and has been successful 13 times, for a strike-rate of 33 per cent and a small level-stakes profit of 2.63pts.

In those past three years, Mullins is 3-66 in Grade 1s without Walsh riding for a loss of -39.38pts.

The overall record of Mullins' festival runners in handicaps since 2015 is just 3-42 but with a 13pts. Without Walsh in the saddle, the record is 3-31 for a healthier 24pts profit.

Barry Geraghty

Leading jockey at the festival in 2003 and 2012, and second on the all-time list with 34 winners, Geraghty is hard to profit from when riding for the high-profile teams of JP McManus and Nicky Henderson, but over the years has been worth noting on his mounts for other yards.

Jessica Harrington, a previous employer, has provided him with 19 winners from 118 rides for a handsome level-stakes profit of 55.25pts and for Jonjo O'Neill his record stands at 4-12 for a profit of 30pts.

When riding for current boss McManus since 2013, Geraghty is just 3-20, although that is for a 4pts profit. Champion Hurdle hot favourite Buveur D'Air looks set to boost that strike-rate, even if it does little for the profit column.

Davy Russell

No longer being tied to a big stable has enabled Russell to become a go-to jockey for many trainers and he has moved to 18 festival winners, with eight in the past four years alone. Overall since 2000 his record is 18-148 for a handsome level-stakes 93.50pts profit. The winners have been spread across 12 different trainers and he is 2-2 (both in the Pertemps Final with Mall Dini and Presenting Percy) for trainer Pat Kelly.

Last year he had just one winner from 17 rides for an overall -2pts loss but he will have rewarded plenty of each-way bets having missed the frame in only five races.

Having renewed a strong relationship with the Gigginstown powerhouse this season, Russell has been riding at the top of his game and is being touted as an outside bet for leading rider honours at the festival.

Richard Johnson

The British champion is a steady accumulator of festival winners, with a total of 22, but profit is hard to find for his followers. Since 2000 his record is 21-238 for a level-stakes loss of -16pts. For main employer Philip Hobbs he is 3-46 since 2013 with a -32pts loss.

Sam Twiston-Davies

Twiston-Davies has partnered seven winners from 105 rides since his festival debut in 2009, resulting in a level-stakes loss of -37pts. That statistic becomes healthier when examining his record for boss Paul Nicholls, as the pair are 4-42 since 2013 for a profit of 10pts.

Twiston-Davies went 0-15 at last year's festival, with third place in the Plate his best result, but he has time on his side and it will be a surprise if he doesn't do better this year.

Amateur jockeys

Crack Irish riders **Derek O'Connor** and **Jamie Codd** usually have their pick in the National Hunt Chase, Foxhunter Chase and Kim Muir Handicap Chase – the three festival races confined to amateurs – and their mounts tend to be closely watched in the market.

Since riding two winners (Chicago Grey and Zemsky) from just three rides in 2011 for a level-stakes profit of 37pts, O'Connor has managed to add only one more win to his tally, aboard Minella Rocco in the 2016 National Hunt Chase.

Codd has fared much better and is 5-13 since 2015. When riding for Gordon Elliott he has a 50 per cent strike-rate at a profit of 19.50pts. Three of the four winners came aboard festival stalwart Cause Of Causes and the pair are expected to take plenty of beating in their defence of this year's Cross Country race.

TOP JOCKEYS

Festival award winners

Year	Jockey	
2017	Ruby Walsh	4
2016	Ruby Walsh	7
2015	Ruby Walsh	4
2014	Ruby Walsh	3
2013	Ruby Walsh	4
2012	Barry Geraghty	5
2011	Ruby Walsh	5
2010	Ruby Walsh	3
2009	Ruby Walsh	7
2008	Ruby Walsh	3

Total festival winners

Jockey	
Ruby Walsh	56
Barry Geraghty	34
Richard Johnson	22
Davy Russell	18
Tom Scudamore	10
Bryan Cooper	8
Timmy Murphy	8
Nina Carberry	7
Jamie Codd	7
Sam Twiston-Davies	7

TOP TRAINERS

Festival award winners

Year	Trainer	
2017	Gordon Elliott	6
2016	Willie Mullins	7
2015	Willie Mullins	8
2014	Willie Mullins	4
2013	Willie Mullins	5
2012	Nicky Henderson	7
2011	Willie Mullins	4
2010	Nicky Henderson	3
2009	Paul Nicholls	5
2008	Paul Nicholls	3

Total festival winners

Nicky Henderson	58
Willie Mullins	54
Paul Nicholls	41
Jonjo O'Neill	26
Philip Hobbs	19
Edward O'Grady	18
Nigel Twiston-Davies	17
Alan King	15
David Pipe	15
Gordon Elliott	14

Derek O'Connor: arrives on a high after recent Grade 1 win with Edwulf

Stuart Riley on some of the trainers and jockeys looking for a first success at the festival

Joseph O'Brien

He has technically done it already, having overseen Ivanovich Gorbatov's preparation for the 2016 Triumph Hurdle, but the horse ran in father Aidan's name and thus the Melbourne Cup-winning trainer is still seeking his first official festival success. With the backing of major owners, the equine talent at his disposal and his talent as a trainer, it is only a matter of time before O'Brien jnr scores at Cheltenham. The Champion Bumper, for which Rhinestone and Alighted are shorter than 14-1 in the ante-post betting, might be his best chance, although Edwulf has a shot at the Gold Cup and the 24-year-old trainer showed his ability in big handicaps with Tigris River's win in this season's Galway Hurdle. Given his proficiency with juveniles, the Fred Winter could be a race he targets.

The Bowen brothers

He may not be able to drive, or vote, or do any number of other age-restricted activities, but there does not seem much runaway conditional

jockeys' championship leader James Bowen cannot do on horseback. Given his reputation as comfortably the best claimer in the weighing room, and the support of Nicky Henderson, Gordon Elliott and his father Peter, the Welsh National and Lanzarote-winning teenager looks sure to feature at this year's festival. He turns 17 the day before the festival starts but he has composure and skill beyond his years and, given the right opportunity, there is no doubting he is a rider for the big occasion.

Older brother Sean, 20, was champion conditional in 2014-15 and is in the top ten overall in Britain this season, but he is the only one of that elite group still waiting for a first festival winner. He

draws strong support from his father's yard, Paul Nicholls and Henderson among others, which will continue to give him plenty of chances.

Olly Murphy

Murphy was celebrating after last year's Cheltenham Festival, having helped his then boss Gordon Elliott do the seemingly impossible and dethrone Willie Mullins as the meeting's top trainer. This year Murphy will turn up with horses of his own and after a stellar first season it would be no surprise to see this shrewd operator walk away with one of the handicaps. Hunters Call is an early fancy for the County Hurdle and Murphy also has a shot at the Champion Bumper with Brewin'Upastorm.

Jedd O'Keeffe and Joe Colliver

O'Keeffe, the trainer who nearly quit due to ill health, and Colliver, the jockey who thought his career was over when he was jailed, could combine for one of those wonderfully romantic winners jump racing can provide. In Sam Spinner they have found a horse who has emerged as a force this season, winning what was the Fixed Brush hurdle by a dominant 17 lengths before proving it was no fluke with a Grade 1 triumph in the Long Walk. He is owned by Caron and Paul Chapman, the couple who talked O'Keeffe out of quitting in his darkest hour, and it would be some story if these connections could land the Stayers' Hurdle.

Fergal O'Brien

O'Brien is based just down the road from Prestbury Park and his yard has become a growing force since he took out a licence in 2011-12. He won his first Grade 1 this season courtesy of Poetic Rhythm in the Challow Novices' Hurdle and the likes of Cap Soleil, Colin's Sister and Barney Dwan help form the spine of a strong team, which also includes a number of promising bumper horses.

Three more to watch

The 2005-06 champion conditional **Will Kennedy** is still awaiting a first festival winner, but his patience could finally pay off as his superb horsemanship has played an integral part in helping Donald McCain revive his operation

Looking to break their duck: (clockwise from main) Joseph O'Brien (second left), Sean Bowen, James Bowen, Olly Murphy, Jedd O'Keeffe, Joe Colliver and Fergal O'Brien

and now Kennedy has some serious ammo.

Nick Gifford has gone close at festivals past – Straw Bear was second in Noland's Supreme as was Tullamore Dew in the 2010 Coral Cup – and in Didtheyleaveuoutto he saddles a major player in the Champion Bumper.

Sean Flanagan is too good a rider, and rides for too good a trainer in Noel Meade, to go much longer without a festival winner and is sure to have plenty of chances.

Marcus Buckland highlights some key lessons from last year's meeting

Check the ratings

Eighteen of the 28 races at the festival are non-handicaps, where horses generally race off level weights, and it is notable that ten of the 18 last year were won by horses ranked in the top two on official ratings. Maybe that is not so surprising, considering the horse with the highest mark is rated the most talented by the handicapper and often goes off favourite in level-weights races, but there were some eyecatching starting prices among last year's high-rated winners.

Top of the list was 16-1 winner Tiger Roll, second top-rated in the National Hunt Chase. Day two turned up another big-priced winner with Willoughby Court at 14-1 in the Neptune (the top two on ratings finished first and second, albeit the opposite way round) and Might Bite (also second top) landed the RSA Chase at 7-2.

Day three was good for favourites and for the top rated with Yorkhill (6-4) in the JLT Novices' Chase, Un De Sceaux (7-4) in the Ryanair Chase and Let's Dance (11-8) in the Mares' Novices' Hurdle. The final day was the least profitable but it still yielded one winner courtesy of Defi

Du Seuil (5-2f) in the Triumph Hurdle.

Blindly backing the horses rated in the top two (including joint) in those 18 non-handicaps would have resulted in a level-stakes profit of 21.38pts, a healthy return.

Front-runners are vulnerable

As with the 2016 festival when only Douvan and Annie Power were successful, front-runners again found life tough. Only three horses who made the running over the 28 races were able to hang

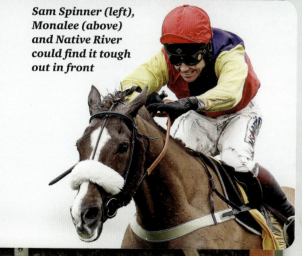

Sam Spinner (left), Monalee (above) and Native River could find it tough out in front

Sam Spinner (Stayers' Hurdle) and Maria's Benefit (Mares' Novices' Hurdle), while it will be interesting to see whether Footpad (Arkle Chase), Monalee (RSA Chase) and Native River (Gold Cup) try to take the hard route to victory or look for a rival to do the early donkey work.

Experience counts

Seventeen of the 28 races were won by horses who had run at the festival at least once before (three of them had appeared in the 2016 Supreme Novices' Hurdle). Of these 17 winners, seven had scored at the festival previously, although Un Temps Pour Tout (Ultima Handicap Chase) was the only one to win the same race for a second time.

Two of the winners were making their Cheltenham Festival debut but had won at the course previously – RSA Chase scorer Might Bite had been a winner over hurdles and Defi Du Seuil won a Triumph Hurdle trial before taking the main event.

The remaining eight winners were making their first appearance at Cheltenham, but six of those came from Ireland. British-trained horses by definition have more opportunity to try out the course and the only ones who won at last year's festival without having done so were Willoughby Court (Neptune) and Flying Tiger (Fred Winter).

on to win and interestingly all came within the space of four races on day two (Willoughby Court at 14-1, Might Bite at 7-2 and Special Tiara at 11-1).

Hold-up horses did best, accounting for ten winners and often at big prices (11-8f, 6-4f, 7-4f, 5-2, 4-1, 7-1, 10-1, 16-1 25-1 and 33-1). Seven of those ten hold-up victories came in hurdle races and one was in the bumper, suggesting that a handier position is more effective over fences.

Among the fancied front-running hurdlers who could be vulnerable this year are

How the 2017 festival unfolded – and what we can learn from the facts and figures of the 28 scorers

IT will come as no surprise that of the 14 Grade 1 winners at last year's meeting ten were trained by either Gordon Elliott, Nicky Henderson or Willie Mullins.

More illuminating is that 16 of the 28 winners in total were aged six or seven and that 23 had a prep run less than 50 days before their chosen target, with 16 less than 40 days before, while all four winning horses coming off a significant break of 70 days or more were trained in Ireland.

The 28 winners averaged four runs beforehand that season, amassing 55 wins between them from 121 races. Half of the 2017 winners had achieved an RPR of 150 that season and, in Grade 1 races such as the Arkle, Champion Hurdle, Champion Chase, Ryanair and Gold Cup, a seasonal Topspeed figure above 130 was a must. In fact, 11 of the 28 had achieved 120 on the Topspeed scale.

Eight of the 28 had never been to Cheltenham before, six of whom were trained in Ireland. A good piece of Navan form, a track with a similar configuration to Cheltenham, may help in assessing course debutants from Ireland. It is also worth noting that nearly all of last year's winners had previous winning form on good or good to soft/yielding ground.

The 20 winners with previous Cheltenham form had amassed 54 runs between them on the track, finishing in the top three 34 times. None of those Cheltenham runners fell or unseated at the track, and there were only two such instances from the 121 races the winners had contested that season.

An ideal Cheltenham candidate will be in his/her prime, arriving in good, recent, usually winning form and will have given an indication of an ability to run fast on decent surfaces over at least the trip in question. Good course form, or on similar left-handed tracks, is an obvious plus and erratic jumpers are likely to struggle.

Labaik *Supreme Novices' Hurdle*
Age 6yo
Trainer Gordon Elliott
Pre-festival form (2016-17) 11RR6
Days since last run 16
Previous Cheltenham form -
Best seasonal pre-race RPR 143
Best seasonal pre-race TS figure 109

Altior *Arkle Chase*
Age 7yo
Trainer Nicky Henderson
Pre-festival form (2016-17) 1111
Days since last run 31
Previous Cheltenham form 11
Best seasonal pre-race RPR 175
Best seasonal pre-race TS figure 153

Un Temps Pour Tout *Ultima Handicap Chase*
Age 8yo
Trainer David Pipe
Pre-festival form (2016-17) 1036
Days since last run 42
Previous Cheltenham form 362416
Best seasonal pre-race RPR 154
Best seasonal pre-race TS figure 135

Buveur D'Air *Champion Hurdle*
Age 6yo
Trainer Nicky Henderson
Pre-festival form (2016-17) 111
Days since last run 38
Previous Cheltenham form 3
Best seasonal pre-race RPR 155
Best seasonal pre-race TS figure 131

Apple's Jade *Mares' Hurdle*
Age 5yo
Trainer Gordon Elliott
Pre-festival form (2016-17) 12212
Days since last run 22
Previous Cheltenham form 2
Best seasonal pre-race RPR 155
Best seasonal pre-race TS figure 123

Tiger Roll *National Hunt Chase*
Age 7yo
Trainer Gordon Elliott
Pre-festival form (2016-17) P114U222133
Days since last run 134

Previous Cheltenham form 1103
Best seasonal pre-race RPR 157
Best seasonal pre-race TS figure 126

Tully East *Novices' Handicap Chase*
Age 7yo
Trainer Alan Fleming
Pre-festival form (2016-17) 162
Days since last run 25
Previous Cheltenham form 4
Best seasonal pre-race RPR 142
Best seasonal pre-race TS figure 106

Willoughby Court *Neptune Novices' Hurdle*
Age 6yo
Trainer Ben Pauling
Pre-festival form (2016-17) 211
Days since last run 32
Previous Cheltenham form -
Best seasonal pre-race RPR 150
Best seasonal pre-race TS figure 109

Might Bite *RSA Chase*
Age 8yo
Trainer Nicky Henderson
Pre-festival form (2016-17) 21F1
Days since last run 34
Previous Cheltenham form 150
Best seasonal pre-race RPR 165
Best seasonal pre-race TS figure 110

Supasundae *Coral Cup Handicap Hurdle*
Age 7yo
Trainer Jessica Harrington
Pre-festival form (2016-17) 0124
Days since last run 24
Previous Cheltenham form 60
Best seasonal pre-race RPR 152
Best seasonal pre-race TS figure 104

Special Tiara *Champion Chase*
Age 10yo
Trainer Henry de Bromhead
Pre-festival form (2016-17) 315
Days since last run 46
Previous Cheltenham form 363335
Best seasonal pre-race RPR 159
Best seasonal pre-race TS figure 144

Cause Of Causes *Cross Country Chase*
Age 9yo
Trainer Gordon Elliott
Pre-festival form (2016-17) 5P05
Days since last run 46
Previous Cheltenham form 302115
Best seasonal pre-race RPR 130
Best seasonal pre-race TS figure 117

Tiger Roll: last season's
National Hunt Chase winner

Flying Tiger
Fred Winter Juvenile H'cap Hurdle
Age 4yo
Trainer Nick Williams
Pre-festival form (2016-17) P614
Days since last run 18
Previous Cheltenham form -
Best seasonal pre-race RPR 132
Best seasonal pre-race TS figure 84

Fayonagh *Champion Bumper*
Age 6yo
Trainer Gordon Elliott
Pre-festival form (2016-17) 11
Days since last run 39
Previous Cheltenham form -
Best seasonal pre-race RPR 129
Best seasonal pre-race TS figure 41

Yorkhill *JLT Novices' Chase*
Age 7yo
Trainer Willie Mullins
Pre-festival form (2016-17) 411
Days since last run 53
Previous Cheltenham form 1
Best seasonal pre-race RPR 153
Best seasonal pre-race TS figure 123

Presenting Percy *Pertemps Final H'cap Hurdle*
Age 6yo
Trainer Patrick Kelly
Pre-festival form (2016-17) 0411541
Days since last run 19
Previous Cheltenham form -
Best seasonal pre-race RPR 147
Best seasonal pre-race TS figure 83

Un De Sceaux *Ryanair Chase*
Age 9yo
Trainer Willie Mullins
Pre-festival form (2016-17) 1611

Days since last run 47
Previous Cheltenham form 121
Best seasonal pre-race RPR 174
Best seasonal pre-race TS figure 155

Nichols Canyon *Stayers' Hurdle*
Age 7yo
Trainer Willie Mullins
Pre-festival form (2016-17) 312F
Days since last run 46
Previous Cheltenham form 33
Best seasonal pre-race RPR 166
Best seasonal pre-race TS figure 135

Road To Respect
Stable Plate Handicap Chase
Age 6yo
Trainer Noel Meade
Pre-festival form (2016-17) 014322
Days since last run 25
Previous Cheltenham form -
Best seasonal pre-race RPR 149
Best seasonal pre-race TS figure 118

Let's Dance *Mares Novices' Hurdle*
Age 5yo
Trainer Willie Mullins
Pre-festival form (2016-17) 21111
Days since last run 46
Previous Cheltenham form 4
Best seasonal pre-race RPR 146
Best seasonal pre-race TS figure 112

Domesday Book
Fulke Walwyn Kim Muir Handicap Chase
Age 7yo
Trainer Stuart Edmunds
Pre-festival form (2016-17) 5603
Days since last run 28
Previous Cheltenham form 0
Best seasonal pre-race RPR 145
Best seasonal pre-race TS figure 128

Defi Du Seuil *Triumph Hurdle*
Age 4yo
Trainer Philip Hobbs
Pre-festival form (2016-17) 111111
Days since last run 48
Previous Cheltenham form 111
Best seasonal pre-race RPR 148
Best seasonal pre-race TS figure 115

Arctic Fire *County Handicap Hurdle*
Age 8yo
Trainer Willie Mullins
Pre-festival form (2016-17) -
Days since last run 407
Previous Cheltenham form 22
Best seasonal pre-race RPR -
Best seasonal pre-race TS figure -

Penhill *Albert Bartlett Novices' Hurdle*
Age 6yo
Trainer Willie Mullins
Pre-festival form (2016-17) 1611141
Days since last run 78
Previous Cheltenham form -
Best seasonal pre-race RPR 148
Best seasonal pre-race TS figure 117

Sizing John *Gold Cup*
Age 7yo
Trainer Jessica Harrington
Pre-festival form (2016-17) 3211
Days since last run 33
Previous Cheltenham form 32
Best seasonal pre-race RPR 170
Best seasonal pre-race TS figure 146

Pacha Du Polder *Foxhunter Chase*
Age 10yo
Trainer Paul Nicholls
Pre-festival form (2016-17) 3341
Days since last run 35
Previous Cheltenham form P065
Best seasonal pre-race RPR 143
Best seasonal pre-race TS figure 104

Champagne Classic
Martin Pipe Conditional Jockeys' Handicap Hurdle
Age 6yo
Trainer Gordon Elliott
Pre-festival form (2016-17) 2123213
Days since last run 22
Previous Cheltenham form -
Best seasonal pre-race RPR 144
Best seasonal pre-race TS figure 97

Rock The World *Grand Annual H'cap Chase*
Age 9yo
Trainer Jessica Harrington
Pre-festival form (2016-17) 2000
Days since last run 146
Previous Cheltenham form 130
Best seasonal pre-race RPR 155
Best seasonal pre-race TS figure 97

Yorkhill parades past the crowds after his JLT victory

1.30 Sky Bet Supreme Novices' Hurdle   ITV/RUK
2m½f   Grade 1   £125,000

Willie Mullins has had the outright favourite or a joint-favourite in each of the past four runnings, winning the first two with Vautour and Douvan (which completed a hat-trick after the victory of Champagne Fever, joint-second favourite, in 2013) but having to settle for second place with Min and Melon in the past two years. This time he looks set to carry early Irish banker hopes again with Getabird, who has raced only twice over hurdles but was impressive in winning a Grade 2 at Punchestown on his second start in January. Samcro, hailed as the best novice in Ireland, looks likely to go for the longer Ballymore, leaving Mengli Khan (runner-up at Punchestown) as Gordon Elliott's most likely challenger. Principal British hopes lie with Harry Fry's If The Cap Fits (unbeaten in three over hurdles but untried in Graded company), Betfair Hurdle winner Kalashnikov and Nicky Henderson's Claimantakinforgan.

Getabird
6 b g; Trainer Willie Mullins
Hurdles form (all right-handed) 11, best RPR 152

Point winner who is unbeaten in two bumpers and two hurdles since joining Willie Mullins and has stamped himself as the most likely contender for the 2m novice crown won in the past by stable/ownermates Champagne Fever, Vautour and Douvan. That arguably came as a surprise to pretty much everyone as he was initially seen as a stayer and started his hurdles career over 2m4f on heavy ground at Punchestown, where he got the trip no problem and powered away for a seven-length win. However, he was dropped back to 2m for the Grade 2 Moscow Flyer at the same track in January and made all to slam Mengli Khan by nine lengths. If you wanted to quibble with the form you could argue that he got an easy lead, the runner-up, conceding 6lb, is quirky and had his share of disappointments on the Flat and the third needs 3m. That said, he was foot-perfect over his obstacles and quickened nicely at the end, so he has every right to be favourite assuming he comes here and Samcro heads for the Ballymore.

Going preference Doesn't seem to have a preference
Star rating ✪✪✪✪✪

Samcro
6 ch g; Trainer Gordon Elliott
Hurdles form 111, best RPR 154
Left-handed 11, best RPR 154
Right-handed 1, best RPR 146

Unbeaten and potentially brilliant novice who won the 2m Deloitte Novice Hurdle in fantastic style at Leopardstown but is still an odds-on favourite for the Ballymore on the Wednesday and is dealt with in more detail there. Needless to say, he'd be a major player here and probably favourite were connections to change their minds.

Going preference Unknown
Star rating ✪✪✪✪✪

If The Cap Fits
6 b g; Trainer Harry Fry
Hurdles form 111, best RPR 145
Left-handed 1, best RPR 138
Right-handed 11, best RPR 145

Decent bumper performer last season, finishing a close fourth in the Aintree Grade 2 in April, and has made great strides as a hurdler this season, winning all three. The first two triumphs came in weak enough company, but his five-length win under a double penalty at Kempton over Christmas came in a competitive heat and it was impressive the way he pulled clear in the end. The runner-up was only fifth in the Lanzarote Hurdle next time, but certainly not disgraced, while the fourth was beaten only a neck by Beyond The Clouds at Musselburgh, the pair in front of Claimantakinforgan, who was until then third favourite for this. Almost certainly needs to improve again to beat the top Irish contenders but has answered every question so far and at least looks one of the best of the home team.

Going preference Seems to act on any, but once a non-runner due to soft
Star rating ✪✪✪

Kalashnikov
5 br g; Trainer Amy Murphy
Hurdles form 1121, best RPR 153
Left-handed 111, best RPR 153
Right-handed 2, best RPR 144

Flagbearer for Amy Murphy, who had run only 13 horses in this sphere this season by the middle of February, but managed to train the winner of the most valuable 2m handicap hurdle in Britain. That was Kalashnikov, who completed his preparation for Cheltenham with a four-and-a-half-length success from the punted-on Bleu Et Rouge in a really strong field of 24 runners in the Betfair Hurdle at Newbury. There were around ten horses within four or five lengths going to the second-last, but by the end there was eight lengths back to third place and nine further back to fourth, so it's hard to see this as anything other than top-class form. What's more, it came on pretty soft ground, which his trainer blamed for his defeat in the Tolworth Hurdle to Summerville Boy the time before, and she remains adamant he wants a better surface. If that's true, he will be a serious danger to all as he has a terrific attitude to go with his

huge engine and it's worth remembering that novices Get Me Out Of Here and My Tent Or Yours both went close in the Supreme following Betfair Hurdle victory. However, it's also worth pointing out that Kalashnikov has an entry in the Ballymore and that's where Murphy was leaning towards before the Betfair Hurdle, although she changed her tune after it. Wherever he goes, he's a player.

Going preference Clearly acts well enough on soft but trainer convinced he wants better ground
Star rating ✪✪✪✪✪

Mengli Khan
5 b g; Trainer Gordon Elliott
Hurdles form 24111RO2, best RPR 150
Left-handed 11RO, best RPR 145
Right-handed 2412, best RPR 150

In-and-out performer on the Flat for Hugo Palmer, finishing last more times than he won, but was also capable of some classy form, notably a victory off a mark of 90 on the all-weather in September 2016. Didn't make an immediate mark over hurdles last season, finishing second in a maiden and then a distant fourth in a Grade 3, but better in second season for Gordon Elliott, winning his first three, including the Grade 1 Royal Bond at Fairyhouse with the minimum of fuss. Wheels came off next time, though, when he ran out through the wing two out in an eventful race won by the remarkably lucky Whiskey Sour. Arguably back on track next time when second to Getabird conceding 6lb, but the winner did it easily by nine lengths, so he has ground to make up. His Flat career makes him more heavily raced than most

JOCKEY'S VIEW
Jack Quinlan on Kalashnikov "We think an awful lot of him and, on good to soft ground, we would have really fancied him [in the Betfair Hurdle on soft]. His class brought him through. He's only five and that was only his fifth start, so he's entitled to mature all the time and he has improved since Sandown" *Stepped up 9lb to RPR of 153 to win the Betfair Hurdle, having gone up 13lb the time before*

(14 starts in all) and not easy to see him improving at the same rate as some of the less exposed types.

Going preference Likes soft, non-runner due to very fast ground once on Flat, but should be okay on spring good over jumps
Star rating ✪✪

Laurina
5 b m; Trainer Willie Mullins
Hurdles form F211, best RPR 148
Left-handed F2, best RPR -
Right-handed 11, best RPR 148

Promising mare who has bolted up in two mares' races for Willie Mullins so far. Fourth favourite in many lists for this, but trainer says mares' novice is the target and hard to see her lining up against the boys.

Going preference Obviously handles deep ground. Rest unknown
Star rating ✪

Claimantakinforgan
6 b g; Trainer Nicky Henderson
Hurdles form 113, best RPR 142
Left-handed 1, best RPR 129
Right-handed 13, best RPR 142
Cheltenham form (bumper) 3, best RPR 127
At the festival 15 Mar 2017 Midfield, headway 3f out, ridden over 1f out, every chance inside final furlong, stayed on under pressure, not quicken and held towards finish, finished third, beaten two and three-quarter lengths by Fayonagh in Champion Bumper

Won only one of five bumpers, but honest gelding who put up some decent performances in defeat, finishing third in the Champion Bumper at Cheltenham and fifth at Aintree. Good start to hurdles career when winning at Newbury in November and followed up in an Ascot Grade 2 the following month, but limitations apparently exposed when only third, beaten a length and three-quarters by Beyond The Clouds at Musselburgh early in February. The talented winner is not entered at Cheltenham and the runner-up was rated just 125 going into the race, having been soundly thumped by If The Cap Fits the time before, so it was a big knock to his form

claims and left Nicky Henderson to say "we'll have to see about Cheltenham now". That said, he appreciates better ground than at Musselburgh and a stronger gallop in a bigger field are almost certainly going to be in his favour, so there's no reason not to roll the dice.

Going preference Winner on soft but likes it quicker
Star rating ✪✪

Paloma Blue
6 br g; Trainer Henry de Bromhead
Hurdles form 3213, best RPR 143
Left-handed 313, best RPR 143
Right-handed 2, best RPR 125

Has long been well regarded by his trainer and finished second to Fayonagh in Grade 1 Punchestown bumper in April on only his second racecourse start last season. Although he didn't break his duck over hurdles until his third start, he has improved with every run and was a fair third to Samcro in the Deloitte, although that was a muddling race in which several key rivals underperformed. That said, he raced too freely himself and will surely be happier given a more searching gallop. Obviously needs to find plenty of improvement but looks to have a good future and no surprise if he makes the frame.

Going preference Proper fast ground an unknown but doesn't look like it will be a problem
Star rating ✪✪✪

Duc Des Genievres
5 gr g; Trainer Willie Mullins
Hurdles form 132, best RPR 146
Left-handed 32, best RPR 146
Right-handed 1, best RPR -

Won sole hurdles start at Moulins in France before being sent to Willie Mullins and has kept red-hot company since, running in two Grade 1s. Not disgraced in either, finishing third to Next Destination over 2m4f at Naas in January and second to impressive winner Samcro in the 2m Deloitte. Did well to get second coming from the back in a slowly run race and not one to underestimate wherever he ends up – has all three novice entries, which is nothing unusual for a Mullins horse.

Going preference Unraced on anything bar soft/heavy
Star rating ✪✪

Summerville Boy

6 b g; Trainer Tom George
Hurdles form 2231, best RPR 150
Left-handed 223, best RPR 137
Right-handed 1, best RPR 150
Cheltenham form 23, best RPR 137

Bought for £130,000 after winning Killarney bumper last season but seemingly had limitations exposed when failing to win any of his first three novice hurdles, although one of them was a Grade 2. Took his form to a completely different level when winning Grade 1 Tolworth Hurdle at Sandown by four lengths from Kalashnikov and, while favourite Western Ryder clearly never gave his running in a well-beaten (31 lengths) fourth, the runner-up had achieved a good level beforehand and subsequently won the Betfair Hurdle, and it didn't look to be a fluke. The race was run on really deep ground, though, and Summerville Boy clearly saw it out very well, so while he has yet to race beyond 2m1f, the chances are he's going to want further soon enough.

Going preference Very effective on heavy, yet to run on good
Star rating ✪✪

Sharjah

5 b g; Trainer Willie Mullins
Hurdles form 11F7, best RPR 147
Left-handed F7, best RPR 147
Right-handed 11, best RPR 136

Briefly threatened to be the Mullins no.1 for this contest after winning first two novices easily and then looking like hosing up in the Grade 1 Future Champions Novice Hurdle at Leopardstown over Christmas only to fall at the last when seemingly travelling all over Real Steel, who also fell independently.

Whether that fall knocked his confidence or he was just out of form next time is hard to tell, but he didn't run much of a race when well beaten in seventh behind Samcro in the Deloitte in February (raced freely early on, beaten turning in). Questions to answer now but worth recalling Patrick Mullins, who rode him in the Future Champions, said before the Deloitte: "No horse, not even Samcro, should be odds-on to beat him." Clearly held in very high regard and shouldn't be written off if making the trip.

Going preference Has raced only on soft or heavy over hurdles, Flat form in France suggests better ground will suit
Star rating ✪✪

OTHERS TO CONSIDER

There are more among the entries who could be forces but have more suitable targets, the obvious one being **Apple's Shakira**, who is 6-1 with a run in a place. She'll go to the Triumph, though, and you'd expect **Next Destination** to head for the Ballymore or even the Albert Bartlett. **Western Ryder** bounced back to some sort of form following his Tolworth flop when second in the Sidney Banks at Huntingdon, although he seemed to be outstayed by the winner. That probably means he's more likely to run here than anywhere and, while he needs improvement to make an impact, his fifth in the Champion Bumper tells you he'll be at home in a strongly run race on decent ground at Cheltenham. **First Flow** has an entry and his odds of 25-1 bear no relation to his form chance, which is much better. They do, however, reflect the likelihood of his participation because unless we get an extremely wet festival Kim Bailey probably won't risk this confirmed mudlark.

VERDICT

Assuming Samcro heads for the Ballymore, Getabird will be favourite for Willie Mullins and Rich Ricci, but it's easy enough to argue KALASHNIKOV'S Betfair Hurdle win is the most solid piece of form and he'll surely be hard to kick out of the frame if he lines up.

SUPREME NOVICES' HURDLE RESULTS AND TRENDS

	FORM	WINNER	AGE & WGT	Adj RPR	SP	TRAINER	BEST RPR LAST 12 MONTHS (RUNS SINCE)
17	11RR6	Labaik D	6 11-7	150-8	25-1	G Elliott (IRE)	won Navan Gd3 nov hdl (2m) (3)
16	61111	Altior CD	6 11-7	163T	4-1	N Henderson	won Kempton class 2 nov hdl (2m) (0)
15	2111	Douvan D	5 11-7	160-3	2-1f	W Mullins (IRE)	won Punchestown Gd2 nov hdl (2m) (0)
14	2-111	Vautour D	5 11-7	157T	7-2j	W Mullins (IRE)	won Gd1 Deloitte Hurdle (2m2f) (0)
13	-1231	Champagne Fever C,D	6 11-7	157-13	5-1	W Mullins (IRE)	won Gd1 Deloitte Hurdle (2m2f) (0)
12	-2111	Cinders And Ashes D	5 11-7	152-6	10-1	D McCain	won Aintree class 4 mdn hdl (2m1f) (2)
11	-F311	Al Ferof D	6 11-7	146-17	10-1	P Nicholls	won Newbury class 3 nov hdl (2m½f) (0)
10	11212	Menorah D, BF	5 11-7	160-3	12-1	P Hobbs	won Kempton class 2 nov hdl (2m) (1)
09	12121	Go Native D	6 11-7	153-8	12-1	N Meade (IRE)	won Punchestown Listed nov hdl (2m) (2)
08	1/711	Captain Cee Bee D	7 11-7	151-2	17-2	E Harty (IRE)	won Punchestown hdl (2m) (0)

WINS-RUNS: 4yo 0-4, 5yo 4-80, 6yo 5-60, 7yo 1-16, 8yo 0-3, 9yo 0-1 **FAVOURITES:** -£4.25

TRAINERS IN THIS RACE (w-pl-r): Willie Mullins 3-3-25, Nicky Henderson 1-9-20, Paul Nicholls 1-1-9, Philip Hobbs 1-1-7, Gordon Elliott 1-0-3, Noel Meade 1-0-3, Donald McCain 1-0-2, Edward Harty 1-0-1, Alan King 0-1-5, David Pipe 0-0-6, Dan Skelton 0-0-2, Harry Fry 0-0-1, Henry de Bromhead 0-1-3, Colin Tizzard 0-0-2

FATE OF FAVOURITES: 2534021122 **POSITION OF WINNER IN MARKET:** 4643621120

Key trends

🐎 Won at least 50 per cent of hurdle starts, nine winners in last ten runnings

🐎 Ran within the last 59 days, 9/10

🐎 Adjusted RPR of at least 150, 9/10

🐎 Won last time out, 8/10

🐎 Previously contested a Graded race, 8/10 (seven won)

🐎 Rated within 8lb of RPR top-rated, 8/10 (only two were top-rated)

Other factors

🐎 Ireland has won this 15 times in the past 27 years

🐎 Only one winner had come via the Flat. Seven of the other nine started their careers in bumpers, where they had earned an RPR of at least 110. The other two started over hurdles in France

🐎 Three winners had previously run in the Champion Bumper (Al Ferof second in 2010, Cinders And Ashes fifth in 2011 and Champagne Fever won in 2012)

🐎 For many years, the shortest priced Irish runner was often beaten by a compatriot. However, of the last ten to win, seven were the most fancied

Notes

2.10 Racing Post Arkle Chase
2m · Grade 1 · £175,000 · ITV/RUK

Footpad is ante-post favourite for Willie Mullins, who won this contest with Un De Sceaux in 2015 and Douvan the following year, although this one is not yet quite such a hot proposition as the Irish champion trainer's previous winners. Last time out he beat main market rival Petit Mouchoir by five lengths in the Irish Arkle – the second of a pair of Grade 1 wins in three starts over fences – but the rematch promises to be closer and potentially one of the races of the festival if they bring the sort of form that saw them finish third and fourth in last year's Champion Hurdle (Petit Mouchoir three lengths ahead of Footpad then). Leading British contender Sceau Royal was also involved in that Champion Hurdle, finishing sixth, and is another who has made a smooth transition to chasing, winning a Grade 1 at Sandown in December and a Grade 2 last time out. Harry Whittington's exciting Saint Calvados bolstered his claims by winning the Grade 2 Kingmaker at Warwick last time but one with questions to answer is Nicky Henderson's Brain Power, who has UF next to his name from his last two starts.

Footpad
6 b g; Trainer Willie Mullins
Chase form (left-handed) 111, best RPR 168
Cheltenham form (hurdles) 34, best RPR 159
At the festival 18 Mar 2016 Behind, ridden after 2 out to go pace, headway soon after, switched left slightly between last 2, went 3rd approaching last, stayed on, not pace to trouble front pair, finished third, beaten seven and a quarter lengths by Ivanovich Gorbatov in Triumph Hurdle
14 Mar 2017 Held up, headway approaching last, soon chasing leaders and ridden, not quicken, kept on under pressure run-in but not pace of leaders, finished fourth, beaten ten and a half lengths by Buveur D'Air in Champion Hurdle

Has already been to two Cheltenham Festivals, finishing third in the Triumph and fourth in the Champion Hurdle, but undoubtedly has his best chance yet of success. Always seemed to lack that extra change of gear as a hurdler and was tried over 3m at the end of last season, although probably didn't really get home when third to Unowhatimeanharry and the ill-fated Nichols Canyon. Transformed as a chaser, though, and with prominent/front-running tactics deployed (was held up as a hurdler) he has quickly developed into a top-class novice, winning all three starts. Has been odds-on for all three outings over fences, but two of them were Grade 1s and he already had the measure of market rival Death Duty when that one fell at the last in the Racing Post Novice Chase at Leopardstown over Christmas. Confirmed himself the one to beat at Cheltenham when winning the Irish Arkle at Leopardstown in February by an easy five lengths from Petit Mouchoir, a rival he had finished behind on all three meetings over hurdles. If there is one small doubt it's that he didn't seem to have the pace for decent ground at Cheltenham in the past two years, but he is ridden differently now, certainly doesn't look to lack speed and jumps quite beautifully, so easy enough to argue he's the complete package and deservedly a short-priced favourite even in this field.

Going preference Acts on any, suspicion he prefers it soft
Star rating ⭐⭐⭐⭐

Petit Mouchoir
7 gr g; Trainer Henry de Bromhead
Chase form 12, best RPR 161
Left-handed 2, best RPR 161
Right-handed 1, best RPR 153
Cheltenham form (all) 83, best RPR 163
At the festival 15 Mar 2016 Tracked leaders, hit 2 out, soon ridden, faded before last, finished

eighth, beaten 15 lengths by Altior in Supreme Novices' Hurdle

14 Mar 2017 Led, hit 2nd, hit 4 out, mistake when pressed 2 out, ridden and headed approaching last, kept on same pace run-in, edged right closing stages, finished third, beaten seven and a half lengths by Buveur D'Air in Champion Hurdle

You can understand why Footpad is such a short price for the Arkle when the second favourite is the one he so soundly thrashed last time out, but if there is a horse with the potential to cause a minor upset it is surely this two-time Grade 1-winning hurdler. He beat Footpad three times over hurdles last season and was a shorter price to do so every time (once odds-on when Footpad was 12-1) and he made a pretty sparkling debut over fences himself with an all-the-way success at Punchestown in October. Unfortunately he picked up a joint injury afterwards and his run in the Irish Arkle early in February was his first run since then. That is probably why he was given a more conservative ride than usual at Leopardstown, sitting in behind Footpad and giving the winner an easy lead rather than making the running himself, as he had done for his two Grade 1 wins last season and his Champion Hurdle third. Petit Mouchoir clearly needed the run and the experience (he dived at the first and third, but warmed up afterwards) and it will be a surprise if he allows Footpad such an easy time of it at Cheltenham. A very talented horse who clearly has the class between the obstacles to trouble Footpad and could be the one to benefit if the favourite doesn't fire.

Going preference Seems happy enough on most surfaces
Star rating ✪✪✪✪

Sceau Royal

6 b g; Trainer Alan King
Chase form 12111, best RPR 166
Left-handed 1211, best RPR 164
Right-handed 1, best RPR 166
Cheltenham form (all) 10162, best RPR 157
At the festival 18 Mar 2016 In touch, effort to chase leading bunch after 2 out, no impression, weakened before last, finished 12th, beaten 25 lengths by Ivanovich Gorbatov in Triumph Hurdle

Footpad: complete package who deservedly heads the market

14 Mar 2017 Held up, headway after 3 out, chasing leaders after 2 out, ridden before last, soon weakened, finished sixth, beaten 13 and a half lengths by Buveur D'Air in Champion Hurdle

In the same ownership as Footpad and very similar profile in that he appeared just short of top class over hurdles, but seems to have improved over fences. Only defeat in five outings came when going down by a neck to North Hill Harvey over the Arkle course and distance in October, but turned that form around with an 11-length defeat of the same horse off levels in the Henry VIII at Sandown in December. That was an eventful race in which favourite Finian's Oscar was beaten before halfway and second favourite Brain Power unseated at the last, but Sceau Royal was already booked for an easy win by the time the latter dipped out and that was by some margin the best performance by a British-trained 2m novice chaser this season until Saint Calvados rocked up at Warwick in February. Indeed, Racing Post Ratings puts him just 2lb off Footpad. Travelled really well in last season's Champion Hurdle but still finished behind Petit Mouchoir and Footpad then, so he needs to have improved by even more than those two to overturn the form. That is not impossible, though, and he will like it if the big two get involved in a battle early on. Wasn't the most fluent in his final warm-up at Doncaster in January, but trainer said he hadn't done much since Sandown and runner-up Shantou Rock is in any case quite a talent.

Going preference Acts on most, arguably doesn't want it too fast
Star rating ✪✪✪✪

Saint Calvados
5 b g; Trainer Harry Whittington
Chase form (left-handed) 111, best RPR 168

Potential superstar for Harry Whittington who is 3-3 since joining from France and has won each of his races in emphatic fashion. The first two came in novice handicaps at Newbury, but off marks of 143 and 147 and he won by nine lengths and ten lengths. Stepped up to Grade 2 company in the Kingmaker at Warwick, he led from pillar to post, jumping as well as any novice has round there, and strolled home by 22 lengths from the 143-rated Diego Du Charmil. It's hard to dress that up as anything other than top-class novice form and it arguably puts him at least on a par with the best of those ahead of him in the betting. With him, Footpad and Petit Mouchoir all prominent racers/front-runners, it could be some sight seeing them match strides in the early stages, but a tear-up probably won't do any of them any good. The one big worry with Saint Calvados is much faster ground because he has never run on anything other than soft or heavy ground and has a very high knee action, which suggests plenty of ease will always suit best. Jockey Aidan Coleman reckons he won't have any problem on a better surface, but we'll have to see.

Going preference Has never raced on anything other than soft/heavy
Star rating ✪✪

Brain Power

7 b g; Trainer Nicky Henderson
Chase form (all right-handed) 1UF, best RPR 162
Cheltenham form (hurdles) 88, best RPR 147
At the festival 14 Mar 2017 Raced keenly, chased leaders, raced in 2nd place briefly 4 out,

every chance 3 out, weakened quickly after 2 out, finished 9th, placed 8th, beaten 30 lengths by Buveur D'Air in Champion Hurdle

No doubt he's a hugely talented horse, but once called "stupid" by his owner for his lack of concentration and that may well have contributed to his late departures on last two starts over fences, having made such a sparkling debut when sauntering home by 28 lengths at Kempton in November. Took on the big boys in the Grade 1 Clarence House after unseating in the Henry VIII and, although he reportedly made a noise, he had moved into second place, around three lengths down on Un De Sceaux, when falling heavily at the last. Has obviously shown high-class form despite those non-completions at Sandown and Ascot, but

Saint Calvados: a star in the making

has something to prove at the same time, not least going left-handed. Did win a bumper at Newcastle on debut, but three subsequent runs on a left-handed track, the last two at Cheltenham, have resulted in defeats by 26, 20 and 30 lengths.

Going preference Comparable form on anything from good to soft
Star rating ✪✪✪

River Wylde

7 b g; Trainer Nicky Henderson
Chase form (left-handed) 12, best RPR 149
Cheltenham form (all) 03, best RPR 148
At the festival 14 Mar 2017 In touch, headway 5th, ridden to lead briefly turning in, held in 3rd when mistake last, no extra, finished third, beaten ten and a quarter lengths by Labaik in Supreme Novices' Hurdle

Third in last season's Supreme Novices' Hurdle, although beaten just over ten lengths, and made a good start to his chase career with a three-length win from subsequent impressive handicap winner Hell's Kitchen (off 137) at Uttoxeter in November. Best form on good/good to soft over hurdles and may have found it too deep when thumped 18 lengths by North Hill Harvey over the Arkle course and distance a couple of weeks later and not seen since. Trainer thinks he'll stay further, but he's never been tried over more than 2m and had only the Arkle as an entry among the Grade 1 novice chases. Mark of 144 could well underestimate him (Hell's Kitchen is now on 145), though, and no surprise if Nicky Henderson takes a look at the Grand Annual.

Going preference Has won on soft but said to hate it and better form when it's quicker
Star rating ✪✪

OTHERS TO CONSIDER

With such strong form contenders at the top of the market, this has all the makings of a small-field contest and I'm not sure anything else would be doing more than making up the numbers. One exception could be **Cyrname**, who is talented but would want it very soft (being by top-class mudlark Nickname) and has proved he stays 2m4f with his excellent second in the Scilly Isles, so would probably go for the JLT in any case. **North Hill Harvey** runs well at Cheltenham but looked to have been well found out by Saint Calvados at Warwick.

VERDICT

For a race with a short-priced favourite a month before the meeting, this contest is remarkably deep with at least four horses boasting form comparable to that of Footpad. Two of them, Saint Calvados and Petit Mouchoir, are also usually front-runners and if the jockeys aren't careful they could risk getting involved in a tear-up early on. I would certainly expect Petit Mouchoir to try to serve it up to Footpad from the off rather than sit behind him as he did at Leopardstown in February, but surely the speed they are likely to go will set things up for a closer, with the obvious one being SCEAU ROYAL.

Long term, I'm far from convinced Alan King's runner will end up the best of these (I can see Saint Calvados being a star on soft ground for Harry Whittington) but his most impressive performance over fences came at Sandown when they went hard in front in the Henry VIII and the make-up of this race might just suit him best of all. He looks a reasonable each-way proposition at around 7-1.

TRAINER'S VIEW

Alan King on Sceau Royal "I've always worried, certainly when Sceau Royal was running over hurdles, that he was 10lb below the very tops, but I think fences have improved him. From the first moment we schooled him he has been electric" *Went into last year's Champion Hurdle 7lb off top-rated on RPR but only 2lb below favourite Footpad and Saint Calvados here*

ARKLE CHASE RESULTS AND TRENDS

	FORM WINNER	AGE & WGT	Adj RPR	SP	TRAINER	BEST RPR LAST 12 MONTHS (RUNS SINCE)
17	-1111 **Altior** C, D	7 11-4	185[T]	1-4f	N Henderson	won Newbury Gd2 ch (2m½f) (0)
16	-1111 **Douvan** C, D	6 11-4	180[T]	1-4f	W Mullins (IRE)	won Leopardstown Gd1 nov ch (2m1f) (1)
15	1-F11 **Un De Sceaux** D	7 11-4	181[T]	4-6f	W Mullins (IRE)	won Leopardstown Gd1 nov ch (2m1f) (0)
14	1-261 **Western Warhorse**	6 11-4	148[-23]	33-1	D Pipe	won Doncaster class 3 nov ch (2m3f) (0)
13	11-11 **Simonsig** C, D	7 11-7	174[T]	8-15f	N Henderson	won Kempton Gd2 nov ch (2m) (0)
12	3-111 **Sprinter Sacre** D	6 11-7	179[T]	8-11f	N Henderson	won Newbury Gd2 ch (2m½f) (0)
11	22221 **Captain Chris** C, D	7 11-7	163[-4]	6-1	P Hobbs	2nd Sandown Gd1 nov ch (2m4½f) (1)
10	41111 **Sizing Europe** C, D	8 11-7	170[T]	6-1	H de Bromhead (IRE)	won Leopardstown Gd1 nov ch (2m1f) (0)
09	-1222 **Forpadydeplasterer** D	7 11-7	160[-6]	8-1	T Cooper (IRE)	2nd Gd1 nov ch (2m5f) (0)
08	-1112 **Tidal Bay** C, BF	7 11-7	160[T]	6-1	H Johnson	won Carlisle class 3 nov ch (2m4f) (2)

WINS-RUNS: 5yo 0-5, 6yo 3-30, 7yo 6-46, 8yo 1-13, 9yo 0-6, 10yo 0-1, 12yo 0-1 **FAVOURITES:** -£2.57

TRAINERS IN THIS RACE (w-pl-r): Nicky Henderson 3-2-10, Willie Mullins 2-1-10, Henry de Bromhead 1-2-6, Alan King 0-0-2, Gordon Elliott 0-0-2, Nigel Twiston-Davies 0-0-1, Paul Nicholls 0-1-9

FATE OF FAVOURITES: 3F04112111 **POSITION OF WINNER IN MARKET:** 2334118111

Key trends

🐎Finished in the first two on all completed chase starts, 10/10

🐎RPR hurdle rating of at least 153, 9/10

🐎SP no bigger than 8-1, 9/10

🐎Aged six or seven, 9/10

🐎Rated within 6lb of RPR top-rated, 9/10 (seven were top-rated)

🐎Adjusted RPR of at least 160, 9/10

🐎Three to five chase runs, 8/10 (both exceptions had fewer)

Other factors

🐎Seven winners had previously won a 2m-2m1f Graded chase

🐎Seven winners had previously run at the festival, showing mixed form in a variety of hurdle races

🐎A French-bred has finished in the first three on seven occasions (three won)

Notes

2.50 Ultima Handicap Chase ITV/RUK
3m1f   Grade 3   £110,000

The most prestigious handicap chase of the meeting has been won by just two favourites since 1977 (Antonin at 4-1 in 1994 and Wichita Lineman at 5-1 in 2009) but 13 of the past 19 winners were sent off 10-1 or lower. The latest was Un Temps Pour Tout, 9-1 last year when he won the race for the second year in a row (the top three in the betting took the first three places). He was the first back-to-back winner since Scot Lane in 1983, with Sentina (1957-1958) the only other to achieve the feat.

With his first victory, Un Temps Pour Tout became the first horse since Dixton House in 1989 to land the prize having not won a race over fences before, although he did continue the recent trend of inexperienced chasers taking this competitive handicap. In the last ten years only two horses, Golden Chieftain (2013) and The Druids Nephew (2015), had run more than ten times over fences before landing the prize.

David Pipe – Un Temps Pour Tout's trainer – and Jonjo O'Neill have the best recent records in the race, winning three times each in the last ten runnings.

Eight-year-olds have won the race eight times since the turn of the millennium, along with five seven year-olds. Together they account for 76 per cent of winners (13-17) in that period.

An official rating of 134 was required to get into last year's race and in the last 11 seasons no horse rated under 129 has qualified. However, in 2017 Un Temps Pour Tout (off 155) became the first winner since 1983 with a mark higher than 150. He carried 11st 12lb, the highest winning weight since Different Class with 11st 13lb in 1967.

While second-season chasers have traditionally done well, Un Temps Pour Tout's success in 2016 meant that a raw novice has landed the race five times in the last 14 runnings.

The only winner in the past 13 years without any previous course form was the Irish-trained Dun Doire, who completed a six-timer over fences in this race for Tony Martin in 2006. While Irish-bred horses account for ten of the last 11 winners, those trained across the Irish Sea have not done so well, having been successful only twice since 1966 with Youlneverwalkalone (2003) and Dun Doire.

Singlefarmpayment – short-head runner-up as favourite last year – could return with a leading chance, while local trainer Fergal O'Brien has an intriguing candidate in Barney Dwan. The eight-year-old Irish-bred novice, runner-up in last year's Pertemps Handicap Hurdle, achieved an RPR of 154 over 3m at Market Rasen in December before following up on his fifth chase start at Musselburgh in February.

Singlefarmpayment: could return in a bid to improve on last year's second place

ULTIMA HANDICAP CHASE RESULTS AND TRENDS

	FORM	WINNER	AGE & WGT	OR	SP	TRAINER	BEST RPR LAST 12 MONTHS (RUNS SINCE)
17	-1036	Un Temps Pour Tout CD	8 11-12	155-10	9-1	D Pipe	won Ultima Handicap Chase (3m1f) (5)
16	-1224	Un Temps Pour Tout D, BF	7 11-7	148-15	11-1	D Pipe	2nd Newbury Gd2 nov ch (2m7½f) (1)
15	-1275	The Druids Nephew	8 11-3	146T	8-1	N Mulholland	2nd Cheltenham Gd3 hcap ch (3m3½f) (1)
14	32U11	Holywell C, D	7 11-6	145-9	10-1	J O'Neill	won Doncaster class 4 nov ch (3m) (0)
13	P3633	Golden Chieftain D	8 10-2	132-1	28-1	C Tizzard	won Worcester class 3 hcap ch (2m4f) (5)
12	-PF75	Alfie Sherrin (1oh) D	9 10-0	129-5	14-1	J O'Neill	7th Kempton class 3 hcap ch (2m4½f) (0)
11	F2-52	Bensalem C, BF	8 11-2	143T	5-1	A King	fell Ultima Handicap Chase (3m½f) (3)
10	-3701	Chief Dan George D	10 10-10	142-6	33-1	J Moffatt	won Doncaster class 2 hcap ch (3m) (0)
09	9-121	Wichita Lineman C, D	8 10-9	142T	5-1f	J O'Neill	won Chepstow class 3 nov ch (3m) (0)
08	3-P61	An Accordion D	7 10-12	143-6	7-1	D Pipe	won Doncaster Listed hcap ch (3m) (0)

WINS-RUNS: 6yo 0-15, 7yo 3-44, 8yo 5-55, 9yo 1-48, 10yo 1-30, 11yo 0-17, 12yo 0-4, 13yo 0-1 **FAVOURITES:** -£4.00

FATE OF FAVOURITES: 312F020002 **POSITION OF WINNER IN MARKET:** 3102703253

OR 121-133 2-2-30, **134-148** 7-23-152, **149-161** 1-5-36

Key trends

🐎 Aged seven to nine, 9/10

🐎 Officially rated 132-148, 8/10

🐎 Ran no more than five times that season, 9/10

🐎 Carried no more than 11st 3lb, 7/10

🐎 Won over at least 3m, 8/10

🐎 No more than 11 runs over fences, 8/10

🐎 Top-three finish on either or both of last two starts, 8/10

Other factors

🐎 Eight winners had run at a previous festival, four recording at least one top-four finish

🐎 Five winners had run well in a handicap at Cheltenham earlier in the season (three placed, one fourth and one sixth). 2011 winner Bensalem and last year's victor Un Temps Pour Tout had run well in a Grade 2 hurdle at the course

🐎 This was once seemingly an impossible task for novices but four of the past ten winners have been first-season chasers

Notes

Hardy Eustace in 2004-05 was the last back-to-back winner of the Champion Hurdle – although Hurricane Fly has been a dual winner since in 2011 and 2013 – but Buveur D'Air is the first in three years to attempt the feat. The short odds-on being offered about Buveur D'Air reflect his strong credentials after easy Grade 1 wins this season in the Fighting Fifth and Christmas Hurdle, followed by a stroll in the same Sandown race used as his festival warm-up last year. Victory here would be his tenth in a row since finishing third to stablemate Altior in the 2016 Supreme Novices' and would confirm him in the superstar class. Opposition has been thin on the ground all season and Willie Mullins appears to be the only trainer with realistic hopes of beating Nicky Henderson, although potential challengers Faugheen, Yorkhill, Melon and Wicklow Brave all have question marks against them. Three-time runner-up My Tent Or Yours would be a popular winner but it is hard to see him getting past stablemate Buveur D'Air.

Buveur D'Air

7 b g; Trainer Nicky Henderson
Hurdles form 1131111111, best RPR 171
Left-handed 131111, best RPR 171
Right-handed 1111, best RPR 160
Cheltenham form 31, best RPR 171
At the festival 15 Mar 2016 Held up in rear, headway from 3 out, not fluent 2 out, soon ridden, went 3rd at the last, kept on but not pace to get on terms, finished third, beaten eight and a half lengths by Altior in Supreme Novices' Hurdle
14 Mar 2017 Held up in midfield, hit 4 out, headway soon after, ridden to lead approaching last, ran on run-in, edged right final 75yds when drawing clear, won Champion Hurdle by four and a half lengths from My Tent Or Yours

Very useful novice if not the complete package when third in a Supreme Novices' Hurdle for the ages in 2016, but originally sent chasing last year and began well enough with two comfortable wins, although did tend to get very low at his fences. A switch back to hurdling followed and he duly won his Cheltenham prep in the four-runner Contenders Hurdle at Sandown, although he didn't have much in the way of competition. That didn't matter, though as, sent off 5-1 second favourite, he came of age in the Champion Hurdle, travelling supremely well and sprinting clear of regular Cheltenham bridesmaid My Tent Or Yours for a four-and-a-half-length win. Confirmed himself the best of his generation with a five-length success over the same horse in the Aintree Hurdle after that and it has all been plain sailing so far this term with three wins out of three. You could argue he hasn't exactly faced much as he officially had 15lb in hand of runner-up Irving in the Fighting Fifth and 6lb over The New One in the Christmas Hurdle at Kempton, which is not a track that suits the latter, but he can only beat what's put in front of him and he toyed with them. Swerved the Irish Champion Hurdle in favour of an easier task in the Contenders Hurdle at

TRAINER'S VIEW

Nicky Henderson on Buveur D'Air "He needs a huge amount of work, so it's not really job done [after Sandown]. He's got to keep working and I wouldn't rule him out of having a canter round Kempton or something nearer the time. He's got to be a very burly horse and he puts weight on very easily"

Sandown once again and didn't need to be at his best to see off John Constable. Stands head and shoulders above the best of the rest in Britain and, with Faugheen beaten in the Irish Champion Hurdle and Melon flopping badly in the same race, it's hard to see where the realistic opposition is going to come from. Just about the shortest price of the whole meeting and impossible to argue that it shouldn't be the case.

Going preference Handles most ground fine
Star rating ✪✪✪✪✪

Faugheen

10 b g; Trainer Willie Mullins
Hurdles form 1111111112111P2, best RPR 177
Left-handed 1111P2, best RPR 177
Right-handed 111111211, best RPR 173
Cheltenham form 11, best RPR 170
At the festival 12 Mar 2014 Prominent, tracked leader after 6th, not fluent next, led and mistake 3 out, drew clear before last, ridden out, won Neptune Investment Management Novices' Hurdle by four and a half lengths from Ballyalton
15 Mar 2015 Made all dictating steady pace, jumped right and not fluent 2 out, quickened off bend between last 2, about 3 lengths clear last, kept on well towards finish, won Champion Hurdle by a length and a half from Arctic Fire

Brilliant hurdler up to a couple of years ago having won 12 of his 13 starts in all, the only defeat coming when surprisingly turned over at odds of 1-6 by stablemate Nichols Canyon. There were seven Grade 1s among those wins, including a Neptune and Champion Hurdle at the festival and two Christmas Hurdles, and he looked set for a stellar career. There was some criticism of the jockeys who gave him an easy lead in the 2015 Champion Hurdle, but he went on to prove himself by far and away the best of his generation, his 15-length Irish Champion Hurdle win over Arctic Fire in January 2016 earning him a Racing Post Rating of 177, a figure that had not been bettered by any horse other than Istabraq in a 2m hurdle over the last 20 years. Unfortunately that also marked his final appearance until November last year, when he returned from injury with

a crushing 16-length victory over former Champion Hurdle winner Jezki. That led many to believe he was as good as ever despite his problems, but it seems to have proved a false dawn because Faugheen went backwards next time and was pulled up after never travelling behind Mick Jazz in the Ryanair Hurdle at Leopardstown in December. He fared better next time in the Irish Champion Hurdle, but a two-and-a-quarter-length defeat by Stayers' Hurdle favourite Supasundae was some way off his previous best and just as far off what will be needed to beat Buveur D'Air. Connections remain hopeful he can step up again, but in reality it was wishful thinking to expect him to be the same horse at the age of ten even without the problems he has had.

Going preference No problems with the going, although will be vulnerable at his age if it's fast
Star rating ✪✪

My Tent Or Yours

11 b g; Trainer Nicky Henderson
Hurdles form 12112111232233242221, best RPR 171
Left-handed 21211232232221, best RPR 171
Right-handed 111342, best RPR 171
Cheltenham form 22221, best RPR 171
At the festival 12 Mar 2013 Raced keenly, tracked leaders, went 2nd between last 2, led narrowly last, headed final 110yds, one pace and held close home, finished second, beaten half a length by Champagne Fever in Supreme Novices' Hurdle
11 Mar 2014 Took strong hold, tracked leaders, not fluent 4 out, tracked leaders 2 out, chased winner last, strong run under pressure run-in, finished well, just failed, finished second, beaten a neck by Jezki in Champion Hurdle
15 Mar 2016 Tracked leaders travelling strongly, went 2nd 3rd, every chance 2 out, ridden and outpaced by winner before last, stayed on under pressure run-in but no chance, just held on for 2nd, beaten fourth and a half lengths by Annie Power in Champion Hurdle
14 Mar 2017 Held up, headway after 4 out, ridden to chase winner last, no impression under pressure run-in, finished second, beaten four and a half lengths by Buveur D'Air in Champion Hurdle

Admirable veteran who landed his first victory since scoring in a jumpers' bumper in February 2014 when beating old rival The New One in the International Hurdle at Cheltenham in December. That was his first victory at Cheltenham, but there's no denying he loves the place as he has been second in a Supreme and three Champion Hurdles, coming closest when going down by a neck to Jezki in 2014. Also finished second to Buveur D'Air in the Aintree Hurdle last season and then to the enterprisingly ridden Wicklow Brave in the Punchestown Champion Hurdle. International win, albeit in receipt of 6lb from The New One, confirms he retains the vast majority of his ability and, given the lack of youngsters coming through, there's every chance he will place again. The fact he is a shorter price as an 11-year-old in February than he was on the day last year tells you how weak the competition is.

Going preference Doesn't want it bottomless, but otherwise acts on any
Star rating ✪✪✪

Melon

6 ch g; Trainer Willie Mullins
Hurdles form 122135, best RPR 160
Left-handed 1235, best RPR 160
Right-handed 21, best RPR 155
Cheltenham form 23, best RPR 160
At the festival 14 Mar 2017 Travelled strongly, tracked leaders, every chance after turning in, ridden when not fluent last, kept on until no extra final 100yds, finished second, beaten two and a quarter lengths by Labaik in Supreme Novices' Hurdle

A ten-length maiden hurdle win on his debut for Willie Mullins was enough to see this one sent off joint-favourite when thrown straight into last season's Supreme Novices' Hurdle and he acquitted himself well enough, finishing second to the quirky Labaik, who had refused to race or only reluctantly set off

Faugheen (right): needs to step up on recent form if he's going to trouble Buveur D'Air

miles behind on his three previous outings. If anything Melon travelled too well and found little off the bridle, and that was also the case when he was backed down to favouritism for the International Hurdle at Cheltenham in December. That was still the best run of his life according to Racing Post Ratings as he was beaten just over two lengths conceding 6lb to winner My Tent Or Yours. In an effort to tame his headstrong tendencies, Mullins reached for a first-time hood in the Irish Champion Hurdle at Leopardstown in February, but he still raced keenly enough in the early stages and, having been a huge market drifter in the closing minutes before racetime, he dropped away tamely to be beaten 12 lengths in fifth. That cannot be his running but it has left him with a question or two to answer and there's always a chance he'll boil over on the big day given the huge crowd.

Going preference Acts on good and soft
Star rating ✪✪

Yorkhill

8 ch g; Trainer Willie Mullins
Hurdles form 11114, best RPR 158
Left-handed 11, best RPR 158
Right-handed 114, best RPR 152
Cheltenham form (all) 11, best RPR 166
At the festival 16 Mar 2016 Took keen hold, held up in rear, not fluent 4th and 7th, not much room bend before 3 out, progressed to track leaders 2 out, squeezed through on inner to lead on bend before last, 3 lengths up and fine jump last, edged right and ridden out, won Neptune Investment Management Novices' Hurdle by a length and three-quarters from Yanworth 16 Mar 2017 Travelled strongly, held up in touch, left tracking leaders 4 out, smooth run on inner turning in, led soon after next, pecked last, kept on, ridden out, won JLT Novices' Chase by a length from Top Notch

Hugely talented horse who has variously been considered Champion Chase/Champion Hurdle/Gold Cup winner in waiting but will go into Cheltenham under a cloud if he does indeed line up, which has to be doutbful.

He was a brilliant novice under both codes, winning the Neptune over hurdles in 2016 and the JLT over fences last season, but things have really gone pear-shaped this term. Any ideas about him being a Gold Cup horse went out the window when he patently failed to stay in the 3m Christmas Chase at Leopardstown and was beaten 59 lengths, but he was even worse dropped to 2m1f for the Dublin Chase, in which he was beaten 81 lengths. He was a late drifter in the market and clearly wasn't himself in the race as he never seemed to travel from the off. That seems to be it for fences, but even if Yorkhill does return to hurdles he still needs to prove he is a 2m horse and that he retains the ability he has already shown on the racecourse, which in any case would not be quite good enough to beat Buveur D'Air. His best form over 2m is his Tolworth Hurdle success in January 2016, but he earned an RPR of only 152 for beating O O Seven (now a 3m handicap chaser). No

Wicklow Brave: has the talent to hit the frame

longer as artificially priced as he has been all season but hardly screaming to be backed at current inflated odds.

Going preference Acts on any, probably doesn't want it too heavy
Star rating ◑

Wicklow Brave

9 b g; Trainer Willie Mullins
Hurdles form 1166F580P103371, best RPR 165
Left-handed 680137, best RPR 158
Right-handed 116F5P031, best RPR 165
Cheltenham form 617, best RPR 158
At the festival 11 Mar 2014 In touch, tracking leaders 3 out, went 2nd approaching last, no impression on winner, lost 2nd 110yds out, weakened towards finish, finished 6th, beaten nine and a half lengths by Vautour in Supreme Novices' Hurdle
13 Mar 2015 Held up towards rear, smooth progress on outer after 3 out, led going strongly after 2 out, clear when hit last, ran on strongly, readily, won Vincent O'Brien County Handicap Hurdle by eight lengths from Sort It Out
14 Mar 2017 Reluctant to jump off, held up, headway approaching 2 out, soon close up chasing leaders, ridden and weakening when mistake last, finished 8th, placed 7th, beaten 14 and a half lengths by Buveur D'Air in Champion Hurdle

Much-travelled nine-year-old who is one of the highest earners in the field, although that is largely down to his exploits on the Flat, which include a Group 1 Irish St Leger victory over hot favourite Order Of St George in September 2016. His four hurdles wins include a County Hurdle at Cheltenham and, last season, the Punchestown Champion Hurdle, in which Patrick Mullins rode his professional rivals to sleep, pinching a long lead from halfway. Flat exploits in the summer suggest he hasn't deteriorated as he was only a half-length second to subsequent Melbourne Cup winner Rekindling at the Curragh in July and fourth in the Goodwood Cup the following month. Although well beaten in the Caulfield and Melbourne Cups (12th and tenth), he was a 70-1 shot for each and not much better could have been expected. Indeed, he fared a lot better than he had in Melbourne the year before, that run preceding last year's crack at the Champion Hurdle. Does have his quirks and lost any chance he had at the start at Cheltenham last year by conceding his rivals around ten lengths jumping off. It's worth remembering, however, that he approached the second-last seemingly travelling as well as anything and traded at little over 3-1 on Betfair (had a Betfair SP of 41) before dropping back in the straight. Forgotten horse in some respects and has the talent to hit the frame if he behaves himself.

Going preference Handles pretty much anything
Star rating ✪✪✪

Mick Jazz
7 b g; Trainer Gordon Elliott
Hurdles form 6232P12313513, best RPR 158
Left-handed 32P213, best RPR 158
Right-handed 6213135, best RPR 151
Cheltenham form P

Spent two seasons as a novice but thrived after returning from injury and switched to Gordon Elliott from Harry Fry and his record of steady improvement has continued this season, albeit he needs a fair chunk more. Won what turned out to be an exceptionally weak Ryanair Hurdle at Leopardstown in December after 2-11 favourite Faugheen pulled up and arguably achieved at least as much when a seven-length third to Supasundae and Faugheen in the Irish Champion Hurdle back at the same track next time. Is going forwards but probably not quickly enough.

Going preference Best form on soft, but hasn't run on anything quicker since December 2016, when he put up then career best on good to yielding
Star rating ✪✪

Elgin
6 b g; Trainer Alan King
Hurdles form 1122741161, best RPR 159
Left-handed 12741, best RPR 152
Right-handed 12161, best RPR 159
Cheltenham form 71, best RPR 152
At the festival 14 Mar 2017 Mid-division, not fluent 3 out, soon pushed along, outpaced 2 out, stayed on approaching last but not pace to get on terms, finished seventh, beaten 23 lengths by Labaik in Supreme Novices' Hurdle

Seemingly well short of top class as a novice, finishing seventh and beaten a long way in the Supreme, but has upped his game big time this term, winning two good handicaps at Cheltenham and Ascot and taking step up in class in his stride when giving 4lb and a two-and-a-half-length beating to Ch'Tibello in the Kingwell at Wincanton. Not entered for the Champion Hurdle but connections will consider supplementing (for £20,000) and no reason why they shouldn't as there's good place money up for grabs.

Going preference Seems versatile
Star rating ✪✪

OTHERS TO CONSIDER

It's hard to see where any other threats are going to come from. **Ch'Tibello** had his chance to stake a claim in the Kingwell but had no excuses and Harry Skelton was talking in terms of the Scottish Champion afterwards. **Call Me Lord** also got found out at Wincanton and can't be considered now. The likes of **Min** and **Apple's Jade** retained entries at the February scratchings stage but would be hugely unlikely runners.

VERDICT

BUVEUR D'AIR really looks a class above unless Faugheen can recover his best form, but that's looking less likely by the day and the favourite should make it two Champion Hurdles with the minimum of fuss. If you're looking for each-way punts, perennial second My Tent Or Yours and Wicklow Brave, if he behaves himself, would be my picks to follow the jolly home.

	FORM	WINNER	AGE & WGT	Adj RPR	SP	TRAINER	BEST RPR LAST 12 MONTHS (RUNS SINCE)
17	1-111	**Buveur D'Air** D	6 11-10	163^{-7}	5-1	N Henderson	Won Gd1 Aintree nov hdl (2m½f) **(1)**
16	1F-11	**Annie Power** C, D	8 11-3	173^{T}	5-2f	W Mullins (IRE)	Won Gd1 Punchestown Mares Hurdle (2m2f) **(1)**
15	1-111	**Faugheen** C, D	7 11-10	173^{-4}	4-5f	W Mullins (IRE)	Won Gd1 Christmas Hurdle (2m) **(0)**
14	-1124	**Jezki** D	6 11-10	169^{-8}	9-1	J Harrington (IRE)	2nd Gd1 Ryanair Hurdle (2m) **(1)**
13	1-111	**Hurricane Fly** CD	9 11-10	177^{T}	13-8f	W Mullins (IRE)	won Gd1 Irish Champion Hurdle (2m) **(0)**
12	23-12	**Rock On Ruby** C, D	7 11-10	170^{-7}	11-1	P Nicholls	2nd Gd1 Christmas Hurdle (2m) **(0)**
11	1-111	**Hurricane Fly** D	7 11-10	172^{-2}	11-4f	W Mullins (IRE)	won Gd1 Irish Champion Hurdle (2m) **(0)**
10	3-531	**Binocular** D	6 11-10	171^{-2}	9-1	N Henderson	won Sandown Listed hdl (2m½f) **(0)**
09	1-1F3	**Punjabi** D, BF	6 11-10	168^{-8}	22-1	N Henderson	won Gd1 Punchestown Champ Hurdle (2m) **(3)**
08	-1321	**Katchit** CD	5 11-10	166^{-8}	10-1	A King	won Gd2 Kingwell Hurdle (2m) **(0)**

WINS-RUNS: 5yo 1-29, 6yo 4-33, 7yo 3-22, 8yo 1-18, 9yo 1-7, 10yo 0-4, 11yo 0-4, 12yo 0-2, 13yo 0-1 **FAVOURITES:** £5.67

TRAINERS IN THIS RACE (w-pl-r): Willie Mullins 4-4-16, Nicky Henderson 3-7-23, Alan King 1-0-8, Paul Nicholls 1-1-8, Nigel Twiston-Davies 0-2-6, Philip Hobbs 0-0-2, Henry de Bromhead 0-1-3, Dan Skelton 0-0-1

FATE OF FAVOURITES: 0301314110 **POSITION OF WINNER IN MARKET:** 5971415112

Key trends

🐎 Adjusted RPR of at least 163, 10/10

🐎 Rated within 8lb of RPR top-rated, 10/10

🐎 No more than 12 hurdle runs, 9/10

🐎 Won a Grade 1 hurdle, 9/10

🐎 Aged between six and eight, 8/10

🐎 Ran within the past 51 days, 8/10

🐎 Won last time out, 7/10

🐎 Topspeed of at least 151, 7/10

Other factors

🐎 Katchit (2008) broke a longstanding trend when he became the first five-year-old to win since See You Then in 1985. In the intervening years 73 failed while 27 have come up short since

🐎 Only two winners had not run since the turn of the year (Rock On Ruby and Faugheen)

Notes

4.10 OLBG Mares' Hurdle   ITV/RUK
2m4f   Grade 1   £120,000

There has long been an Irish stranglehold on this contest, principally with Willie Mullins' six-time heroine Quevega and his subsequent winners Glens Melody and Vroum Vroum Mag. Gordon Elliott pushed Mullins aside last year by relegating him to the minor places as Apple's Jade – who had been with Mullins until the split with Gigginstown – defeated Vroum Vroum Mag and Limini. Apple's Jade, who ranks alongside peak-form Quevega and above the other previous winners on Racing Post Ratings, has demonstrated her class this season with Grade 1 victories over Nichols Canyon (last year's Stayers' Hurdle winner) and Supasundae (ante-post favourite for this year's Stayers') and is set to return as odds-on favourite. Mullins is likely to field the main challenger in Let's Dance, who took the novice version of this race last year but has yet to win in five attempts at Grade 1 level – including a nine-length defeat by erstwhile stablemate Apple's Jade when they were juvenile hurdlers. Mullins also has Benie Des Dieux, Vroum Vroum Mag and Augusta Kate in his potential team, while British hopes appear to lie with Colin's Sister and La Bague Au Roi.

OLBG MARES' HURDLE RESULTS AND TRENDS

	FORM WINNER	AGE & WGT	Adj RPR	SP	TRAINER	BEST RPR LAST 12 MONTHS (RUNS SINCE)
17	12212 **Apple's Jade** D, BF	5 11-5	171^T	7-2	G Elliott (IRE)	won Aintree Gd1 juv hdl (2m1f) (5)
16	1-111 **Vroum Vroum Mag** D	7 11-5	160^T	4-6f	W Mullins (IRE)	won Ascot Gd2 hdl (2m7½f) (0)
15	7521 **Glens Melody** D	7 11-5	162^{-11}	6-1	W Mullins (IRE)	won Warwick Listed hdl (2m5f) (0)
14	1/11- **Quevega** CD	10 11-5	171^T	8-11f	W Mullins (IRE)	won Gd1 Punchestown World Hdl (3m) (0)
13	/111- **Quevega** CD	9 11-5	168^T	8-11f	W Mullins (IRE)	won Gd1 Punchestown World Hdl (3m) (0)
12	1/1-1 **Quevega** CD	8 11-5	168^T	4-7f	W Mullins (IRE)	won Gd1 Punchestown World Hdl (3m) (0)
11	3911- **Quevega** CD	7 11-5	166^T	5-6f	W Mullins (IRE)	won Gd2 Mares' Hurdle (2m4f) (1)
10	11-39 **Quevega** CD	6 11-5	168^T	6-4f	W Mullins (IRE)	3rd Gd1 Punchestown Champ Hdl (2m) (1)
09	19-31 **Quevega** D	5 11-3	156^{-4}	2-1f	W Mullins (IRE)	won Punchestown hdl (2m4f) (0)
08	23121 **Whiteoak**	5 11-0	139^{-23}	20-1	D McCain	won Ascot class 3 nov hdl (2m) (0)

WINS-RUNS: 4yo 0-3, 5yo 3-26, 6yo 1-48, 7yo 3-45, 8yo 1-33, 9yo 1-11, 10yo 1-3, 11yo 0-1 **FAVOURITES:** £4.03

TRAINERS IN THIS RACE (w-pl-r): Willie Mullins 8-3-14, Gordon Elliott 1-0-2, Alan King 0-1-7, Ben Case 0-0-2, Harry Fry 0-1-4, Fergal O'Brien 0-0-1, Martin Keighley 0-0-1, Neil Mulholland 0-0-5, Nicky Henderson 0-3-10, Nigel Twiston-Davies 0-0-4, Oliver Sherwood 0-0-3, Gary Moore 0-0-1, Warren Greatrex 0-0-1, Gavin Cromwell 0-0-1

FATE OF FAVOURITES: 3111111F13 **POSITION OF WINNER IN MARKET:** 7111111213

Key trends

- Top-three finish in a Grade 1 or 2 hurdle, 10/10
- At least nine career starts, 10/10
- Adjusted RPR of at least 156, 9/10
- Won last time out, 8/10
- Trained by Willie Mullins, 8/10

Other factors

- Nicky Henderson has yet to win this but has had three places from ten runners (two seconds, one third)
- A runner priced 16-1 or bigger has finished in the first three in nine of the ten renewals
- Quevega used to come here fresh when defending her crown but the other four winners had between three and five outings that season

4.50 National Hunt Chase · RUK
4m · Grade 2 · Amateur riders' novice chase · £125,000

This is the longest and oldest race at the festival. The structure of the race has changed and it has gradually lost its reputation for producing shocks, with last year's winner Tiger Roll (16-1) being the only one to score at double-figure odds in the last seven runnings. Before 2002, horses who had won over hurdles were excluded and since 2010 chase winners have not had to carry penalties. It was awarded Listed status in 2014, and raised to Grade 2 last year, and is now more of a four-mile RSA Chase in quality.

This means the big yards have a greater chance of producing the winner. In the last seven years, three favourites have obliged and three others were sent off at 8-1. It is notable that three of those past seven winners had the highest official rating, while Shotgun Paddy (top-rated in 2014) was beaten only a neck and, despite his odds, Tiger Roll was second-highest on official ratings last year.

NATIONAL HUNT CHASE RESULTS AND TRENDS

FORM	WINNER	AGE & WGT	Adj RPR	SP	TRAINER	BEST RPR LAST 12 MONTHS (RUNS SINCE)
17	22133 **Tiger Roll** C	7 11-6	159-6	16-1	G Elliott (IRE)	won Limerick hcap ch (3m) (2)
16	-3P62 **Minella Rocco**	6 11-6	159-7	8-1	J O'Neill	2nd Ascot Gd2 nov ch (3m) (0)
15	20-75 **Cause Of Causes**	7 11-6	159-2	8-1	G Elliott (IRE)	2nd Kim Muir hcap ch (3m1½f) (3)
14	61U21 **Midnight Prayer**	9 11-6	154-12	8-1	A King	won Warwick class 3 nov ch (3m2f) (0)
13	/2111 **Back In Focus**	8 11-6	161T	9-4f	W Mullins (IRE)	won Leopardstown Gd1 nov ch (3m) (0)
12	321P1 **Teaforthree**	8 11-6	161T	5-1f	R Curtis	won Chepstow class 3 nov ch (3m) (2)
11	11F25 **Chicago Grey** C	8 11-6	163T	5-1f	G Elliott (IRE)	2nd Cheltenham class 2 nov ch (3m1½f) (1)
10	-2951 **Poker De Sivola**	7 11-6	145-8	14-1	F Murphy	2nd Kelso class 3 hcap ch (3m1f) (3)
09	42212 **Tricky Trickster**	6 11-11	140-18	11-1	N Twiston-Davies	2nd Cheltenham class 2 nov hcap ch (2m5f) (0)
08	27322 **Old Benny**	7 11-7	135-18	9-1	A King	2nd Newbury class 2 nov ch (3m) (0)

WINS-RUNS: 5yo 0-1, 6yo 2-25, 7yo 4-71, 8yo 3-52, 9yo 1-21, 10yo 0-7, 12yo 0-1 **FAVOURITES:** £5.25

TRAINERS IN THIS RACE (w-pl-r): Gordon Elliott 3-0-5, Alan King 2-1-10, Nigel Twiston-Davies 1-0-9, Rebecca Curtis 1-0-5, Willie Mullins 1-3-11, Colin Tizzard 0-1-2, David Pipe 0-2-8, Nicky Henderson 0-1-4, Tony Martin 0-1-2, Charlie Longsdon 0-0-3, Noel Meade 0-0-3, Paul Nicholls 0-1-7, Warren Greatrex 0-1-3, Fergal O'Brien 0-0-2, Henry de Bromhead 0-0-1, Mark Bradstock 0-0-2, Neil Mulholland 0-0-1, Philip Hobbs 0-0-2, Donald McCain 0-0-7, Charlie Mann 0-0-3, Bob Buckler 0-0-2

FATE OF FAVOURITES: 5451110045 **POSITION OF WINNER IN MARKET:** 4571114359

Key trends

- Ran at least three times over fences, 10/10
- Hurdles RPR of at least 118, 10/10
- Finished first or second in a chase over at least 3m, 10/10
- Top five-finish last time out, 9/10 (exception unplaced in Class 1 chase)
- Top-three finish on either or both of last two starts, 9/10
- Had won over at least 3m (hurdles or chases), 8/10
- Aged seven or eight, 7/10

Other factors

- The three winners from 2008 to 2010 had adjusted RPRs of 135-145. The last seven were 154-163
- The 2011, 2012 and 2013 winners were outright favourites – the last to oblige before them was Keep Talking in 1992
- Jonjo O'Neill landed this contest five times between 1995 and 2007 and again in 2016
- Paul Nicholls has never won this race despite strong representation

5.30 Close Brothers Novices' Handicap Chase   RUK
🐎2m4½f   🐎Listed   🐎£70,000

In its first six years this race was run on the New course over 2m5f but it was then moved to the Old course over half a furlong less and there has been a growing accent on quality. The last seven winners carried the biggest weights so far successful. Six of the seven had an official rating of 137 or more, whereas only one of the first seven winners was rated above 135.

The ceiling rating is now 145, raised from 140 last year, and in last year's 20-runner contest a rating of 137 was required to get in. It is therefore hardly surprising that strong recent form is important. Ten of the 13 winners had secured a top-two finish last time out, with six winning.

Seven-year-olds enjoy the best record in the race, with seven wins. The 2016 scorer Ballyalton (aged nine) was the oldest winner in the race's 13-year history, breaking a run of three consecutive six-year-old winners.

Winners have been prominent in the betting, with 11 sent off at odds between 9-2 and 12-1. The biggest-priced winner was 20-1 scorer L'Antartique in 2007.

One to note is the Paul Nicholls-trained Movewiththetimes, a 142-rated seven-year-old son of Presenting who finished a promising second to Finian's Oscar over this course and distance on good to soft in November.

CLOSE BROTHERS NOVICES' HANDICAP CHASE RESULTS AND TRENDS

	FORM WINNER	AGE & WGT	OR	SP	TRAINER	BEST RPR LAST 12 MONTHS (RUNS SINCE)
17	4-162 **Tully East**	7 11-8	138-10	8-1	A Fleming (IRE)	2nd Navan Gd3 nov ch (2m1f) (0)
16	/U62F **Ballyalton** C	9 11-10	140-6	12-1	I Williams	2nd Market Rasen class 2 ch (2m5½f) (1)
15	7-323 **Irish Cavalier**	6 11-7	137-4	11-1	R Curtis	3rd Cheltenham class 2 nov hcap ch (2m5f) (0)
14	32121 **Present View** D	6 11-7	137-1	8-1	J Snowden	won Kempton class 3 hcap ch (2m4½f) (0)
13	-2F17 **Rajdhani Express** D	6 11-7	140T	16-1	N Henderson	won Kempton class 3 hcap ch (2m4½f) (1)
12	12111 **Hunt Ball** D	7 12-0	142-4	13-2f	K Burke	won Kempton class 3 hcap ch (2m4½f) (0)
11	31591 **Divers** D	7 11-4	132-6	10-1	F Murphy	won Musselburgh class 3 nov ch (2m4f) (0)
10	-1321 **Copper Bleu**	8 11-1	139-3	12-1	P Hobbs	won Exeter class 4 ch (2m1½f) (0)
09	9-F21 **Chapoturgeon**	5 10-11	135-2	8-1	P Nicholls	won Doncaster class 2 nov ch (2m½f) (0)
08	-3F22 **Finger Onthe Pulse** D	7 10-12	135-7	9-1	T Taaffe (IRE)	2nd Leopardstown Gd2 nov ch (2m5f) (0)

WINS-RUNS: 5yo 1-15, 6yo 3-41, 7yo 4-75, 8yo 1-48, 9yo 1-17, 10yo 0-3 **FAVOURITES:** £-2.50

FATE OF FAVOURITES: F00515026F **POSITION OF WINNER IN MARKET:** 3254183653

OR 123-130 0-2-8, **131-140** 9-26-179, **141-148** 1-2-12

Key trends

🐎Officially rated 132-142, 10/10

🐎Top-three finish on last completed start, 9/10

🐎Won over at least 2m2f, 8/10

🐎Carried no more than 11st 8lb, 8/10

🐎Aged six or seven, 7/10

🐎Finished in the first four in all completed starts over fences, 6/10

Other factors

🐎Four winners had fallen at least once over fences

🐎Four winners ran over hurdles at a previous festival

🐎Three winners had hurdle RPRs of at least 140, three in the 130s and two in the 120s

🐎Only one winner started bigger than 12-1

PAUL KEALY ON THE KEY CONTENDERS

1.30 Ballymore Novices' Hurdle ITV/RUK
2m5f • Grade 1 • £125,000

Samcro is the most talked-about novice of the season and will be favourite wherever he runs, although this has long seemed the preferred option over the Supreme or Albert Bartlett. He has tackled 2m4f only once under rules, which brought a 12-length Grade 3 win in November, and dropped back to the Grade 1 Deloitte's new 2m trip for another comfortable victory last time, but there seems little doubt about his suitability for this longer distance. He has the potent mix of stamina and speed that will make him extremely hard to beat, with his task likely to be eased by some potential rivals being sent for the Albert Bartlett instead. One who seems likely to stand his ground is Nicky Henderson's highly promising On The Blind Side and Willie Mullins has options with Next Destination, Getabird and Duc Des Genievres, but many people expect this race to be all about Samcro.

Samcro
6 ch g; Trainer Gordon Elliott
Hurdles form 111, best RPR 154
Left-handed 11, best RPR 154
Right-handed 1, best RPR 146

Was a talking horse before he set foot on the racecourse, but has been doing all the talking on it since and is unbeaten in a point, three bumpers and three hurdles without ever really being tested. Kept away from Cheltenham last season, but a Racing Post Rating of 136 he earned at Fairyhouse in April was the highest by any bumper horse during that campaign and nothing he has done since suggests he's anything but top class. Was considered a stayer and, long term, the Gold Cup is the ultimate target, but showed he is more than just a galloper when cruising to victory in the 2m Grade 1 Deloitte Novice Hurdle at Leopardstown. There is a suspicion some of the other form horses did not perform, but a steadily run 2m contest turning into a sprint should not really have suited Samcro and he won as he liked. Afterwards trainer Gordon Elliott confirmed the Ballymore as the target, but some believe the end-to-end gallop of the Supreme would suit more than the usual stop-start of the longer race and nothing is set in stone. Would almost certainly be favourite for either and not hard to see Getabird switching to the longer race if Elliott was to change his mind. It all makes things tricky for ante-post punters. Wherever he goes – and the Ballymore is clearly odds-on at the time of writing – Samcro will start a warm order and deservedly so as he has reached a high level without even being tested.

Going preference Obviously handles soft/heavy fine but also hacked up in a bumper on good to yielding
Star rating ✪✪✪✪✪

TRAINER'S VIEW

Gordon Elliott on Samcro "He's opened up a lot of doors and I'd say we can go any road with him [after the Deloitte]. He was bought to be a big three-mile chaser, and that's what he is, but he showed a lot of class there and he could be anything. I don't know where we'll go at Cheltenham. Coming here I would have said we'd be going for the Ballymore but the way he's done that, I'd say he could go for any race" *Recorded 152 on RPR in the 2m Deloitte, having previously stamped himself the season's top novice with 154 over 2m4f*

On The Blind Side

6 b g; Trainer Nicky Henderson
Hurdles form 111, best RPR 152
Left-handed 11, best RPR 150
Right-handed 1, best RPR 152
Cheltenham form 1

Unbeaten in a point and three hurdles from 2m4f-2m5f and looks very much the strongest of the British contenders. Made to work for first two hurdles successes, particularly the second over the Ballymore course and distance, when he appeared to be struggling at the top of the hill but powered through late after trading at just over 40-1 in running. That race has worked out very well, though, with runner-up Momella winning a Class 2 handicap easily off a mark of 134 next time and third-placed Poetic Rhythm battling to victory in the Grade 1 Challow at Newbury. Things were plain sailing by comparison in the Grade 2 Winter Novices' Hurdle at Sandown in early December, when he strolled to a nine-length success over the useful Springtown Lake (has won since, but at odds of 1-12 in a match), but will be heading to Cheltenham off a four-month break if not getting out sometime between now and the big day. No recent winner has had such a long layoff, but quite a few had their last race at the end of December and trainer Nicky Henderson has won festival races with horses off for even longer. Faces a tough cookie in Samcro, but only 2lb between them on RPR.

Going preference All hurdles wins on good to soft, point on soft
Star rating ✪✪✪✪

Getabird

6 b g; Trainer Willie Mullins
Hurdles form (all right-handed) 11, best RPR 152

Dealt with in far more detail in Tuesday's section as he's hot favourite for the Supreme, but easy enough to see him switching to this if connections of Samcro have a change of heart and run him there. Will go off favourite for this if so.

Going preference Doesn't seem to have a preference
Star rating ✪✪✪✪✪

Next Destination

6 b g; Trainer Willie Mullins
Hurdles form (left-handed) 111, best RPR 152
Cheltenham form (bumper) 4, best RPR 127
At the festival 15 Mar 2017 Chased leaders, pushed along over 2f out, ridden and not quicken over 1f out, stayed on final 100yds, not pace of leaders, finished fourth, beaten three lengths by Fayonagh in Champion Bumper

On The Blind Side: 2lb behind Samcro on RPR

Fared best of two Champion Bumper runners for Willie Mullins last season, finishing a three-length fourth to Fayonagh and beaten at odds-on on final start in that sphere. Quickly developed into very useful hurdler upped in trip, hacking up in maiden hurdle at Naas in November before winning a Grade 2 at Navan and a Grade 1 back at Naas, beating the decent Cracking Smart into second each time. Had to work harder for his Grade 1 success, scoring by only a length, but no denying it's solid form as the third finished runner-up to Samcro in the Deloitte and the fourth was beaten only a head in a 2m6f Grade 1 at the Dublin Festival. Has a good attitude and trainer is convinced he'll be seen to better effect off a searching gallop, so warrants respect.

Going preference Handles soft/heavy fine but Champion Bumper fourth, on only second start after winning a five-runner bumper, shows he's versatile
Star rating ✪✪✪✪

Duc Des Genievres

5 gr g; Trainer Willie Mullins
Hurdles form 132, best RPR 146
Left-handed 32, best RPR 146
Right-handed 1, best RPR -

Dealt with in more detail in the Supreme section on Tuesday as he was runner-up to Samcro in 2m Deloitte on his latest start, but also has form over further, has entries in all three novices and is a similar price for all. Hard to know where he is going to go.

Going preference Unraced on anything bar soft/heavy
Star rating ✪✪

Black Op

7 br g; Trainer Tom George
Hurdles form (left-handed) 412, best RPR 144
Cheltenham form 2, best RPR 144

Only made his debut in February 2017 and wasn't unbacked when beating Claimantakinforgan at Doncaster just a few weeks before that one went on to finish third to Fayonagh in the Champion Bumper at the festival. Sent off favourite on the back of

that in the big Aintree bumper but probably found things happening too quickly over that sharp 2m, and that looked the case again when he was fourth on his hurdles debut to Lostintranslation at Newbury in December. Won a weakish maiden hurdle over 2m5f at Doncaster the following month, but did so very easily and stepped up again in a first-time tongue-tie when second to Santini on Trials Day at Cheltenham later in January. Arguably better than the result there, too, as he tanked through the race and looked by far the most likely winner two out and approaching the last (traded at 1.04 in running) but gave it a fair belt and lost his balance a bit. The pair were 29 lengths clear, so it could prove solid form.

Going preference Seems to handle anything
Star rating ✪✪✪

Vinndication

5 b g; Trainer Kim Bailey
Hurdles form (right-handed) 111, best RPR 149

Won a bumper in November and three hurdles since, all on right-handed tracks. The first two hurdles victories were in straightforward novice races and much his best form came last time in the Listed Sidney Banks at Huntingdon, where he pressed the early lead from the off, took it up not far past halfway and kept on finding to beat Tolworth Hurdle flop Western Ryder by three and a quarter lengths, the pair 23 lengths clear of the rest, among them two 140-plus rated rivals. Plenty to like about his attitude, but trainer says he's still a big baby and would prefer to wait until Aintree, although readily concedes the owners want to go to Cheltenham. Certainly wouldn't underestimate him if he goes there.

Going preference Hurdles form on soft but won bumper on good
Star rating ✪✪✪

Tower Bridge

5 b g; Trainer Joseph O'Brien
Hurdles form 041, best RPR 141
Left-handed 41, best RPR 141
Right-handed 0, best RPR 59

Reasonable bumper form, winning twice on

good ground in the summer, but slow starter over hurdles and tailed off first try on soft ground at Down Royal in November. Much better next time when fourth in a maiden hurdle at Leopardstown over Christmas but was still the outsider of seven when lining up for a Grade 1 at the Dublin Festival. Things hardly looked promising when he walked through the third-last and was scrubbed along in last place approaching two out, but he really put his head down turning for home and just got up on the line. That form is probably some way off what is going to be needed at Cheltenham and he looked all about stamina there, but only holds a Ballymore entry. However, trainer Joseph O'Brien expects him to prove much better suited to faster ground and the fact he ran in summer bumpers and won them easily is a strong pointer that he is right.

Going preference Handles soft but may well prefer better ground
Star rating ✪✪✪

Ok Corral

8 b g; Trainer Nicky Henderson
Hurdles form 121, best RPR 138
Left-handed 2, best RPR 131
Right-handed 11, best RPR 138

Very useful albeit fragile performer who was beaten only two and a quarter lengths by Yorkhill in a Punchestown bumper in April 2015 but then wasn't seen at the track until May last year. Has made a fine belated start to his hurdling career, winning easily at odds of 1-3 on his debut at Kempton, running stablemate Whatswrongwithyou to three-quarters of a length at Newbury and then bolting up again at Kempton in February. With his bumper success also coming at Kempton it's clear he likes it there, but it's hard to say he didn't act on the course for his two defeats as one was to Yorkhill and the other came against a horse who cruised to victory next time out. Form as it stands is still miles off what will be needed, but trainer has long raved about him. He also can't wait to get him over fences, though, and no certainty he'll line up for this,

his sole novice entry, as handicap mark of 144 could be tempting, assuming he stays sound.

Going preference No obvious issues
Star rating ✪✪

OTHERS TO CONSIDER

As always with the novice events there are a few more who could prove a factor if connections decided to switch them from their more obvious targets. I've no doubt **Kalashnikov** will stay for Amy Murphy, who was talking about this after the Tolworth but had changed her mind after he won the Betfair Hurdle, while Tolworth winner **Summerville Boy** shapes like he wants a trip, but the owner also has Black Op, who seems the better fit. **Cracking Smart** is pretty good, but he's much shorter for the Albert Bartlett and in the same ownership as Samcro, so it's hard to see him heading this way.

VERDICT

It's very easy to get taken in by the hype and I'm very tempted to do so when it comes to Samcro as there is plenty of substance to go with the style, but the more I look at all the novice events the more I think they are far more open than the betting suggests. That might be because bookmakers start betting on these events so early and fall over themselves to go as short as they dare as they don't really want to lay a bet ante-post. This race has seen its share of upsets in recent years, with four beaten favourites at 2-1 or shorter since 2011, and on Racing Post Ratings there is no more than 2lb between the top three most likely runners. On The Blind Side and Next Destination are both worthy of huge respect, but the more I look at BLACK OP'S Cheltenham run on Trials Day the more I think he has to be an each-way play at around 16-1. Similar to when The New One just got outstayed by subsequent Albert Bartlett winner At Fishers Cross on Trials Day in 2013, Black Op probably went for home too soon and wasn't helped by a mistake at the last. The pair were miles clear and I think Santini is potentially very smart, so I'm going to have to play at the odds on offer here.

BALLYMORE NOVICES' HURDLE RESULTS AND TRENDS

	FORM	WINNER	AGE & WGT	Adj RPR	SP	TRAINER	BEST RPR LAST 12 MONTHS (RUNS SINCE)
17	5-211	**Willoughby Court** D	6 11-7	154-5	14-1	B Pauling	won Warwick Gd2 nov hdl (2m5f) **(0)**
16	1-111	**Yorkhill**	6 11-7	159-8	3-1	W Mullins (IRE)	won Sandown Gd1 nov hdl (2m) **(0)**
15	-1142	**Windsor Park**	6 11-7	154-3	9-2	D Weld (IRE)	2nd Leopardstown Gd1 nov hdl (2m2f) **(0)**
14	1111	**Faugheen**	6 11-7	156T	6-4f	W Mullins (IRE)	won Limerick Gd3 nov hdl (3m) **(0)**
13	-1112	**The New One** CD, BF	5 11-7	162-1	7-2	N Twiston-Davies	2nd Cheltenham Gd2 nov hdl (2m4½f) **(0)**
12	1121	**Simonsig**	6 11-7	160T	2-1f	N Henderson	2nd Sandown Gd2 nov hdl (2m4f) **(1)**
11	-4131	**First Lieutenant**	6 11-7	152-8	7-1	M Morris (IRE)	won Leopardstown Gd1 nov hdl (2m) **(0)**
10	111	**Peddlers Cross**	5 11-7	155-1	7-1	D McCain	won Haydock Gd2 nov hdl (2m½f) **(0)**
09	21111	**Mikael D'Haguenet**	5 11-7	160-4	5-2f	W Mullins (IRE)	won Punchestown Gd2 nov hdl (2m) **(0)**
08	153-1	**Fiveforthree**	6 11-7	141-9	7-1	W Mullins (IRE)	won Fairyhouse mdn hdl (2m) **(0)**

WINS-RUNS: 4yo 0-2, 5yo 3-44, 6yo 7-69, 7yo 0-19 **FAVOURITES:** +£2

TRAINERS IN THIS RACE (w-pl-r): Willie Mullins 4-5-20, Ben Pauling 1-0-1, Nicky Henderson 1-0-13, Nigel Twiston-Davies 1-0-3, Noel Meade 0-1-4, Colin Tizzard 0-0-2, Jonjo O'Neill 0-0-1, Gordon Elliott 0-0-2, Harry Fry 0-1-1, Henry de Bromhead 0-0-1, Jessica Harrington 0-0-2, Emma Lavelle 0-0-1, Evan Williams 0-0-1

FATE OF FAVOURITES: 0133131322 **POSITION OF WINNER IN MARKET:** 4144121325

Key trends

🏇Aged five or six, ten winners in last ten runnings

🏇Rated within 9lb of RPR top-rated, 10/10

🏇Started career in Irish points or bumpers, 9/10

🏇Adjusted RPR of at least 152, 9/10

🏇Won at least 50 per cent of hurdle runs, 9/10

🏇Scored over at least 2m4f, 8/10

🏇Finished first or second on all completed starts over hurdles, 8/10

🏇Won a Graded hurdle, 8/10

🏇At least three runs over hurdles, 7/10

Other factors

🏇Three of the last ten favourites have obliged (Mikael D'Haguenet 2009, Simonsig 2012, Faugheen 2014) and in that period only one winner has started bigger than 7-1 (Willoughby Court at 14-1 last year)

Notes

2.10 RSA Novices' Chase ITV/RUK
3m½f ⚜ Grade 1 ⚜ £175,000

Ireland has the two leading fancies in Presenting Percy and Monalee, who have solid credentials but have taken different routes here this season. Last year's Pertemps Handicap Hurdle winner Presenting Percy has gone from winning a 3m5f handicap chase to a Grade 2 hurdles success and then back over fences for a Grade 2 second in senior company, while Monalee (runner-up in last year's Albert Bartlett Novices' Hurdle) has been running in Grade 1 novice chases, falling at Leopardstown over Christmas before winning the Flogas there. Willie Mullins has options with Invitation Only and Al Boum Photo, while Alan King's Yanworth could lead the home defence (but is also in the JLT and Stayers' Hurdle) and might be joined by stablemate Mia's Storm. Black Corton, who has struck up such a fruitful partnership with Bryony Frost, is another leading British hope.

Presenting Percy

7 b g; Trainer Patrick Kelly
Chase form (all right-handed) 1312, best RPR 160
Cheltenham form (hurdles) 1, best RPR 156
At the festival 16 Mar 2017 Held up, headway approaching 2 out, led and wanted to lug left before last, a little disorganised after flight, stayed on strongly to go clear final 100yds, won Pertemps Network Final Handicap Hurdle by three and three-quarter lengths from Barney Dwan

Looked better than a handicapper when running away with the Pertemps Final last year and, while he flopped when just 5-2 for the Grade 1 Irish Daily Mirror Novice Hurdle at Punchestown the following month, his exploits this season have confirmed that is very much the case. Put in an assured round to make a winning debut in a high-class beginners' chase at Galway in October, but it was his jumping that let him down when he was third, beaten 13 lengths by Jury Duty and Shattered Love, in a Grade 2 at Punchestown 20 days later. Any thoughts that the race had come too soon were quickly dispelled as he reappeared just 14 days after that to win a high-quality Fairyhouse handicap with his head in his chest off a mark of 145. That promoted him to favouritism for this event and, while he has yet to win at Graded level over fences, his next run in the Grade 2 Galmoy Hurdle confirmed him a high-class

performer under either code as he powered clear to win by five and a half lengths. Beaten in his final warm-up but only by a length over 2m4f by serious Gold Cup hope Our Duke (who gave 7lb) and that is not his trip. What has been so impressive about this campaign is that all his runs have come on soft or heavy ground, while he is known to have relished a decent surface when hacking up at Cheltenham last year. Hard to argue with him being favourite.

Going preference Acts on any but clearly loved decent ground in the Pertemps Final
Star rating ✪✪✪✪✪

Monalee

7 b g; Trainer Henry de Bromhead
Chase form 1F1, best RPR 156
Left-handed, F1, best RPR 156
Right-handed 1, best RPR 155
Cheltenham form (hurdles) 2, best RPR 150
At the festival 17 Mar 2017 Raced keenly, chased leaders, led on bend between last 2, ridden and headed approaching last, kept on under pressure run-in, unable to go with winner final 100yds, finished second, beaten three and a half lengths by Penhill in Albert Bartlett Novices' Hurdle

Decent staying novice hurdler last year but might have raced just a bit too keenly in the Albert Bartlett and had no answer to the finishing kick of Penhill after the second-last, although he did finish well clear of the rest.

Already looks a better chaser, having won two of his three starts, beginning by making all and jumping well to beat Any Second Now in comfortable fashion at Punchestown in November. Was made evens favourite to win a hot-looking Grade 1 Neville Hotels Novice Chase at Leopardstown over Christmas and was jumping superbly until making a mess of the tenth and falling. He proved that hadn't affected his confidence, though, by making all to score by three-quarters of a length in the Grade 1 Flogas Novice Chase over 2m5f at the Dublin Festival at Leopardstown, where once again his sure-footed jumping was a delight. Second favourite for this and much bigger for the JLT, but certainly does not look short of speed and will be among the market leaders for the shorter race if connections have a change of heart.

Going preference Can handle any ground but best form last season was on good at Cheltenham
Star rating ✪✪✪✪

Black Corton

7 br g; Trainer Paul Nicholls
Chase form 21211111211, best RPR 161
Left-handed 12111112, best RPR 161
Right-handed 211, best RPR 161
Cheltenham form 11, best RPR 161

Very heavily raced for a novice chaser (11 starts) but that's because he was considered nowhere near good enough for top company, started by winning tinpot races in the summer and even managed to get beat in one at Worcester in June by a horse still rated 134. However, he turned that form around in August and hasn't looked back since, taking his record this term to eight wins and two

seconds (was beaten the small matter of 63 length by Altior on chase debut in November 2016). Indeed, both defeats this term have been avenged, with Black Corton reversing Newbury form with three-quarter-length winner Elegant Escape in December by beating the same horse by a length and a half in the Kauto Star at Kempton over Christmas. What would have happened if the ill-fated Fountains Windfall hadn't have come down when travelling powerfully in a three-length lead four out is another matter, but it's hard to fault his appetite for a battle and thirst for victory and he has won both starts at Cheltenham. Confirmed himself a serious player with smooth eight-length success in Grade 2 Reynoldstown at Ascot in February and very hard to knock a horse who keeps winning and showing high-class form. Bryony Frost won't be able to utilise her 3lb claim, but that has been the case in six chases since October and he won't lack for confidence or assistance in the saddle.

Going preference Acts on soft but the quicker the better
Star rating ✪✪✪✪

Yanworth

8 ch g; Trainer Alan King
Chase form 1F21, best RPR 155
Left-handed 21, best RPR 155
Right-handed 1F, best RPR 153
Cheltenham form (all) 412D1, best RPR 160
At the festival 11 Mar 2015 Held up towards rear, progress over 3f out, not clear run over 2f out and lost place, driven and ran on from over 1f out, nearest finish, finished fourth, beaten three and a quarter lengths by Moon Racer in Champion Bumper

TRAINER'S VIEW

Henry de Bromhead on Monalee "He had a bad fall at Christmas and it took him a week to get over it, but he's a hardy horse. To come back straight to a Grade 1 was throwing him in at the deep end, his preparation was far from ideal, but it's a testament to the horse that he did this [won the Flogas last time out]. The RSA Chase looks the obvious target" *Four of the last nine RSA winners had run in the Flogas (two won, one was second and the other was third) and, of those, only Cooldine in 2009 recorded a higher RPR at Leopardstown than Monalee*

16 Mar 2016 Held up in rear, progress on wide outside after 7th, close up when mistake 3 out, challenged after 2 out, chased winner before last, stayed on but not pace to challenge, finished second, beaten one and three-quarter lengths by Yorkhill in Neptune Investment Management Novices' Hurdle
14 Mar 2017 In touch, hit 3rd, lost place and outpaced after 3 out, plugged on under pressure run-in when no danger, finished 7th, disqualified (banned substance in sample) from Champion Hurdle won by Buveur D'Air

Dealt with in more detail in the JLT section on Thursday as he has yet to attempt 3m over fences, but in this and the Stayers' Hurdle and hard to know where he will go. The fact that Supasundae, whom he beat over 3m in the Liverpool Hurdle at Aintree last spring, is now favourite for the Stayers', must tempt connections.

Going preference Acts on any, but 6-7 on soft or heavy and 6-11 on faster
Star rating ✪✪✪

Invitation Only
7 b g; Trainer Willie Mullins
Chase form F113, best RPR 154
Left-handed 13, best RPR 154
Right-handed F1, best RPR 153

Another yet to try 3m over fences, but nudged out of second close home behind Monalee at Leopardstown over 2m5f in February, the furthest he has tackled so far, so dealt with in the JLT section. That's no more than a guess, though, and he's also in the four-miler, so Willie Mullins may have more confidence in his stamina.

Going preference All best form on soft/ heavy but did win a maiden hurdle on good/yielding
Star rating ✪✪✪

Al Boum Photo
6 b g; Trainer Willie Mullins
Chase form 1F2, best RPR 154
Left-handed 12, best RPR 154
Right-handed F, best RPR 151

Decent novice hurdler who missed Cheltenham last year and finished behind Monalee but in front of Presenting Percy in 3m Grade 1 novice hurdle at Punchestown in April, although all three were below their best in fourth, fifth and sixth behind outsider Champagne Classic. Made a good impression on chase debut when scoring easily over 2m1f at Navan, but was another to fall next time upped to Graded company. He got as far as the last at Limerick and was cantering at the time, so would surely have won. Hard to say that dented his confidence as he was beaten only three-quarters of a length in the Grade 1 Flogas by Monalee at Leopardstown next time, but he did make a few mistakes and was untidy at the last. Rallied strongly to grab second off stablemate Invitation Only and shaped as though worth another try at 3m. Is slightly shorter for the JLT in the ante-post market, but that's just as much to do with the strength of competition and you have to think Willie Mullins will split him and Invitation Only. This is the way I'd go, but who knows?

Going preference Best form on soft or heavy
Star rating ✪✪

Shattered Love
7 b m Trainer Gordon Elliott
Chase form 11211, best RPR 151
Left-handed 1, best RPR 151
Right-handed 1121, best RPR 149
Cheltenham form (hurdles) 0, RPR 97
At the festival 15 Mar 2017 Held up, pushed along briefly approaching 4 out, struggling when not fluent 3 out, soon eased, finished 12th, beaten 52 and three-quarter lengths by Willoughby Court in Neptune Investment Management Novices' Hurdle

Winner of eight of 14 starts and 4-5 over fences, all those runs coming between October and December. Took advantage of Monalee's fall to record best effort when taking the Grade 1 Neville Hotels Novice Chase at Leopardstwon over Christmas, her first run over 3m, and clearly got the trip very well as she reversed earlier Punchestown form with Jury Duty. Entitled to serious consideration on the book getting the 7lb sex allowance but was beaten miles in the Neptune (now Ballymore) last season, so needs to prove her aptitude for Cheltenham. Shorter for the four-miler too and stamina doesn't look like it's going to be an issue.

Going preference Some form on decent ground but handles soft/heavy very well
Star rating ✪✪

Dounikos

7 b g; Trainer Gordon Elliott
Chase form 114, best RPR 153
Left-handed 4, best RPR 153
Right-handed 11, best RPR 151

Won first two novice chases before the turn of the year, including when springing a 14-1 shock in Grade 2 at Limerick when Al Boum Photo came down at the last. Proved that run no fluke, though, when beaten only a length and three-quarters into fourth by Monalee in the Grade 1 Flogas at Leopardstown in February. Has won over 2m7f over hurdles and shaped as though he wants at least that far over fences. Another who also has the National Hunt Chase as an option.

Going preference Hurdles win on good but handles deep ground well
Star rating ✪✪

Mia's Storm

8 b m; Trainer Alan King
Chase form 11F, best RPR 155
Left-handed 1, best RPR 144
Right-handed 1F, best RPR 155
Cheltenham form (hurdles) 9, RPR 102

Potentially very smart mare who made quite an impression on her first two chase starts. On the first occasion she needed only hands and heels riding to see off the now 150-rated Elegant Escape by just over three lengths at Chepstow, while next time she cruised home in a Listed mares' chase at Market Rasen, where she was really fluent apart from making one minor mistake. That was enough to see her go off 5-2 favourite against the boys in the Grade 1 Kauto Star at Kempton over Christmas, but after a mistake at the third she was never travelling and she was already well beaten when she came down at the 14th. That was her first run on soft ground since she was beaten 36 lengths at Cheltenham over hurdles in December 2016 and it could simply be that she can't handle it. Five of her six career wins have come on good and the other on good to soft and if she can bounce back given the right surface at Cheltenham she should not be underestimated with her sex allowance.

Going preference Decent ground seems key
Star rating ✪✪✪

Black Corton: goes very well at Cheltenham and will relish quicker ground

Benatar

6 b g; Trainer Gary Moore
Chase form 111, best RPR 154
Left-handed 1, best RPR 144
Right-handed 11, best RPR 154

Dealt with in more detail in Thursday's JLT section as he's shorter for that, but trainer seems in two minds about which race to aim him at. Certainly worth trying over 3m at some point, but JLT looks an easier race.

Going preference Has won on soft and good, suspicion he likes better ground
Star rating ✪✪

Ballyoptic

8 b g; Trainer Nigel Twiston-Davies
Chase form 1241, best RPR 161
Left-handed 21, best RPR 159
Right-handed 14, best RPR 161
Cheltenham form 2, RPR 159

Very useful staying hurdler who made sparkling chase debut when thrashing Elegant Escape by 13 lengths at Exeter in November, but couldn't justify odds-on quote when beaten four lengths by Black Corton over the RSA course and distance just 11 days later. Worse was to come when he flopped badly in the Kauto Star at Kempton over Christmas, finishing a 27-length fourth to Black Corton (Elegant Escape was a close second), a run that no doubt prompted his trainer to enter him in the Stayers' Hurdle to keep all options open. However, he wasn't the only Twiston-Davies horse to underperform that week and he seemed to be back on track with a strong-staying performance to beat Welsh National fourth Vintage Clouds in the Grade 2 Towton at Wetherby, a race his trainer also won with 2016 RSA Chase winner Blaklion. Similar type to Blaklion in that he's tough and tries his heart out, and peak form doesn't put him far off the best.

Going preference Does handle good but best chance probably lies with a wet week
Star rating ✪✪

OTHERS TO CONSIDER

Others who would be entitled to take a hand should they switch from more obvious targets include **Willoughby Court** and **Finian's Oscar**, although the former has been confirmed as going for the JLT, while it's anyone's guess what happens with Finian's Oscar. He flopped when returned to hurdles and tried over 3m on Trials Day, so I'd say he's more likely to try fences again and, despite being far from a natural, he has still run to a high level. The JLT is probably a better fit, though. Anthony Honeyball wants to run **Ms Parfois** in the four-miler, but only if it's soft ground, while **Barney Dwan**, runner-up to Presenting Percy in last season's Pertemps, has the option of this, the four-miler or the novice handicap on the first day and the assessor has dangled a carrot for the latter by dropping him 2lb to 143 (same mark as last year over hurdles) following his Musselburgh win. He has a tendency to get low at his fences but that might be ironed out on better ground. **Keeper Hill** certainly wasn't done with when coming down in that Musselburgh race and is a horse his trainer believes stays very well and wants good ground, while the likes of **Jury Duty** and **Elegant Escape** are tough and consistent and certainly wouldn't be making up the numbers if they lined up. They also have other options, though.

VERDICT

With Racing Post Ratings suggesting there's no more than 2lb between the top seven and 5lb between the top dozen at the entry stage, it's easy enough to argue this is more competitive than the odds suggest. I'm not normally one for a shortish-priced favourite at the festival unless they are truly impossible to oppose (in which case I won't bet) but PRESENTING PERCY has impressed me no end this season. He has achieved a good level of form on heavy ground and we know he prefers a better surface and acts on this track. He'll be hard to beat. I'd be really tempted to send Monalee to the JLT as he could run them ragged with his sure-footed jumping but might be susceptible to a stronger stayer. Black Corton is so likeable and can be a big player for Britain.

RSA CHASE RESULTS AND TRENDS

	FORM WINNER	AGE & WGT	Adj RPR	SP	TRAINER	BEST RPR LAST 12 MONTHS (RUNS SINCE)
17	-21F1 **Might Bite** C, D	8 11-4	175ᵀ	7-2f	N Henderson	Fell Kempton Gd 1 nov ch (3m) (1)
16	4F121 **Blaklion** C, D	7 11-4	172⁻¹	8-1	N Twiston-Davies	won Wetherby Gd 2 nov ch (3m) (0)
15	1-211 **Don Poli** C, D	6 11-4	165⁻²	13-8f	W Mullins (IRE)	won Leopardstown Gd1 nov ch (3m) (0)
14	4-2P1 **O'Faolains Boy** D	7 11-4	160⁻⁹	12-1	R Curtis	won Gd2 Reynoldstown Nov Ch (3m) (0)
13	22123 **Lord Windermere**	7 11-4	155⁻¹⁰	8-1	J Culloty (IRE)	3rd Gd1 Dr PJ Moriarty Nov Ch (2m5f) (0)
12	1-132 **Bobs Worth** C, D	7 11-4	172⁻⁶	9-2	N Henderson	3rd Gd1 Feltham Nov Ch (3m) (1)
11	21411 **Bostons Angel** D	7 11-4	160⁻¹³	16-1	J Harrington (IRE)	won Gd1 Dr PJ Moriarty Nov Ch (2m5f) (0)
10	3F122 **Weapon's Amnesty** C, D	7 11-4	160⁻¹⁵	10-1	C Byrnes (IRE)	2nd Leopardstown Gd1 nov ch (3m) (1)
09	-8131 **Cooldine**	7 11-4	166⁻³	9-4f	W Mullins (IRE)	won Gd1 Dr PJ Moriarty Nov Ch (2m5f) (0)
08	-1211 **Albertas Run** CD	7 11-4	164⁻³	4-1f	J O'Neill	won Gd2 Reynoldstown Nov Ch (3m) (0)

WINS-RUNS: 5yo 0-4, 6yo 1-18, 7yo 8-59, 8yo 1-20, 9yo 0-9 **FAVOURITES:** £5.38

TRAINERS IN THIS RACE (w-pl-r): Willie Mullins 2-3-15, Nicky Henderson 2-4-11, Nigel Twiston-Davies 1-1-4, Paul Nicholls 0-1-10, Alan King 0-1-2, Colin Tizzard 0-0-4, David Pipe 0-0-4, Gordon Elliott 0-1-3, Donald McCain 0-0-3, Noel Meade 0-1-2, Emma Lavelle 0-0-1, Philip Hobbs 0-1-2, Gary Moore 0-0-1, Sue Smith, 0-0-2, Henry de Bromhead 0-0-2

FATE OF FAVOURITES: 1155442131 **POSITION OF WINNER IN MARKET:** 1157248131

🐎Did not run on the Flat, 10/10

🐎Top-three finish last time out, 10/10

🐎Contested a Graded chase, 10/10 (seven won)

🐎Adjusted RPR of at least 160, 9/10

🐎Six to 12 hurdles and chase runs, 9/10

🐎Last ran between 24 and 53 days ago, 9/10

🐎Ran at least three times over fences, 9/10

🐎Aged seven, 8/10

🐎Rated within 10lb of RPR top-rated, 8/10 (only one was top-rated)

Other factors

🐎Of the combined 45 chase starts of winners, only 2016 scorer Blaklion had finished outside the first three (four had fallen). However, only Don Poli was unbeaten over fences

🐎Eight winners had previously run at the festival – five ran in the Albert Bartlett (1P14P), one in the Martin Pipe (1) and two in the Bumper two years earlier (07)

🐎Ten five-year-olds have run in the last 23 years – one won, four placed, three were unplaced and two fell

Notes

2.50 Coral Cup Handicap Hurdle ITV/RUK
2m5f Grade 3 £100,000

Only one outright and one joint-favourite have won this tricky handicap hurdle in its 24-year history and there have been just two winners at single-figure odds since 2005. Eleven of the past 12 winners were in the first seven in the betting, however, so the market is not such a bad guide.

The race has tended to suit younger, less exposed types, with ten of the past 17 winners aged five or six and just three winners in the last 18 renewals aged eight or older. Nine of the last ten victors arrived at Cheltenham with single figures of runs over hurdles.

Ireland has had nine winners and only Xenophon, 4-1 favourite in 2003, was heavily fancied. The other eight Irish winners were returned at between 11-1 and 16-1.

CORAL CUP RESULTS AND TRENDS

	FORM WINNER	AGE & WGT	OR	SP	TRAINER	BEST RPR LAST 12 MONTHS (RUNS SINCE)
17	48124 **Supasundae**	7 11-4	148-2	16-1	J Harrington (IRE)	won Punchestown hdl (2m4f) (2)
16	P-421 **Diamond King**	8 11-3	149-5	12-1	G Elliott (IRE)	won Punchestown hdl (2m4f) (0)
15	1-31 **Aux Ptits Soins**	5 10-7	139-4	9-1	P Nicholls	won Auteuil hdl (2m1½f) (0)
14	-3312 **Whisper** C, D, BF	6 11-6	153-4	14-1	N Henderson	2nd Ffos Las class 2 hcap hdl (2m4f) (0)
13	-2241 **Medinas**	6 11-10	148-3	33-1	A King	won Ffos Las class 2 hcap hdl (2m4f) (0)
12	-9090 **Son Of Flicka**	8 10-6	135T	16-1	D McCain	2nd Martin Pipe Cond Hcp Hdl (2m4½f) (5)
11	2-102 **Carlito Brigante** (2ow)	5 11-0	142-10	16-1	G Elliott (IRE)	2nd Fairyhouse hdl (2m) (0)
10	1-510 **Spirit River** C	5 11-2	141-1	14-1	N Henderson	won Cheltenham class 3 hcap hdl (2m1f) (1)
09	-4511 **Ninetieth Minute**	6 10-3	140T	14-1	T Taaffe (IRE)	won Thurles Listed hdl (2m) (0)
08	12-71 **Naiad Du Misselot** D	7 10-13	130-7	7-1	F Murphy	won Haydock class 2 hcap hdl (2m4f) (0)

WINS-RUNS: 5yo 3-54, 6yo 3-75, 7yo 2-62, 8yo 2-36, 9yo 0-18, 10yo 0-12, 11yo 0-3, 12yo 0-1 **FAVOURITES:** -£10

FATE OF FAVOURITES: 0000205300 **POSITION OF WINNER IN MARKET:** 2667705266

Key trends

- Not run for at least 32 days, 9/10
- Won a race earlier in the season, 9/10 (five won last time out)
- No more than four runs that season, 9/10
- No more than nine hurdle runs, 9/10
- Won between 2m2f and 2m6f over hurdles, 8/10

- Officially rated 135 to 149, 8/10
- Aged five to seven, 8/10
- Carried no more than 11st 3lb, 7/10

Other factors

- The only winner to have had more than nine hurdle runs had 22 starts (Son Of Flicka in 2012)

Notes

3.30 Betway Queen Mother Champion Chase ITV/RUK
2m · Grade 1 · £400,000

Altior, long touted as the successor to the great Sprinter Sacre for Nicky Henderson, takes his shot at the two-mile championship, having climbed the ranks in time-honoured fashion with wins in the Supreme Novices' Hurdle and Arkle Chase on his two previous visits to the festival. His return path has not been entirely smooth this season as he had a wind operation in November that was cloaked in controversy, but he was impressive on his belated reappearance with a comfortable victory over Tingle Creek winner Politologue at Newbury. Things have gone even more awry with Douvan, not seen since his flop at odds of 2-9 in this race last year, and in his absence Min – representing the same team of Willie Mullins and Rich Ricci – has developed into a top-class two-miler with the talent to give Altior a proper test. Politologue and last year's winner Special Tiara are admirable performers but do not look in the same class as the big two.

Altior

8 b g; Trainer Nicky Henderson
Chase form 1111111, best RPR 177
Left-handed 111, best RPR 177
Right-handed 1111, best RPR 177
Cheltenham form (all) 111, best RPR 168
At the festival 15 Mar 2016 Travelled and jumped well, mid-division, headway after 5th, challenged after 2 out, ridden to lead before last, quickened clear, impressive, won Supreme Novices' Hurdle by seven lengths from Min
14 Mar 2017 Tracked leaders, went 2nd before 5th, ½ length down and pressing leader when left in lead 2 out, ridden out after last, ran on to draw clear inside final 100yds, won Racing Post Arkle Chase by six lengths from Cloudy Dream

Brilliant eight-year-old who can lay claim to being the best jumper in training in Britain or Ireland. Unbeaten novice hurdle campaign culminated in scintillating Supreme Novices' Hurdle victory as he streaked seven lengths clear of Min in a race that produced three Cheltenham Festival winners the next season. He was one of those as he took to fences like a duck to water, winning four times before Cheltenham and taking apart some top-class established chasers when slamming Fox Norton and Traffic Fluide in the Game Spirit at Newbury. Was arguably a little bit below par in the Racing Post Arkle at Cheltenham but still won by six lengths from Charbel, his change of gear at the end of his races taking him clear. That change of gear was also evident when he fairly laughed at shock Champion Chase winner Special Tiara on the final day of the season in the Grade 1 Celebration Chase at Sandown, a race in which he bounded clear after the last to win by eight lengths. Has been a hot favourite for this ever since as he bids to fill the shoes of the brilliant Sprinter Sacre – Altior was better than him as a hurdler but still has some way to go over fences – but things haven't been plain sailing this term as he reportedly made a noise during his build-up to the Tingle Creek and missed the race in favour of a wind operation. After that he faced a race with time to get a run in before Cheltenham, but Nicky Henderson got him to the Game Spirit and he picked up where he left off with a hands-and-heels four-length win from Politologue, who went to Newbury unbeaten in three this term, including the Tingle Creek. The wind op clearly had the desired effect and Altior looks every bit as good as he did last season, so there's no arguing with his position as odds-on favourite, although he'll do well to beat Min by as far as he did in the Supreme.

Going preference Handles all, prefers good
Star rating ●●●●○

Min

7 b g; Trainer Willie Mullins
Chase form 11121, best RPR 174
Left-handed 1121, best RPR 174
Right-handed 1, best RPR 165
Cheltenham form (hurdles) 2, RPR 160
At the festival 15 Mar 2016 Tracked leader, mistake 3rd, challenged after 2 out, soon ridden, kept on but readily outpaced by winner, finished second, beaten seven lengths by Altior in Supreme Novices' Hurdle

The match many people have long wanted to see was Douvan v Altior, but one between Min and Altior need be no less mouthwatering, not least because they have a bit of history – and if Douvan also makes the gig, then so much the better. Min was no match for his big rival in the Supreme Novices' Hurdle two years ago, but it's worth remembering he'd run just twice over hurdles and never been tested, while Altior had more experience (four runs) against better horses. It's also worth remembering he remains the only other horse to finish ahead of Buveur D'Air in a hurdle race, so his class is undoubted. He also took very well to chasing in his first season, jumping like an old hand when winning at Navan in November and Leopardstown in December, where he won the Grade 1 Racing Post Novice Chase by nine lengths in a canter from Ordinary World (went on to be third in the Racing Post Arkle at Cheltenham, albeit beaten 15 lengths). Unfortunately injury struck afterwards and he wasn't seen again until dishing out a 36-length defeat to Flaxen Flare at odds of 1-9 in a race that told us little more than he was still alive. Unbeaten chase record disappeared next time when he short-headed Simply Ned in a Grade 1 at Leopardstown over Christmas, but was rightly disqualified for leaning on his rival after the last. That led some to assume he wasn't as good as hoped and may need further, but connections were adamant it wasn't him and he went a long way to proving them right when slamming the same rival by 12 lengths in the Dublin Chase at Leopardstown in February. With last year's Champion Chase winner Special Tiara setting a fierce pace, the time was good and you can't put it down as anything other than a top-class performance, one that puts him within spitting distance of Altior's best. A Racing Post Rating of 174 is just 3lb shy of Altior's peak and, with Special Tiara sure to take no prisoners again, the front two could treat us to something special.

Going preference Seems to handle any
Star rating ❍❍❍❍

Politologue

7 gr g; Trainer Paul Nicholls
Chase form 11214F1112, best RPR 170
Left-handed 124F2, best RPR 170
Right-handed 11111, best RPR 170
Cheltenham form (all) U04, best RPR 154
At the festival 16 Mar 2016 Tracked leaders, challenged from 3 out until weakened quickly soon after 2 out, finished 20th, beaten 20 and a quarter lengths by Diamond King in Coral Cup
16 Mar 2017 Tracked leaders, disputing close 4th after 3 out, ridden and held between last 2, kept on same pace, finished fourth, beaten ten lengths by Yorkhill in JLT Novices' Chase

Very useful if a little highly

strung as a novice chaser but only defeat in four outings in the run-up to Cheltenham came against rising star Waiting Patiently, who remains unbeaten over fences. Was hooded for final three starts last season in a bid to calm him down a bit, but despite having won twice at 2m5f, didn't seem to get home in top company over 2m4f in the JLT, finishing a ten-length fourth to Yorkhill. Proved he was better than that dropped to 2m for the first time over fences at Aintree in April and was shaping like the winner of the Grade 1 Maghull Novices' Chase before falling at the last, which was a surprise given he is usually so sure-footed. He improved again kept to around 2m this season, winning the Haldon Gold Cup off a mark of 154 and then showing fine battling qualities to hold off Fox Norton in the Grade 1 Tingle Creek. He then had a fairly straightforward gallop round Kempton in the Desert Orchid Chase (won by 13 lengths) before finishing second to Altior in the Game Spirit. He may not have been suited by making his own running that day and Paul Nicholls had warned he wouldn't be fully tuned up, but doubtful the winner was either and he breezed past him. Arguably best chance if ground became very soft as he's a staying two-miler, but needs to find more to challenge the big two.

Going preference Handles all, arguably wants it soft
Star rating ✪✪✪

Douvan

8 b g; Trainer Willie Mullins
Chase form 1111111117, best RPR 178
Left-handed 1111117, best RPR 178
Right-handed 111, best RPR 178
Cheltenham form (all) 117, best RPR 165
At the festival 10 Mar 2015 Mid-division, smooth headway after 3 out, shaken up to lead before last, ran on strongly, driven out, won

Politologue: needs to improve to get involved in the finish

Supreme Novices' Hurdle by four and a half lengths from Shaneshill

15 Mar 2016 With leader, led 3rd, made rest, always travelling strongly, powered clear between last 2, mistake last, ran on well, comfortably, won Racing Post Arkle Chase by seven lengths from Sizing John

15 Mar 2017 Led until 2nd, tracked leaders, reached for 3rd, not fluent next, hit 3 out, soon outpaced, ridden between last 2, found little, lame, finished seventh, beaten 11 and three-quarter lengths in Queen Mother Champion Chase by Special Tiara

For all the top-class horses Willie Mullins has had through his hands, it seems Douvan has long been regarded the best of all and he has spent most of his life reinforcing the point. He was unbeaten and rarely tested in his first 13 starts for the yard, which included a Supreme Novices' Hurdle and the Punchestown equivalent, and a Grade 1 spring festival treble at Cheltenham, Aintree and Punchestown over fences. Continued to make serene progress in his first season out of novice company last term, winning all three outings with ridiculous ease, and it was hard to argue that he didn't deserve to be as short as 2-9 to land a first Champion Chase for his trainer. Unfortunately he never seemed to be travelling from an early stage and trailed in seventh of the ten runners having finished lame. Since then it has been a long road to getting him back and if he does make the line-up it will be his first run since. Connections obviously have a serious shot at Altior with Min, so you would imagine they will need to be 100 per cent convinced Douvan is back to his very best to risk him. Confirmed as on target for this by Willie Mullins in February despite entry in Ryanair.

Going preference Doesn't seem to have any problems
Star rating ✪✪✪

Great Field

7 b g; Trainer Willie Mullins
Chase form 1111, best RPR 160
Left-handed 1, best RPR 158
Right-handed 111, best RPR 160
Cheltenham form (hurdles) P

At the festival 18 Mar 2016 Raced freely, soon led, headed after 2 out (usual 3 out), soon weakened, pulled up after next in County Handicap Hurdle won by Superb Story

Lightly raced but has won seven of eight completed starts over obstacles, including four chases last season. Best effort obviously on final start when handing out 11-length thrashing to Arkle third Ordinary World in the Grade 1 Ryanair Novice Chase and looked to have a huge future. Unfortunately he is another Mullins horse to have had his problems and we are yet to see him this season. This is his only Cheltenham entry and it's hard to see him running in the Grand Annual off 161, but obviously going to have loads to prove if getting there.

Going preference Acts on soft/heavy, pulled up on good in 2016 County Hurdle
Star rating ✪✪

Special Tiara

11 b g; Trainer Henry de Bromhead
Chase form 12513U3463341314236315123F3, best RPR 170
Left-handed 51U3643433513, best RPR 170
Right-handed 123433112612F3, best RPR 170
Cheltenham form 36333513, best RPR 170
At the festival 12 Mar 2014 Led, hit 3rd, blundered and headed 4th, led again before next, headed 6th, stayed pressing leaders until led again after 4 out, headed approaching 3 out, weakened 2 out, finished sixth, beaten 15 and a half lengths by Sire De Grugy in Queen Mother Champion Chase

11 Mar 2015 Led, clear 4th, joined after 3 out, soon ridden, headed on landing last, kept on bravely but no extra final 110yds, finished third, beaten three lengths by Dodging Bullets in Queen Mother Champion Chase

16 Mar 2016 Led, mistake 3rd, headed after 4 out, ridden and every chance after 3 out, held by winner before next but kept pressing for 2nd, stayed on same pace, finished third, beaten three and a half lengths by Sprinter Sacre in Queen Mother Champion Chase

15 Mar 2017 Led 2nd, clear after 5th, kicked on again after 3 out, ridden after next, 2 lengths up last, held on gamely, all out, won Queen Mother Champion Chase by a head from Fox Norton

Really game trailblazer who earned his just

rewards for a string of valiant efforts when winning the Champion Chase by a head from Fox Norton last year. That was his fourth attempt at the race and he obviously benefited from Douvan's failure to fire, but it's hard to begrudge a horse who wears his heart on his sleeve, as he undoubtedly will do in his defence. Probably went off too fast on ground softer than he likes when well beaten by Min at Leopardstown in February and will appreciate better going should we get any, but still hard to see him fending off some very talented youngsters.

Going preference The quicker the better
Star rating ✪✪

OTHERS TO CONSIDER

The likes of **Ar Mad** and **Charbel** could line up and help to make it a searching gallop

alongside Special Tiara, but it's hard to see them taking a hand. **Fox Norton** and **Un De Sceaux** also feature among the entries but are surely heading towards the Ryanair along with **Top Notch**, while **God's Own** looks to have had his day now.

VERDICT

With or without Douvan this could be one of the races of the meeting, with two chasers who have already shown enough to win an average Champion Chase going head to head in a rematch of their Supreme Novices' Hurdle meeting two years ago. ALTIOR proved much the best on that occasion and the head says he'll come out on top again, but Min could well get a lot closer and they could serve up a classic. I'd expect them to come well clear of the rest (unless Douvan is at his best) but wouldn't mind betting Special Tiara sneaks third.

CHAMPION CHASE RESULTS AND TRENDS

	FORM WINNER	AGE & WGT	Adj RPR	SP	TRAINER	BEST RPR LAST 12 MONTHS (RUNS SINCE)
17	-6315 **Special Tiara** D	10 11-10	174-8	11-1	H de Bromhead (IRE)	3rd Gd 1 Champion Chase (2m) (4)
16	P2-11 **Sprinter Sacre** CD	10 11-10	177-1	5-1	N Henderson	won Kempton Gd2 ch (2m) (0)
15	5-311 **Dodging Bullets** CD	7 11-10	178-6	9-2	P Nicholls	won Gd1 Clarence House Ch (2m1f) (0)
14	12111 **Sire De Grugy** D	8 11-10	178ᵀ	11-4f	G Moore	won Gd1 Clarence House Ch (2m1f) (0)
13	11-11 **Sprinter Sacre** CD	7 11-10	182ᵀ	1-4f	N Henderson	won Gd1 Victor Chandler Ch (2m1f) (0)
12	21-12 **Finian's Rainbow** D, BF	9 11-10	171-9	4-1	N Henderson	2nd Gd1 Victor Chandler Ch (2m1f) (0)
11	3-223 **Sizing Europe** CD	9 11-10	170-9	10-1	H de Bromhead (IRE)	3rd Punchestown Gd2 ch (2m) (0)
10	-2141 **Big Zeb** D	9 11-10	171-19	10-1	C Murphy (IRE)	won Navan Gd2 ch (2m) (2)
09	12-11 **Master Minded** CD	6 11-10	191ᵀ	4-11f	P Nicholls	won Gd1 Champion Chase (2m) (3)
08	-2U11 **Master Minded** D	5 11-10	173-4	3-1	P Nicholls	won Gd2 Game Spirit Ch (2m1f) (0)

WINS-RUNS: 5yo 1-1, 6yo 1-7, 7yo 2-16, 8yo 1-24, 9yo 3-23, 10yo 2-14, 11yo 0-7, 12yo 0-2, 13yo 0-1 **FAVOURITES:** -£3.64

TRAINERS IN THIS RACE (w-pl-r): Paul Nicholls 3-0-14, Nicky Henderson 3-1-9, Henry de Bromhead 2-4-9, Gary Moore 1-0-4, Tom George 0-2-5, Alan King 0-1-2, Willie Mullins 0-1-7, Colin Tizzard 0-1-2, Kerry Lee 0-0-1, Nigel Twiston-Davies 0-0-2

FATE OF FAVOURITES: 2140211P20 **POSITION OF WINNER IN MARKET:** 2145211324

Key trends

🐎 Won over at least 2m1f, 10/10

🐎 At least seven runs over fences, 10/10

🐎 Adjusted RPR of at least 170, 10/10

🐎 No older than nine, 8/10

🐎 No more than 9lb off RPR top-rated, 9/10

🐎 Grade 1 chase winner, 9/10

🐎 Won Graded chase last time out, 7/10

Other factors

🐎 Four winners had previously won at the festival

🐎 In the past ten years 34 French-breds have run, yielding five wins, four seconds and four thirds

4.10 Glenfarclas Cross Country Chase ITV/RUK
3m6f £65,000

This unusual event is in its third year as a conditions race, having previously been a handicap, but there have been some interesting pointers to note over the years.

Ireland has won 11 of the 13 runnings, helped largely by the success of Enda Bolger, widely regarded as the cross-country master. He trained four of the first five winners up to 2009 and had 2016 winner Josies Orders, who was awarded the race when the original winner Any Currency was disqualified after a banned substance was detected in a post-race test. Philip Hobbs is the only trainer to have won for Britain, with Balthazar King in 2012 and 2014.

It has paid to back horses at the head of the market, with nine of the 13 winners returned at 11-2 or shorter. The biggest-priced winner was A New Story at 25-1 in 2010.

Last year's winner Cause Of Causes is set to return in an attempt to land a fourth consecutive success at the festival, having previously won the National Hunt Chase in 2015 and the Kim Muir in 2016.

CROSS COUNTRY RESULTS AND TRENDS

FORM		WINNER	AGE & WGT	OR	SP	TRAINER	BEST RPR LAST 12 MONTHS (RUNS SINCE)
17	-5P05	**Cause Of Causes** C	9 11-4	166-3	4-1	G Elliott (IRE)	won Kim Muir hcap ch (3m2f) (5)
16	18119	**Josies Orders** CD	8 11-4	148-7	15-8f	E Bolger (IRE)	won Cheltenham cross-country ch (3m6f) (1)
15	4172F	**Rivage D'Or**	10 10-10	134-4	16-1	T Martin (IRE)	2nd Kilbeggan hcap ch (3m1f) (2)
14	P-111	**Balthazar King** CD	10 11-12	150-5	4-1	P Hobbs	won Cheltenham cl 2 hcap ch (3m½f) (1)
13	-F742	**Big Shu**	8 10-5	136-10	14-1	P Maher (IRE)	2nd Punchestown cross-country ch (3m) (0)
12	15P00	**Balthazar King** C	8 10-9	139-3	11-2	P Hobbs	won Cheltenham cl 2 hcap ch (3m½f) (4)
11	4-138	**Sizing Australia**	9 10-9	140-7	13-2	H de Bromhead (IRE)	3rd Cheltenham cross-country ch (3m7f) (0)
10	70454	**A New Story** (4oh)	12 9-7	135-3	25-1	M Hourigan (IRE)	3rd Cork National hcap ch (3m4f) (4)
09	1-421	**Garde Champetre** CD	10 11-12	150-4	7-2	E Bolger (IRE)	won Cheltenham cross-country ch (3m7f) (0)
08	9-9F1	**Garde Champetre**	9 10-13	129-T	4-1	E Bolger (IRE)	won Punchestown cross-country ch (3m) (0)

WINS-RUNS: 6yo 0-4, 7yo 0-8, 8yo 3-19, 9yo 3-33, 10yo 3-29, 11yo 0-26, 12yo 1-23, 13yo 0-11, 14yo 0-4, 15yo 0-2

FAVOURITES: -£7.13 **FATE OF FAVOURITES:** 6254P03013 **POSITION OF WINNER IN MARKET:** 2293372712

Key trends

🐎 Won over at least 3m, 10/10

🐎 Trained in Ireland, 8/10

🐎 Won or placed in a cross-country race at Cheltenham or Punchestown, 7/10 (one exception carried out when set to place)

🐎 At least 13 chase runs, 7/10

🐎 Top-four finish in last completed start, 6/10

Other factors

🐎 The inaugural running was in 2005 and JP McManus and Enda Bolger teamed up for four of the first five winners. They also had 2016 winner Josies Orders following his promotion on the disqualification of Any Currency

🐎 Two winners had landed the PP Hogan at Punchestown in February, while 2013 winner Big Shu was runner-up in that event

🐎 Only nine British-trained runners have made the first four, although in 2014 the home team had first, second and fourth

🐎 Ireland has had the first four on four occasions and in 2009 had the first nine finishers

4.50 Boodles Fred Winter Juvenile Hcap Hurdle RUK
2m½f   Grade 3   £80,000

A fiercely competitive handicap hurdle that went to 33-1 shot Flying Tiger last year, giving trainer Nick Williams his first festival winner.

The big stables are always worth noting. Paul Nicholls has been responsible for three winners, as well as several placed horses, and Nicky Henderson, David Pipe and Gordon Elliott have had a winner apiece.

Nicholls' three winners were French-breds, who have done extremely well in this juvenile contest with six wins in 13 runnings (a French-bred has finished first or second in the last six renewals, with Henderson's 9-2 favourite Divin Bere beaten just a neck into second last year).

Nine of the 13 winners had won on one of their last two starts. No winner has carried top weight, with Crack Away Jack (11st 10lb in 2008) the only one to carry more than 11st 4lb.

It is important to look for runners rated in a certain bracket – 12 of the 13 winners were rated between 124 and 134 (the exception was 2011 winner What A Charm off 115, although that wouldn't happen now as a mark of 124 was required to get in last year's race).

Claiming jockeys can be significant, with three of the 13 winners having been partnered by conditional or amateur riders, most recently Henderson's Une Artiste in 2012 by then 5lb claimer Jeremiah McGrath.

FRED WINTER HANDICAP HURDLE RESULTS AND TRENDS

	FORM	WINNER	AGE & WGT	OR	SP	TRAINER	BEST RPR LAST 12 MONTHS (RUNS SINCE)
17	2P614	**Flying Tiger** D	4 11-5	134-2	33-1	N Williams	won Newbury class 4 hdl (2m½f) **(1)**
16	322	**Diego Du Charmil** BF	4 11-1	133-17	13-2	P Nicholls	2nd Enghien hdl (2m½f) **(0)**
15	3-421	**Qualando**	4 11-0	131-9	25-1	P Nicholls	4th Auteuil Listed hdl (2m1½f) **(2)**
14	1216	**Hawk High** D	4 11-1	130-12	33-1	T Easterby	won Warwick class 4 hdl (2m) **(1)**
13	125	**Flaxen Flare** D	4 10-8	127-5	25-1	G Elliott (IRE)	5th Leopardstown Gd1 nov hdl (2m) **(0)**
12	11114	**Une Artiste** D	4 10-8	127-6	40-1	N Henderson	won Haydock class 2 hdl (2m) **(1)**
11	757	**What A Charm**	4 10-6	115-3	9-1	A Moore (IRE)	7th Fairyhouse Gd2 nov hdl (2m) **(0)**
10	531	**Sanctuaire** D	4 11-2	127-9	4-1f	P Nicholls	3rd Auteuil hdl (2m2f) **(1)**
09	52111	**Silk Affair** (5x)	4 10-4	125-12	11-1	M Quinlan	won Sandown cl 3 nov hcap hdl (2m4f) **(1)**
08	531	**Crack Away Jack** D	4 11-10	133-22	14-1	E Lavelle	won Sandown class 3 nov hdl (2m½f) **(0)**

FAVOURITES: -£5.00 **FATE OF FAVOURITES:** 2414300002 **POSITION OF WINNER IN MARKET:** 4415000020

Key trends

- Officially rated 125 to 134, 9/10
- Top-three finish in at least one of last two starts, 9/10
- Had lost maiden tag over hurdles, 8/10
- Won at least one of last two starts, 7/10
- Sired by a Group 1 winner on the Flat, 7/10
- Beaten in first two starts over hurdles, 6/10

Other factors

- Four of the five winners who had run on the Flat had earned an RPR of at least 87; the other five were unraced on the Flat
- Four winners were French-bred

As usual this race will not take shape until festival week but what we do know is that this is no longer an Irish-dominated affair, with the score standing at 4-4 between the home team and the raiders in the past eight runnings. Ireland's champion trainer Willie Mullins is the major influence on the market once again with a host of potential challengers led by the unbeaten Grade 2 winner Blackbow. Nowadays he often trims his team right back (last year he had two runners) and plans are far from finalised with his other options including Hollowgraphic, Colreevy, Carefully Selected and Tornado Flyer. Joseph O'Brien has a couple with good credentials in Rhinestone, runner-up to Blackbow last time, and Leopardstown Christmas winner Alighted. Among the fancied home contenders are Nick Gifford's Didtheyleaveuoutto, Anthony Honeyball's Acey Milan and Fergal O'Brien's Time To Move On – all representing trainers who have yet to win at the festival.

Blackbow
5 b g; Trainer Willie Mullins
Bumper form (left-handed) 11, best RPR 142

Unbeaten in three starts overall (one point, two bumpers) and it was a very good Grade 2 he won at Leopardstown's Dublin Festival in February, when he and runner-up Rhinestone put up huge figures as they pulled 15 lengths clear of the rest. The winner's Racing Post Rating of 142 has been bettered in this sphere only a handful of times in the past ten years and, to put it into perspective, is 17lb superior to that awarded to Fayonagh for her Champion Bumper success last season and 6lb better than Samcro, who was RPR's top bumper horse last term. Not all horses who put up big numbers pre-Cheltenham confirm them at the festival, but obviously he's in the right hands to land this race and sets some standard.

Going preference Has won on yielding and soft, and won point on good
Star rating ✪✪

Hollowgraphic
5 ch g; Trainer Willie Mullins
Bumper form (right-handed) 21, best RPR 132

Neck second to Vision Des Flos (disappointing until winning after a wind operation in February) in valuable Punchestown bumper last April and confirmed the impression he left there with easy 13-length win back at the same course in December. Runner-up won next time but was beaten out of sight by Blackbow at Leopardstown in February. Still looks very promising and adds another powerful string to the bow for a trainer who is a serial winner of this event.

Going preference Win was on heavy but second on good/yielding hardly shabby
Star rating ✪✪✪

Didtheyleaveuoutto
5 ch g; Trainer Nick Gifford
Bumper form 11, best RPR 124
Left-handed 1, best RPR 112
Right-handed 1, best RPR 124

Had some clockwatchers purring after finishing effort to win Lingfield bumper by ten lengths on his debut and confirmed that promise when again quickening up quite smartly to land seemingly well-contested 14-runner Listed event at Ascot next time. Put away for this afterwards and you'd have to think he's one of the leading British hopes.

Going preference Said not to want it soft
Star rating ✪✪✪✪

Rhinestone

7 b g; Trainer Joseph O'Brien
Bumper form 212, best RPR 140
Left-handed 2, best RPR 140
Right-handed 21, best RPR 134

Chinned on debut at odds-on at Punchestown in November but left that form way behind when running out 19-length winner at Thurles the following month and bettered that form when beaten just a length and a half by Blackbow in what was surely the hottest bumper of the season so far at Leopardstown in February. There were some who thought he was given an over-confident ride by Derek O'Connor then, but it's red-hot form anyway and, being by an Arc winner out of a half-sister to a Dewhurst winner, he's certainly bred to go a bit.

Going preference All runs on soft/heavy, trainer expects better on decent ground
Star rating ✪✪✪✪

Acey Milan

4 b g; Trainer Anthony Honeyball
Bumper form 2111, best RPR 132
Left-handed 11, best RPR 132
Right-handed 21, best RPR 112

Progressive form in bumpers, winning last three, and was pretty impressive with 11-length success on latest start at Newbury on Betfair Hurdle day in a race won by 2016 Champion Bumper winner Ballyandy. Obviously very decent but is a four-year-old and only three from that age group – Rhythm Section and top-class pair Dato Star and Cue Card – have managed to win this in 25 runnings.

Going preference All wins on soft but related to multiple good-ground winners and pedigree gives hope
Star rating ✪✪✪✪

Alighted

5 b g; Trainer Joseph O'Brien
Bumper form (left-handed) 1, RPR 125

Won well-contested bumper at Leopardstown (runner-up beaten again since, but ran well in another good race) and quoted by a couple of firms, but owned by Gigginstown and said to be a big baby, so it will be a surprise if he's even entered.

Going preference Win came on soft
Star rating ✪

Colreevy

5 b m; Trainer Willie Mullins
Bumper form 13, best RPR 110
Left-handed 1, best RPR 106
Right-handed 3, best RPR 110

Fell at the last when challenging on point debut but won first start in a bumper before being beaten into third at odds-on in Grade 2 at Leopardstown in February. The bookies are on guard with the Mullins string, but this is a total guess as on Racing Post Ratings she hasn't achieved anywhere near enough to figure.

Going preference All runs on soft/heavy
Star rating ✪

Time To Move On

5 ch g; Trainer Fergal O'Brien
Bumper form (right-handed) 11, best RPR 127

Deeply impressive ten-length winner first time up at Exeter in December when accounting for a previous winner who looked very useful beforehand but he was then a little workmanlike when defying a penalty at long odds-on back at the same track in February. However, connections put that down to the lack of a gallop and it's hard to win impressively when the ground is as deep as it was at that stiff track. Trainer has superb overall record in bumpers and raves about this half-brother to Pertemps Final runner-up Barney Dwan.

Going preference Both runs on soft/heavy but half-brother likes decent ground
Star rating ✪✪✪✪

Downtown Getaway

5 b g; Trainer Nicky Henderson
Bumper form (right-handed) 1, RPR 130

Big-field 14-1 winner from a 20-1 shot at Fairyhouse in December for Mags Mullins, but there didn't seem to be any fluke about it and he was knocked down to Nicky Henderson for £350,000. The 12-length runner-up has since been sold to David Pipe and won at odds-on on his next start at Chepstow, while the third has since been a close third in a Listed bumper at Punchestown. From the same family as Chomba Womba, whom Henderson also trained and picked up from Mullins.

Going preference Win came on soft
Star rating ✪✪✪

Carefully Selected
6 b g; Trainer Willie Mullins
Bumper form (left-handed) 1, RPR 132

Won second of two points by 30 lengths under Katie Walsh, who then recommended him to Willie Mullins. Looked a decent enough purchase when running out easy eight-length winner of 2m4f bumper at Leopardstown over Christmas, but staying is evidently his game and trainer already talking about next year's Albert Bartlett. Could be run off his feet dropped to 2m on decent surface.

Going preference Win on soft, point form on yielding
Star rating ✪✪

Bullionaire
5 b g; Trainer Harry Fry
Bumper form 12, best RPR 118
Left-handed 1, best RPR 116
Right-handed 2, best RPR 118

Won what is often an informative 20-runner bumper at Newbury last March – won twice by Diamond Harry – when said to be green and he still looked far from the finished article on his reappearance in a Listed bumper at Ascot in December. Sent off 3-1 favourite, he proved no match for the finishing kick of Didtheyleaveuoutto, going down by two and three-quarter lengths. However, he raced keenly for well over a mile and a half and there has to be a chance he'll do better if he settles.

Going preference Both runs on good to soft
Star rating ✪✪

Tornado Flyer
5 b g; Trainer Willie Mullins
Bumper form (right-handed) 1, RPR 115

Out of a half-sister to Hurricane Fly and made fine start to career with battling head victory in nine-runner Fairyhouse bumper in January. That form some way off the pick of the contenders and Cheltenham wasn't mentioned afterwards.

Going preference Win on soft
Star rating ✪

Crooks Peak
5 b g; Trainer Philip Hobbs
Bumper form (left-handed) 11, best RPR 123

Unbeaten in two bumpers in the autumn, the second a Listed affair at Cheltenham, when he coped better with the soft ground than his trainer expected. That form worked out well with the runner-up winning easily next time and third finishing second to Acey Milan in that good Newbury bumper in February. Not seen since, presumably to avoid winter ground.

Going preference Acts on good and soft, said to prefer the former
Star rating ✪✪✪

OTHERS TO CONSIDER

It's an achievement just to feature the winner on these pages so far in advance and I can confirm that last year's book did not include the winner or third! That's how much of a guess-up this race is and Mullins' **Stay Humble** is as short as 14-1 in a place even though he is yet to run in a bumper.

VERDICT

I've only ever backed the winner of this once and that was when having a blind stab at Total Enjoyment in 2004 as I was having a good day. I can't take it too seriously as a betting heat but would give RHINESTONE a shot at overturning form with Blackbow. It looks like connections have been trying to work him out as he made the running when he won but was then buried in a big field when second to Blackbow. Given his Flat pedigree, you'd think better ground will suit.

CHAMPION BUMPER RESULTS AND TRENDS

	FORM	WINNER	AGE & WGT	Adj RPR	SP	TRAINER	BEST RPR LAST 12 MONTHS (RUNS SINCE)
17	811	Fayonagh D	6 10-12	140^T	7-1	G Elliott (IRE)	won Fairyhouse Listed bumper (2m) (0)
16	1121	Ballyandy CD	5 11-5	146^T	5-1	N Twiston-Davies	won Newbury Listed bumper (2m½f) (0)
15	-11	Moon Racer CD	6 11-5	140^{-7}	9-2f	D Pipe	won Cheltenham bumper (2m½f) (0)
14	3/2-1	Silver Concorde D	6 11-5	132^{-15}	16-1	D Weld (IRE)	won Leopardstown bumper (2m) (0)
13	1	Briar Hill D	5 11-5	117^{-27}	25-1	W Mullins (IRE)	won Thurles bumper (2m) (0)
12	21	Champagne Fever D	5 11-5	144^{-1}	16-1	W Mullins (IRE)	won Fairyhouse bumper (2m) (0)
11	21	Cheltenian D	5 11-5	126^{-13}	14-1	P Hobbs	won Kempton cl 5 mdn bumper (2m) (0)
10	1	Cue Card	4 10-12	126^{-15}	40-1	C Tizzard	won Fontwell class 6 bumper (1m6f) (0)
09	2-11	Dunguib D	6 11-5	147^T	9-2	P Fenton (IRE)	won Navan Gd2 bumper (2m) (0)
08	1	Cousin Vinny	5 11-5	118^{-23}	12-1	W Mullins (IRE)	won Punchestown bumper (2m) (0)

WINS-RUNS: 4yo 1-26, 5yo 5-146, 6yo 4-56 **FAVOURITES:** -£4.50

TRAINERS IN THIS RACE (w-pl-r): Willie Mullins 3-4-40, Gordon Elliott 1-0-3, Philip Hobbs 1-1-9, Nigel Twiston-Davies 1-0-6, Anthony Honeyball 0-1-2 **FATE OF FAVOURITES:** 3306222170 **POSITION OF WINNER IN MARKET:** 5206006123

Key trends

🐎 Won last time out, 10/10

🐎 Aged five or six, 9/10

🐎 Adjusted RPR of at least 126, 8/10 (both exceptions were once-raced winners trained by Willie Mullins)

🐎 Off the track for at least 32 days, 8/10 (three not seen since Christmas or earlier)

🐎 Won a bumper with at least 13 runners, 7/10

🐎 Won a bumper worth at least £4,000 or €4,000 to the winner, 7/10

Other factors

🐎 Ireland has won six of the last ten and 18 of the 25 runnings

🐎 Willie Mullins has the best record with eight victories (three in the last ten years) but is often mob-handed. On four of the occasions he has won it, he saddled just one runner. On the other four, the winner was not his most fancied in the market

🐎 The 25 winners have been sired by 25 different stallions. Those are Montelimar, Where To Dance, Strong Gale, Accordion, Welsh Term, Florida Son, Glacial Storm, Mister Lord, River Falls, Broken Hearted, Teenoso, Flemensfirth, Overbury, Shernazar, Fasliyev, Bob Back, Presenting, King's Theatre, Astarabad, Stowaway, Shantou, Dansili, Saffron Walden, Kayf Tara and Kalanisi

🐎 Five of the last ten winners were bred in Ireland

Notes

THURSDAY, MARCH 15 (NEW COURSE)
PAUL KEALY ON THE KEY CONTENDERS

1.30 JLT Novices' Chase — ITV/RUK
⚐2m4f ⚐Grade 1 ⚐£150,000

Like the Ryanair Chase for the seniors, this novice chase over the intermediate distance has quickly become a legitimate target in its own right, rather than simply an easier alternative than the Arkle or RSA, especially since its promotion to Grade 1 status in 2014. Ireland has won six of the seven runnings and more particularly four have gone to Willie Mullins, including the last three with Vautour, Black Hercules and Yorkhill. Mullins has several options again, notably Footpad, Invitation Only and Al Boum Photo, but for a change the ante-post market leader is British-trained in the shape of Ben Pauling's Willoughby Court. Last year's Neptune Novices' Hurdle winner established his chasing credentials with a Grade 2 victory at Newbury in December but then had that form reversed by Yanworth on heavy ground at Cheltenham's New Year's Day meeting. Yanworth is a potential rival again, along with Grade 1 winners Monalee and Terrefort, but as usual the picture will not become clear until festival week.

Willoughby Court
7 br g; Trainer Ben Pauling
Chase form 113, best RPR 157
Left-handed 13, best RPR 157
Right-handed 1, best RPR 148
Cheltenham form (all) 13, best RPR 152
At the festival 15 Mar 2017 Made all, pushed along when hard pressed approaching last, drifted right under pressure run-in, drifted left towards finish, gamely kept finding for pressure, won Neptune Investment Management Novices' Hurdle by a head from Neon Wolf

Really tough and game novice hurdler last season who broke the hearts of favourite backers in the Neptune when repelling the challenge of the ill-fated Neon Wolf by a head. Has taken well enough to chasing, although jumped alarmingly left at times during debut win at Huntingdon (reportedly had never done so at home). No problem with his jumping at Newbury next time, though, as he was virtually foot-perfect and stayed on strongly to beat Yanworth by three lengths in the Grade 2 Berkshire Novices' Chase. The 5lb penalty he picked up for that was always going to make things harder for him in the Grade 2 Dipper at Cheltenham on New Year's Day, but he was still a bit disappointing in finishing third, this time beaten eight and a quarter lengths by Yanworth. The heavy ground shouldn't have been a problem, but stable form was an issue at the time with Ben Pauling going through a particularly bad time from late December through January. Has the target on his back now as favourite, but only because he's one of few guaranteed runners. Has not yet achieved the level of form required to win any running of this, so needs to step up. That's entirely possible, but short enough on racecourse evidence.

Going preference Seems to act on any ground
Star rating ✪✪✪✪✪

Yanworth
8 ch g; Trainer Alan King
Chase form 1F21, best RPR 155
Left-handed 21, best RPR 155
Right-handed 1F, best RPR 153
Cheltenham form (all) 412D1, best RPR 160
At the festival 11 Mar 2015 Held up towards rear, progress over 3f out, not clear run over 2f out and lost place, driven and ran on from over 1f out, nearest finish, finished fourth, beaten three and a quarter lengths by Moon Racer in Champion Bumper
16 Mar 2016 Held up in rear, progress on wide outside after 7th, close up when mistake 3 out, challenged after 2 out, chased winner before last, stayed on but not pace to challenge, finished second, beaten one and three-quarter

lengths by Yorkhill in Neptune Investment Management Novices' Hurdle
14 Mar 2017 In touch, hit 3rd, lost place and outpaced after 3 out, plugged on under pressure run-in when no danger, finished 7th, disqualified (banned substance in sample) from Champion Hurdle won by Buveur D'Air

Has always been a high-quality performer but also a beaten favourite at the last two festivals, going down at 11-10 to Yorkhill in the Neptune two years ago and running no sort of race as 2-1 jolly in last season's Champion Hurdle. Even had the ignominy of being disqualified from his tame seventh place due to a banned substance in his sample, but bounced back at Aintree when stepped up to 3m for the first time and beating Supasundae by a length in the Grade 1 Liverpool Hurdle. Chasing has not been plain sailing as he has looked far from a natural in four starts, falling at Exeter on his second outing, but on balance Alan King was right to be angry at everyone telling him to go back over hurdles. His argument that those who have never ridden a horse do not have valid opinions obviously doesn't wash, but at the same time if we stuck every horse who took time to click over fences back over hurdles there wouldn't be many chasers around. The one thing Yanworth hasn't done in his three completed starts is shirk a challenge and he's closely matched with Willoughby Court yet double the price. Trainer did seem to bow to public opinion by getting him an entry for the Stayers' Hurdle – may be tempting given Supasundae is favourite – but I'd go here as it will be the easier assignment.

Going preference Acts on any, but 6-7 on soft or heavy and 6-11 on faster
Star rating ✪✪✪✪

Invitation Only

7 b g; Trainer Willie Mullins
Chase form F113, best RPR 154
Left-handed 13, best RPR 154
Right-handed F1, best RPR 153

Willie Mullins' usual scattergun approach means this one is entered in all three Grade 1s

plus the four-miler, but he has been exclusively campaigned over 2m4f-2m5f for well over a year and there doesn't seem to be any need to go further. Indeed, he lost second place close home in the 2m5f Flogas Novice Chase at Leopardstown in February. That piece of form is up there with the best of the likely runners, but while he won a maiden hurdle on decent ground, he has faced only soft/heavy since and his trainer once referred to him as a winter horse.

Going preference All best form on soft/heavy but did win maiden hurdle on good/yielding
Star rating ✪✪

Al Boum Photo

6 b g; Trainer Willie Mullins
Chase form 1F2, best RPR 154
Left-handed 12, best RPR 154
Right-handed F, best RPR 151

Shorter for this than the RSA, but shapes like he wants further to me and dealt with in RSA section on Wednesday.

Going preference Best form on soft/heavy
Star rating ✪✪

Benatar

6 b g; Trainer Gary Moore
Chase form 111, best RPR 154
Left-handed 1, best RPR 144
Right-handed 11, best RPR 154

I must admit I nearly choked on my cornflakes when I read Gary Moore was targeting the RSA for this one as his form is over the JLT trip and the race will be much easier to win (and I've backed him). It seems the trainer is in two minds, but the market says he's much more likely to play a hand in this contest and he could well be a force. Always highly regarded by Moore, he was a 33-1 fourth to Finian's Oscar in a Grade 1 hurdle at Aintree last season but always looked a chaser in the making and has taken off over fences. If he hadn't run in that Aintree hurdle he would have been able to run in his opening handicap chase off a mark of 130 at Ascot, but his 12lb rise meant he had to shoulder 12st off 142 and it made no difference as he won readily. He then slammed subsequent Grade 2 winner Keeper Hill by nine lengths at Plumpton and finished his preparation in December when just hanging on from Finian's Oscar in a Grade 2 back at Ascot. The runner-up was conceding 5lb and much was made of his sometimes shoddy jumping, but he'd warmed up after the first few and it was still a good piece of form. Benatar shapes like he will benefit from a strongly run race and, while he will need to improve, that's entirely possible.

Going preference Has won on soft and good, suspicion he likes better ground
Star rating ✪✪✪✪

Terrefort
5 gr g; Trainer Nicky Henderson
Chase form 22613311, best RPR 160
Left-handed 633, best RPR 128
Right-handed 22111, best RPR 160

Joined Nicky Henderson from France this winter with the novice handicap chase at the festival as the original target, but blew that out the window by earning a stone rise from his initial mark of 137 when slamming the previously in-form Bentelimar by ten lengths. Any thoughts of handicaps were surely dispelled next time when he won the Grade 1 Scilly Isles Novices' Chase at Sandown, making the most of the 3lb weight-for-age he was getting from Cyrname to win by a neck, the pair 30 lengths clear. A Racing Post Rating of 160 is better than most in the likely line-up, although weight-for-age will be just 1lb at Cheltenham and there are a couple of other things to ponder too. First, in 12 starts in France and Britain he has yet to run on anything other than soft or heavy ground. The second concern might prove to be nothing at all, but both his wins in France came on right-handed tracks, as did both in Britain, and as well as three chase defeats going left-handed he also has three losses to his name over hurdles that way round, two of them heavy and one of those when a

short-priced favourite. Overall form figures left-handed are 285633, compared to 221111 right-handed.

Going preference Has run only on soft or heavy
Star rating ✪✪✪

Monalee
7 b g; Trainer Henry de Bromhead
Chase form 1F1, best RPR 156
Left-handed, F1, best RPR 156
Right-handed 1, best RPR 155
Cheltenham form (hurdles) 2, best RPR 150
At the festival 17 Mar 2017 Raced keenly, chased leaders, led on bend between last 2, ridden and headed approaching last, kept on under pressure run-in, unable to go with winner final 100yds, finished second, beaten three and a half lengths by Penhill in Albert Bartlett Novices' Hurdle

Dealt with in more detail in the RSA section as he's second favourite for that, but is well worth discussing here too as it would be much easier to make all in this than the RSA and he is obviously not short of pace, having won the 2m5f Flogas from the front last time. There is often a last-minute switch of target – although we usually associate them with Willie Mullins – with one horse or another and this is one that wouldn't surprise at all. I think he'd go off favourite if he did.

Going preference Can handle any ground, but best form last year when hitting Cheltenham on good
Star rating ✪✪✪✪✪

Finian's Oscar
6 b g; Trainer Colin Tizzard
Chase form 1132, best RPR 160
Left-handed 11, best RPR 160
Right-handed 32, best RPR 160
Cheltenham form (all) 1P, best RPR 160

High-class novice hurdler last season who had to miss Cheltenham but won a Grade 1 at Aintree and went down by only a short head when trying to follow up at Punchestown. Much was expected of him as a chaser, but he's another for whom it hasn't been all plain sailing and trainer Colin Tizzard came in for some unfair stick for the way he handled him. He won and put up decent figures on his first two starts over fences and those who, with the benefit of hindsight, said he shouldn't have dropped to 2m for the Henry VIII at Sandown ought to have remembered that he cantered to a 2m Tolworth Hurdle win on the track and doesn't lack speed. However, his jumping fell apart after a mistake early down the back and he finished a tailed-off third of three finishers. Tizzard then ran him in a three-runner Grade 2 just two weeks later, which many thought was too soon after his Sandown experience, but after jumping stickily in the early stages he warmed to the task and it was no disgrace to go down by a short head to Benatar, who is rated highly by Gary Moore. That is arguably some of the best chase form on offer in this contest, but Tizzard was another to bow to public pressure and he decided to switch him to hurdles with a tilt at the Stayers' on the horizon. That backfired, though, as Finian's Oscar was pulled up in the Cleeve Hurdle, shaping like a non-stayer in the deep ground on his first try at 3m, although the yard was in poor form at the time as well. Where he goes now is anyone's guess, but he is another who has achieved a high level of form over fences without being a natural. It hasn't affected his appetite for a battle judging by his Ascot run and no reason to shelve chase career yet.

Going preference Acts on soft and good
Star rating ✪✪✪✪

Cyrname

6 b g; Trainer Paul Nicholls
Chase form 1212, best RPR 162
Left-handed 2, best RPR 147
Right-handed 112, best RPR 162

Bit of a tearaway as a hurdler when often too keen to do himself justice, but fences seem to have been the making of him and he's threatening to become a high-class performer. His neck defeat against Terrefort, for which he'd be 2lb better off if they met at Cheltenham, certainly doesn't entitle him to be twice the price of the winner. However, built into those odds is the fact Paul Nicholls said he thinks he's better going right-handed, doesn't want good ground and might miss the meeting.

Going preference Has won on good but best form on soft
Star rating ✪✪

OTHERS TO CONSIDER

It would obviously be the shock of all time if **Footpad** was switched to this race and as usual there are others among the entries with much more likely targets, including the Arkle favourite's rivals **Saint Calvados** and **Petit Mouchoir**. **Shattered Love** beat **Jury Duty** in a 3m Grade 1 at Leopardstown over Christmas and both have this entry, but they are also shorter for the 4m National Hunt Chase. Paul Nicholls has a couple of candidates in **Modus** and **Capitaine**. The former has won all three completed chase starts and, as a Greatwood Hurdle runner-up and Coral Cup sixth, is entitled to respect. He is capable of some prodigious leaps, but also prone to the odd howler. Capitaine has yet to race over the JLT trip, but doesn't look good enough for a red-hot Arkle and would likely get the drier ground he loves on the Thursday, although you could also see him doing some damage in the Grand Annual off 149.

VERDICT

This is always the hardest race in which to predict the line-up. If I could be sure Monalee would run here I'd be lumping on as I think he'd lead them all a merry dance, but he's seemingly on target for the RSA. BENATAR was one of two ante-post bets, the other being FINIAN'S OSCAR, who was 14-1 non-runner no bet and that was just miles too big. Yes, he has his issues with jumping but in terms of pure ability he's probably the most talented in the likely field. I do think Benatar will appreciate a strong gallop at this trip, but his trainer is seemingly in two minds where to go. Willoughby Court is too short, but at least he looks certain to line up.

JLT NOVICES' CHASE RESULTS

	FORM WINNER	AGE & WGT	Adj RPR	SP	TRAINER	BEST RPR LAST 12 MONTHS (RUNS SINCE)
17	1-411 **Yorkhill** C, D	7 11-4	163-7	6-4f	W Mullins (IRE)	won Fairyhouse nov ch (2m) (1)
16	7-11F **Black Hercules** D, BF	7 11-4	169-2	4-1c	W Mullins (IRE)	won Warwick Listed nov ch (3m) (1)
15	-1121 **Vautour** C, D	6 11-4	165-10	6-4f	W Mullins (IRE)	won Leop Gd2 nov ch (2m3f) (0)
14	11321 **Taquin Du Seuil** C, D	7 11-4	167-6	7-1	J O'Neill	won Haydock Gd2 nov ch (2m5f) (0)
13	21241 **Benefficient** D	7 11-4	161-8	20-1	A Martin (IRE)	won Leop Gd1 Arkle nov ch (2m1f) (0)
12	1-111 **Sir Des Champs** C, D	6 11-4	161-8	3-1	W Mullins (IRE)	won Limerick Gd2 nov ch (2m3½f) (1)
11	4-122 **Noble Prince** D	7 11-4	164-6	4-1	P Nolan (IRE)	2nd Leop Gd1 Arkle nov ch (2m1f) (0)

WINS-RUNS: 5yo 0-4, 6yo 2-26, 7yo 5-28, 8yo 0-9, 9yo 0-4 **FAVOURITES:** -£0.34

TRAINERS IN THIS RACE (w-pl-r): Willie Mullins 4-1-12, Alan King 0-1-1, Colin Tizzard 0-0-1, Dan Skelton 0-0-1, David Pipe, 0-1-3, Harry Fry 0-0-1, Henry de Bromhead 0-1-3, Noel Meade 0-2-3, Nicky Henderson 0-2-9, Nigel Twiston-Davies 0-3-6, Paul Nicholls 0-0-8, Philip Hobbs 0-1-4, Nick Williams 0-1-1

FATE OF FAVOURITES: 2024111 **POSITION OF WINNER IN MARKET:** 2274111

Key trends

🐎Distance winner, 7/7

🐎Ran over hurdles at a previous festival, 7/7

🐎Adjusted RPR of at least 161, 7/7

🐎Rated within 8lb of RPR top-rated, 6/7

🐎Won a Graded chase, 5/7

🐎Graded winner over hurdles, 5/7

Other factors

🐎Five winners won last time out – of the two exceptions, one was beaten a short head on their previous start while the other fell when likely to win

🐎Three winners had won over hurdles at a previous festival and all three were trained by Willie Mullins (Sir Des Champs, Vautour and Yorkhill)

Notes

2.10 Pertemps Final (Handicap Hurdle) ITV/RUK
🐎3m 🐎Listed 🐎£100,000

Cheltenham has taken steps to rectify a perceived lack of quality in this staying handicap hurdle by changing the conditions – as of 2016, horses are eligible to run in the final only if they finished in the first six in one of the qualifiers.

Over the longer term last-time-out winners have a strong record (12 winners in the past 22 years), although five of the exceptions have been in the past eight years.

Favourites have a poor record, with Fingal Bay in 2014 only the second market leader to have won in the past 20 runnings. Call The Cops at 9-1 in 2015 was the only other winner since 2003 to be sent off less than double-figure odds.

The bottomweight tends to run off a mark around the mid-130s nowadays (137 in 2017) and the best place to find the winner is from there up to 144, although Presenting Percy was slightly higher on 146 last year and so was Fingal Bay on 148 in 2014. More specifically, five of the last seven winners have been rated between 138 and 142.

The home team has dominated since the turn of the millennium, with 13 of the 17 winners, but Irish trainer Pat Kelly has won the last two runnings with Mall Dini and Presenting Percy. This can be a race for the older hurdler (seven of the last 12 winners were eight or older), although most winners are relatively lightly raced in any case with nine of the last 11 having had no more than ten previous runs over hurdles.

PERTEMPS FINAL RESULTS AND TRENDS

	FORM	WINNER	AGE & WGT	OR	SP	TRAINER	BEST RPR LAST 12 MONTHS (RUNS SINCE)
17	11541	**Presenting Percy**	6 11-11	146-4	11-1	P Kelly (IRE)	won Fairyhouse hcap hdl (2m4f) (0)
16	31433	**Mall Dini**	6 10-11	139-7	14-1	P Kelly (IRE)	won Thurles mdn hdl (2m6½f) (3)
15	21-41	**Call The Cops** (5x) D	6 10-12	138-5	9-1	N Henderson	won Doncaster class 2 hcap hdl (3m½f) (0)
14	120-1	**Fingal Bay** C, D	8 11-12	148T	9-2f	P Hobbs	won Exeter class 2 hcap hdl (2m7½f) (0)
13	-2222	**Holywell**	6 11-4	140-5	25-1	J O'Neill	2nd Warwick class 2 hcap hdl (3m1f) (0)
12	5P504	**Cape Tribulation** D	8 10-11	142-3	14-1	M Jefferson	5th Haydock Gd3 hcap hdl (3m) (1)
11	28700	**Buena Vista** CD	10 10-3	138-4	20-1	D Pipe	won Pertemps Final (3m) (6)
10	-8508	**Buena Vista**	9 10-1	133-1	16-1	D Pipe	5th Haydock Listed hcap hdl (3m1f) (2)
09	26211	**Kayf Aramis** D	7 10-5	129-7	16-1	V Williams	won Warwick class 3 nov hdl (3m1f) (0)
08	-1271	**Ballyfitz** D	8 10-8	132-3	18-1	N Twiston-Davies	won Haydock class 2 hcap hdl (3m) (0)

WINS-RUNS: 5yo 0-16, 6yo 4-56, 7yo 1-68, 8yo 3-48, 9yo 1-20, 10yo 1-14, 11yo 0-11, 12yo 0-1, 13yo 0-1 **FAVOURITES:** -£4.50

FATE OF FAVOURITES: 2000001000 **POSITION OF WINNER IN MARKET:** 0059601365

Key trends

🐎Winning form between 2m4f and 2m6f, 9/10

🐎Carried no more than 11st 4lb, 8/10

🐎Aged six to eight, 8/10

🐎Six to ten runs over hurdles, 8/10 (exceptions 22-plus)

🐎Officially rated 132 to 142, 7/10

🐎Won a Class 2 or higher, 7/10

🐎Off track between 19 and 48 days, 7/10

🐎Won over at least 3m, 6/10

Other factors

🐎Four winners had run at the festival before

🐎Pragada in 1988 is the only winning five-year-old in the race's 43-year history, while Buena Vista in 2011 was the first aged older than nine to oblige since 1981

2.50 Ryanair Chase

ITV/RUK

≈2m5f   ≈Grade 1   ≈£350,000

Last year's victor Un De Sceaux is on course for his bid to emulate Albertas Run, who in 2010 and 2011 became the only dual winner of this race since its inception in 2005. He has followed a similar path to last season with two pre-festival outings, including a comfortable victory (like last year) over the shorter trip of the Grade 1 Clarence House Chase. He has lost only three of his completed starts over fences – twice against Sprinter Sacre but on the other occasion in last season's Punchestown Champion Chase against Fox Norton, who could well oppose him again. Having been a head runner-up in the Queen Mother Champion Chase at last year's festival, Fox Norton has been running over a variety of distances with mixed results but trainer Colin Tizzard might settle on this mid-range trip. Last year's JLT Novices' Chase runner-up Top Notch is a leading fancy for Nicky Henderson, while the most poignant winner would be Waiting Patiently, whose trainer Malcolm Jefferson died in February, with his daughter Ruth taking over the licence.

Un De Sceaux

10 b g; Trainer Willie Mullins
Chase form F1111F122111211, best RPR 174
Left-handed 11F211, best RPR 174
Right-handed F11121211, best RPR 172
Cheltenham form 1211, best RPR 174
At the festival 10 Mar 2015 Raced with zest, made most, shaken up approaching last, quickened clear final 110yds, ran on well, won Racing Post Arkle by six lengths from God's Own
16 Mar 2016 Tracked leader, hit 4th, led after 4 out, ridden when headed before 2 out, soon held by winner, kept on same pace, finished second, beaten three and a half lengths by Sprinter Sacre in Queen Mother Champion Chase
16 Mar 2017 Jumped boldly, held up in touch, racing keenly when progress to lead 5th, 5 lengths clear from 8th, reached for 11th, ridden after last, kept on gamely, won Ryanair Chase by one and a half lengths from Sub Lieutenant

Admirable ten-year-old who has become a bit of a legend over the years for his consistency, enthusiasm and exuberance as much for his undoubted class. Has won 20 of 24 completed starts and been out of the first two only once when getting round, when sixth and palpably not staying in the 3m1½f French Champion Hurdle of 2016. Big-race victories over fences include all the 2m Grade 1s in Britain except the Champion Chase, in which he proved no match for a resurgent Sprinter Sacre when odds-on in March 2016. There was always the suspicion he didn't really like good ground as most of his running was done on soft or heavy in Ireland, but he did win an Arkle on good to soft and dispelled that notion once and for all when tackling this race last season. Although Ruby Walsh tried to ride him with restraint, he'd tanked his way to the front passing the stands. Apart from one mistake when he came up far too soon, he put in some brilliant leaps – including at the last two fences – and although a five-length lead at the last was down to one and a half at the line he was never really in any danger. No evidence that he's on the downgrade this season either, with a 25-length win at Cork followed by a seven-length success in the Clarence House Chase at Ascot – his third victory in that race. That race was probably not up to its usual standard (runner-up Speredek went there rated only 145) but Un De Sceaux still won easily enough. Probably still entitled to be favourite despite his age, although this is shaping up to be a better race than last year.

Going preference Handles everything
Star rating ✪✪✪✪✪

Waiting Patiently

7 b g; Trainer Ruth Jefferson
Chase form 111111, best RPR 174
Left-handed 111, best RPR 158
Right-handed 111, best RPR 167

The rising star in the chasing division having now won six out of six and improved his Racing Post Rating with every start. Didn't have much to beat on first run out of novice company at Carlisle in November, but passed first serious test with smooth eight-length success in Listed chase at Kempton in January and followed that up with another deeply impressive victory in the Grade 1 Betfair Ascot Chase in February. A back-to-form Cue Card had helped set or press a really decent gallop that had most in trouble by the time they turned into the straight but not Waiting Patiently, who was obviously travelling the best approaching the second-last. Cue Card, as is his wont, refused to lie down but there was only going to be one winner and even though Waiting Patiently had to get down to work to make sure, he was still nearly three lengths up at the line. What was most impressive was the fact the pair were only a couple of lengths or so ahead of progressive pair Frodon and Top Notch at the second-last, but that pair, who had their own battle for third, were eventually beaten around 18 and 20 lengths. The problem for ante-post punters is that Ruth Jefferson says her late father's pride and joy won't run unless the ground is soft and might not even if it is. If he does go he's arguably the one to beat now.

Going preference Always said to want winter ground
Star rating ✪✪✪

Fox Norton

8 b g; Trainer Colin Tizzard
Chase form 1123333111221112P, best RPR 174
Left-handed 233331112211, best RPR 174
Right-handed 1112P, best RPR 170
Cheltenham form 2311121, best RPR 172
At the festival 15 Mar 2016 Tracked leaders, pushed along and lost place after 3 out, outpaced after, slightly hampered 2 out, kept on to take 3rd final 75yds, no chance, finished third, beaten ten and three-quarter lengths by Douvan in Racing Post Arkle
15 Mar 2017 Tracked leaders, slightly outpaced after 3 out, headway between last 2, strong run from last to press winner close home, just held, finished second, beaten a head by Special Tiara in Queen Mother Champion Chase

Top class at his best and came within a head of completing a spring festival treble last season. Unfortunately he went down in the first leg when unable to battle his way past Special Tiara in the Champion Chase, but he then ran the race of his life upped to 2m4f for the first time in the Melling Chase at Aintree, storming clear to beat Sub Lieutenant by six lengths. That was four and a half lengths further than Un De Sceaux had beaten the same horse in the Ryanair, but the market still fancied the Mullins runner when the two winners clashed in the Punchestown Champion Chase, with Un De Sceaux a shade of odds-on. Collateral form held up, though, as Fox Norton closed down the favourite after the last and went away for a length and three-quarters victory. He returned in November and looked every bit as good as ever as he turned the Shloer Chase into a procession, winning by eight lengths under a penalty, and although beaten at odds-on in the Tingle Creek at Sandown, he wasn't far off his 2m best in going down by half

TRAINER'S VIEW

Ruth Jefferson on Waiting Patiently "Cheltenham is a unique track, it's quite sharp, quite undulating and they go very quick. He's quite a young horse. He just made the odd mistake here and there [at Ascot] and whether the test of Cheltenham will suit him now is up for debate. That's the doubt we have. He's done most of his winning on a flat or more galloping track" *Only one winner in the Ryanair's 13-year history had not already won at Cheltenham*

a length to new kid on the block Politologue. Whether his run in the King George came too soon afterwards (hard to argue given he'd run so well three times in six weeks in the spring) or there was another reason, it wasn't stamina that proved his undoing as he was in trouble a mile from home and already well beaten long before he pulled up three out. Trainer's horses were not in best form at the

Fox Norton (3): second in last year's Champion Chase is his only defeat in his last five outings at Cheltenham

time and if he comes back fresh and at the level of his Shloer win he will be a handful for all of them. Obviously does come in under a bit of a cloud, but likes decent ground and only defeat in last five Cheltenham starts was in that Champion Chase last year.

Going preference Acts on soft, arguably likes it better
Star rating ✪✪✪✪

Top Notch
7 b g; Trainer Nicky Henderson
Chase form 3111123114, best RPR 171
Left-handed 31123, best RPR 165
Right-handed 11114, best RPR 171
Cheltenham form (all) 2552, best RPR 165
At the festival 13 Mar 2015 In touch, hit 5th, led over 2f out on long run to last, headed final 100yds, continued to challenge and stayed on, always held, finished second, beaten a neck by Peace And Co in Triumph Hurdle
15 Mar 2016 Midfield, headway approaching 3 out, 5th when mistake 2 out, ridden and outpaced before last, stayed on same pace run-in, finished fifth, beaten nine and three-quarter lengths by Annie Power in Champion Hurdle
16 Mar 2017 Tracked leaders, left upsides leader 4 out, every chance when mistake 2 out and dropped 3 lengths, ran on after last but always being held by winner final 100yds, finished second, beaten a length by Yorkhill in JLT Novices' Chase

Talented little chaser who seems to have been around a while but is still only seven and has improved again this season. Was a good novice, having run Yorkhill to a length in last season's JLT, but stepped up on that to thrash subsequent King George second Double Shuffle by eight lengths in the Christy 1965 Chase at Ascot in November and followed up in the rescheduled Peterborough at Taunton the following month, although he was a bit below that Ascot form. Trainer probably left a bit to work on when running him in the Grade 1 Betfair Chase at Ascot in February, but he surrendered his unbeaten course record rather tamely, finishing a 20-length fourth. Didn't jump as well as he can off the searching pace that day, but it's not likely to be any slower at Cheltenham and has a bit to prove now. That said, he's twice been second

at the festival and it would be no surprise to see him run well again.

Going preference Handles any ground
Star rating ✪✪✪✪✪

Balko Des Flos
7 ch g; Trainer Henry de Bromhead
Chase form 2133F31232, best RPR 168
Left-handed 33F2, best RPR 168
Right-handed 213123, best RP 155
Cheltenham form (all) 5F, best RPR 135
At the festival 18 Mar 2016 Held up, headway before 6th, tracked leaders approaching 2 out, ridden before last and not quicken, one pace after, finished fifth, beaten 15 and a half lengths by Unowhatimeanharry in Albert Bartlett Novices' Hurdle
16 Mar 2017 Led until 5th, led 7th, fell 4 out in JLT Novices' Chase won by Yorkhill

Backed in from a morning 50-1 to 16-1 when lining up for the JLT 12 months ago and, while he fell four out, he had raced keenly and jumped well on or near the lead throughout and hadn't been asked a question before his mistake, which was quite a bad one. The confidence in him being better than his odds and rating suggested was not totally misplaced as two starts later he bolted up in the Galway Plate off a mark of 146. He couldn't maintain that improvement in a couple of races in September and November, being well held as favourite each time, but they came on soft/heavy ground and he was back on an upward curve when a 66-1 second to ownermate Road To Respect in the Leopardstown Christmas Chase on a livelier surface. That has now earned him a mark of 164, which is not far off the best of these, and he's only seven so could still be reaching his peak. He's also in the Gold Cup, but while he wasn't disgraced when fifth in the Albert Bartlett a couple of years ago, it didn't look like he stayed 3m then. He just about does now, but any further is doubtful and this is his obvious race. Talent and profile to be a player.

Going preference Definitely doesn't want it too soft, fine on good
Star rating ✪✪✪✪

Djakadam

9 b g; Trainer Willie Mullins
Chase form 11F81221F23213422P3, best RPR 177
Left-handed 11F82F2334P3, best RPR 177
Right-handed 1212122, best RPR 175
Cheltenham form F2F24, best RPR 177
At the festival 13 Mar 2014 Chased leaders, not fluent 3rd, hit 9th, disputing 3 lengths 2nd and going okay when fell 4 out in JLT Novices' Chase won by Taquin Du Seuil
13 Mar 2015 Mid-division, smooth headway 16th, tracked leaders travelling well 18th, ridden in close 3rd approaching 2 out, hit last, stayed on to go 2nd run-in, held when drifted right final 70yd, finished second, beaten one and a half lengths by Coneygree in Gold Cup
16 Mar 2016 In touch, tracked leaders 10th, upsides after 16th, narrow lead after next, ridden and headed after 3 out, not fluent next, stayed on from last but no impression on winner, finished second, beaten four and a half lengths by Don Cossack in Gold Cup
17 Mar 2017 Travelled well most of way, tracked leaders, challenged after 4 out, narrow advantage when mistake 2 out, soon ridden and headed, kept pressing but held from last, no extra close home, finished fourth, beaten three and a quarter lengths by Sizing John in Gold Cup

There have been plenty over the years who have wanted Djakadam to run in this rather than the Gold Cup and the way he has tanked around in the longer race but just failed to get home suggests they might be right. However, he has compiled Gold Cup form figures of 224 and this year's contest doesn't look any stronger, so with his owner wanting a runner in the big one, that's likely where he'll go. Unfortunately, Djakadam has not looked anywhere near as good as he was on his last two starts and his chance in either race may have gone now.

Going preference Acts on any
Star rating ✪✪

Frodon

6 b g; Trainer Paul Nicholls
Chase form 411101F115323213, best RPR 173
Left-handed 41101531, best RPR 173
Right-handed 1F112323, best RPR 162

Cheltenham form (all) 38011, best RPR 173
At the festival 18 Mar 2016 In touch, ridden and outpaced on bend between last 2, kept on under pressure run-in but no danger, finished eighth, beaten 16 and three-quarter lengths by Ivanovich Gorbatov in Triumph Hurdle

Tough six-year-old who has improved markedly this season despite winning only one of his six chase starts. Below form on first of them at Newton Abbot in October but then showed career-best form on his next three starts, finishing second to Might Bite at Sandown, third to Top Notch at Ascot and second to Gold Present in 3m handicap at Ascot. Took form to a new level with massively impressive handicap win over the Ryanair course and distance on Trials Day, winning by 17 lengths off mark of 154. That suggested he was well worth stepping up to Grade 1 company and, while he could manage only a distant third to Waiting Patiently and Cue Card in the Betfair Ascot Chase, that run did come just three weeks after his Cheltenham win on very deep ground. Certainly worth another chance to prove he is up to Grade 1 company and we know he has no problems with this course and distance.

Going preference Clear best form on heavy now but handles better ground okay
Star rating ✪✪✪

Bachasson

7 b g; Trainer Willie Mullins
Chase form (right-handed) F2111, best RPR 165
Cheltenham form (hurdles) U, best RPR 124
At the festival 18 Mar 2016 Held up in rear, hampered 8th, headway approaching 2 out, ridden to go pace after flight, disputing 5th about 6 lengths off the pace and keeping on for pressure when blundered and unseated rider last in Albert Bartlett Novices' Hurdle won by Unowhatimeanharry

Progressive second-season chaser who, unusually for a horse trained by Willie Mullins, may be creeping in under the radar for Cheltenham. First season over fences was cut short as he didn't run after breaking his duck at the third attempt at Gowran in February, but he did that very easily over

2m4f (favourite Mall Dini nearly 11 lengths back in third) and two runs this term have seen him produce considerably better form. Both came in Listed chases and in the first at Thurles he thrashed the 150-rated Val De Ferbet by 24 lengths while in the second at Tramore he hammered the 156-rated A Toi Phil by 13 lengths. Both races were run on deep ground, but Bachasson was a four-time winner over hurdles on a much quicker surface and trainer thinks better ground suits. He also travelled strongly at the back of the field for a long way and wouldn't have been beaten that far in Unowhatimeanharry's Albert Bartlett two years ago when only a five-year-old. He probably didn't quite stay then, but is in the Gold Cup as well and, should he get the go-ahead in either race, might not be one to underestimate.

Going preference Acts on any
Star rating ✪✪✪

Cue Card

12 b g; Trainer Colin Tizzard
Chase form 1U2121511231244524111F143121 F2F22, best RPR 180
Left-handed 1U2121214211F131F2F2, best RPR 180
Right-handed 1513245414212, best RPR 180
Cheltenham form (all) 1124U21FF, best RPR 180
At the festival 17 Mar 2010 Took keen hold, held up well in rear, scythed through field from 5f out, tracked leader over 2f out and still cruising, led over 1f out, hung left briefly but romped clear, won Champion Bumper by eight lengths from Al Ferof
15 Mar 2011 Took keen hold, held up in midfield, progress before 3 out, joined leader 2 out, ridden soon after, hanging and not quicken before last, faded, finished fourth, beaten six and a half lengths by Al Ferof in Supreme Novices' Hurdle
13 Mar 2012 Led until mistake and headed 9th, chased winner from 4 out, stayed on well to try to close on winner after 2 out and 4 lengths down soon after, readily outpaced from last but stayed on well for clear 2nd, finished second, beaten seven lengths by Sprinter Sacre in Racing Post Arkle
14 Mar 2013 Made all, not fluent 3rd, reached for 8th, asserted approaching last, soon clear,

ran on well and in command after, won Ryanair Chase by nine lengths from First Lieutenant
18 Mar 2016 In touch, hit 9th, tracked leaders 14th, disputing lead and travelling well when fell 3 out in Gold Cup won by Don Cossack
17 Mar 2017 Mid-division, not clearest of runs and switched 15th, pushed along after 4 out, yet to make an impression when fell 3 out in Gold Cup won by Sizing John

Absolute legend of a horse who was a Grade 1 performer at the age of four and still is at the age of 12 judging by his second to Waiting Patiently in the Betfair Ascot Chase in February. The nine-time Grade 1 winner did not start this season too well, already being niggled along when falling at the 15th in the Charlie Hall at Wetherby and finishing a 57-length second to Bristol De Mai when the winner was the only one to handle the deep ground in the Betfair Chase at Haydock but, freshened up, he returned to warm the hearts of Ascot's racegoers with an aggressively ridden second to Waiting Patiently when going for a third Ascot Chase success. Arguably jumping as well as he ever has, he had all but the exciting winner in trouble turning for home and it confirmed he can still cut it at this level. Trainer doesn't know if he'll go for this or the Gold Cup, but he won this in 2013 after his first Ascot Chase win and, at his age, it's probably the right call. Whether his ageing legs will recover in time is another matter as he was below par before falling in last season's Gold Cup following his 15-length win at Ascot. Outsider now, but fully entitled to go and would bring the house down if he could win.

Going preference Seems to like it soft these days but never used to have a problem on faster
Star rating ✪✪

OTHERS TO CONSIDER

It's always hard to work out the final line-up for this and some of those deliberately left out who are shorter than some of the above are **Douvan**, **Min**, **Road To Respect**, **Yorkhill**, **Killultagh Vic** and **Benie Des**

Dieux. With the exception of the latter, all of the others would clearly warrant respect. Willie Mullins confirmed Douvan as being on target for the Champion Chase in mid February, but he did have him entered for a 2m4f race in February and there's always the chance he could change his mind. **Coney Island** was a relatively short price for this and the Gold Cup before flopping in the Ascot Chase (bad mistake, pulled up) and you'd have to wonder whether he'll be going anywhere now. Then there's the likes of **Outlander** and **Sub Lieutenant**, who was second last year but hasn't been seen since December.

VERDICT

Only eight went to post last year, with three of them not getting a mention in this book, but on paper it looks like being a much more competitive heat this time and we might just get a big field. Obviously Willie Mullins could throw a spanner in the works by switching Douvan or even Min to this event – he has some previous – and that would change the shape of things. The two who interest me at the prices for now are BALKO DES FLOS, who was running so well when coming down four out in the JLT last year, and BACHASSON. The latter has crept right under the radar for Mullins and may prove to be top class.

RYANAIR CHASE RESULTS AND TRENDS

	FORM WINNER	AGE & WGT	Adj RPR	SP	TRAINER	BEST RPR LAST 12 MONTHS (RUNS SINCE)
17	-1611 **Un De Sceaux** C, D	9 11-10	178^T	7-4f	W Mullins (IRE)	won Cheltenham Gd1 chase (2m½f) (0)
16	11-12 **Vautour** CD	7 11-10	184^T	Evensf	W Mullins (IRE)	2nd Gd1 King George VI Chase (3m) (0)
15	-418U **Uxizandre** C	7 11-10	170^{-5}	16-1	A King	Won Cheltenham Listed chase (2m) (2)
14	21-25 **Dynaste** C, D, BF	8 11-10	179^T	3-1f	D Pipe	2nd Gd1 Betfair Chase (3m1f) (1)
13	2-151 **Cue Card** C, D	7 11-10	174^{-2}	7-2	C Tizzard	won Gd1 Ascot Chase (2m5½f) (0)
12	121-1 **Riverside Theatre** D	8 11-10	176^T	7-2f	N Henderson	won Gd1 Ascot Chase (2m5½f) (0)
11	1-4FP **Albertas Run** CD	10 11-10	176^{-1}	6-1	J O'Neill	won Gd1 Melling Chase (2m4f) (3)
10	P1362 **Albertas Run** C, D	9 11-10	171^{-3}	14-1	J O'Neill	won Ascot Gd2 chase (2m3f) (3)
09	14-16 **Imperial Commander** C, D	8 11-10	165^{-19}	6-1	N Twiston-Davies	won Paddy Power Gold Cup (2m4½f) (1)
08	23-22 **Our Vic** CD, BF	10 11-10	176^{-2}	4-1	D Pipe	2nd Gd1 King George VI Chase (3m) (1)

WINS-RUNS: 6yo 0-3, 7yo 3-18, 8yo 3-40, 9yo 2-30, 10yo 2-12, 11yo 0-5, 12yo 0-3 **FAVOURITES:** £3.25

TRAINERS IN THIS Willie Mullins 2-2-10, Alan King 1-2-8, Colin Tizzard 1-0-4, Nicky Henderson 1-2-13, Nigel Twiston-Davies 1-0-3, Paul Nicholls 0-2-10, Gordon Elliott 0-1-2, Noel Meade 0-1-1, Dan Skelton 0-0-1, Tom George 0-0-1, Venetia Williams 0-1-1, Henry de Bromhead 0-1-2

FATE OF FAVOURITES: 5224121311 **POSITION OF WINNER IN MARKET:** 2282121811

Key trends

🐎Adjusted RPR of at least 165, 10/10

🐎Course winner, 9/10

🐎No more than four runs since October, 9/10

🐎At least seven runs over fences, 8/10

🐎Top-two finish in at least one of last two starts, 8/10

🐎From the first two in the market, 8/10

Other factors

🐎Three of the six beaten favourites had won a Grade 1 chase last time out

🐎Five winners had recorded a top-four finish in a Grade 1 or 2 chase over 3m-plus (three of the other five achieved that subsequently)

🐎The first five winners (2005-2009) had either won or been placed in the BetVictor Gold Cup or Caspian Caviar Gold Cup, but none of the last eight had run in either

The fatal fall of last year's winner Nichols Canyon at Leopardstown's Christmas meeting has left a hole at the top of the staying division and it is far from clear who will fill it, which makes this a fascinating and open race. The leading British candidate is Sam Spinner, whose rise to prominence for trainer Jedd O'Keeffe and jockey Joe Colliver has been one of the stories of the season, while on the Irish side the principal hope is likely to be Supasundae, last year's Coral Cup winner who caused an upset last time out with victory over Faugheen in the Irish Champion Hurdle. Apple's Jade would be favourite if she were confirmed for this race, but the signals all season have been that she will defend her Mares' Hurdle title instead. There is plenty of quality among the other possibles, who include Penhill, Bacardys, L'Ami Serge, The New One and last year's beaten odds-on favourite Unowhatimeanharry, but plenty of questions to answer as well.

Supasundae

8 b g; Trainer Jessica Harrington
Hurdles form 3174812412321, best RPR 165
Left-handed 178241221, best RPR 165
Right-handed 3413, best RPR 153
Cheltenham form (all) 671, best RPR 157
At the festival 11 Mar 2015 Took keen hold, led after 3f to just over 1f out, faded, finished sixth, beaten seven and a half lengths by Moon Racer in Champion Bumper
15 Mar 2016 Tracked leaders, hit 5th, ridden after 2 out, soon outpaced, 5th and held when hit last, no extra, finished seventh, beaten 14 lengths by Altior in Supreme Novices' Hurdle
15 Mar 2017 Chased leaders, not fluent 4 out, challenging 2 out, ridden to lead approaching last, stayed on well, won Coral Cup by two lengths from Taquin Du Seuil

Originally looked just below top class but really blossomed from the second part of last season and made his third visit to the Cheltenham Festival a winning one when taking the Coral Cup. He then proved himself worthy of Grade 1 company when running a length second to Yanworth in the Liverpool Hurdle at Aintree, just being run out of it after the last, and he has progressed again this term. He obviously wasn't quite fit enough to do himself justice when a well-beaten third to Apple's Jade on his return in December, but he ran that mare to just under half a length in the 3m Christmas Hurdle at Leopardstown

a few weeks later and then caused a minor surprise when dropping to 2m and landing the Irish Champion Hurdle, beating Faugheen by two and a quarter lengths. With the former Champion Hurdle winner being obviously short of his glorious best you could argue the race didn't take that much winning, but it was some effort for him at that trip. It's a rare horse who can win Grade 1s at 2m and 3m and in two runs over the latter trip Supasundae has just been run out of it late on, so he does need to fully prove his stamina, but he obviously has to be taken very seriously.

Going preference Acts on any, likes it good
Star rating ✪✪✪✪✪

Sam Spinner

6 b g; Trainer Jedd O'Keeffe
Hurdles form 1211211, best RPR 164
Left-handed 121121, best RPR 162
Right-handed 1, best RPR 164

Has long been highly regarded by trainer and never out of the first two, but only really announced himself as a potential staying star when routing his field stepped up to nearly 3m for the first time in what used to be the Fixed Brush Hurdle at Haydock. Given that was on heavy ground, off a mark of just 139 and Haydock form is not always reliable, he still had questions to answer when lining up for the Grade 1 Long Walk Hurdle at

Ascot in December, but he answered them emphatically. Always in the front rank, he fought off one challenge after another and when L'Ami Serge produced the final threat going to the last, he pulled out more again and won going away by two and three-quarter lengths. With just seven hurdles starts under his belt, there could easily be more to come and he certainly doesn't need much more to be a major player. His one advantage over Supasundae is that he definitely stays very well, but he'd have something to prove on good ground as he's never tried anything that fast. Hasn't run since the Long Walk, but that was the plan and said to take no getting fit.

Going preference Obviously likes it deep, yet to race on good
Star rating ✪✪✪✪

Penhill

7 b g; Trainer Willie Mullins
Hurdles form 161114112, best RPR 155
Left-handed 6111, best RPR 155
Right-handed 11412, best RPR 150
Cheltenham form 1, best RPR 155
At the festival 17 Mar 2017 Held up, headway when slightly hampered 2 out and forced wide, good progress entering straight between last 2, led approaching last, ran on strongly to draw clear final 100yds, won Albert Bartlett Novices' Hurdle by three and a half lengths from Monalee

Former hard-pulling Flat performer in Britain who sometimes didn't get home over middle distances but was somehow turned into a staying hurdler by Willie Mullins and won the Albert Bartlett going away by three and a half lengths from Monalee last March. Extended superiority over the runner-up (now a leading RSA hope) in the Irish version at Punchestown but was still beaten, going down by just over

two lengths to Martin Pipe winner Champagne Classic, and hasn't been sighted since. Doubt that can have been the plan and needs to find at least another 10lb to figure, but layers keen to keep him on side given he is owned by Tony Bloom, who has been known to land some huge gambles, the latest one being with Withhold in the Cesarewitch.

Going preference No real issues
Star rating ✪

Bacardys

7 b g; Trainer Willie Mullins
Hurdles form F11P1, best RPR 155
Left-handed 11P, best RPR 149
Right-handed F1, best RPR 155

Pulled up in last season's Neptune, but then inflicted first hurdles defeat on Finian's Oscar in Grade 1 at Punchestown, confirming he's a horse of some talent. However, only two runs this season, over fences, and he was beaten ten lengths when an even-money favourite at Naas in November and then fell five out when odds-on at Leopardstown, having not been too fluent beforehand. Had a hurdles entry in February but didn't take it up and can only be considered hugely underpriced on this season's form. Last season's still needs improving upon too.

Going preference Handles most ground
Star rating ✪

L'Ami Serge

8 b g; Trainer Nicky Henderson
Hurdles form 32362211142332512122, best RPR 161
Left-handed 323622142332521, best RPR 156
Right-handed 11122, best RPR 161
Cheltenham form (all) 4322, best RPR 159
At the festival 10 Mar 2015 Not that fluent,

TRAINER'S VIEW

Jedd O'Keeffe on Sam Spinner "He was rated 136 at Chepstow and 139 at Haydock. He's shot up the rankings. His jumping [in the Long Walk] wasn't as slick as I've seen it. Hopefully we can tidy that up and we might get another pound or two of improvement. He's a very easy horse to keep fit and fresh" *The six-year-old has gone up from an official mark of 136 to 164 this season*

held up, hampered 4th, soon nudged along, headway 3 out, hampered before next where mistake, soon ridden, went 4th before last but not going pace to get on terms, finished fourth, beaten 10 and a quarter lengths by Douvan in Supreme Novices' Hurdle
17 Mar 2016 Tracked leaders, jumped into wing upright 1st, led after 3 out, went badly left next, soon ridden, headed last, kept on until no extra final 75yds, finished third, beaten four lengths by Black Hercules in JLT Novices' Chase
17 Mar 2017 Mid-division, not clear run briefly turning in, soon switched left and headway, ran on well from last, went 2nd final 50yds, closing on winner at finish, finished second, beaten a neck by Arctic Fire in County Handicap Hurdle

Has been called a few names by some, but has also won nearly £500k in prize-money so has done plenty right in his career, including winning seven times and earning Cheltenham Festival form figures of 432. Latest second was in the 2m1f County Hurdle, when he went down by only a neck, but in June he won the French Champion Hurdle over a mile further and there's little doubt a stamina test suits him best now. Has mixed hurdling with chasing this season, finishing runner-up to Sam Spinner in the Long Walk at Ascot (looked dangerous at the last but winner found more) and then a closing third when a heavily backed favourite for the Sky Bet Chase at Doncaster. Bit of a strange prep for the Stayers' Hurdle, and there's the likelihood he'll find one or two too good, but always seems to run his race at this meeting and easy to see him in the firing line at the last.

Going preference Handles any, particularly soft
Star rating ✪✪✪

The New One
10 b g; Trainer Nigel Twiston-Davies
Hurdles form 11121211231111151214F1215 3414221, best RPR 171
Left-handed 111212131111514F115341421, best RPR 171
Right-handed 1212242, best RPR 171
Cheltenham form (all) 16121131541542, best RPR 171
At the festival 14 Mar 2012: tracked leaders, ridden and outpaced 2f out, hung left over 1f out, rallied final 100yds, no impression on front three, finished sixth, beaten six lengths by Champagne Fever in Champion Bumper
13 Mar 2013 Tracked leaders, not fluent 2 out, driven to lead approaching last, ran on strongly run-in, won Neptune Investment Management Novices' Hurdle by four lengths from Rule The World
11 Mar 2014 Tracking leaders when badly hampered and dropped to 7th 3rd, effort to close after 3 out, ridden approaching 2 out and one pace, rallied under pressure approaching last, stayed on well for 3rd final 50yds, closing on leading duo but always held, finished third, beaten two and three-quarter lengths by Jezki in Champion Hurdle
10 Mar 2015 Raced keenly, jumped right a few times, not fluent 2nd, chased winner until 3 out but still upsides, ridden and outpaced approaching last, hung left after and one pace, finished fifth, beaten eight and three-quarter lengths by Faugheen in Champion Hurdle
15 Mar 2016 Led to 1st, remained prominent, shaken up when every chance 2 out, ridden and outpaced before last, edged left under pressure run-in, kept on but not pace of leaders, finished fourth, beaten eight and three-quarter lengths by Annie Power in Champion Hurdle
14 Mar 2017 Chased leader until hit 4 out, soon regained 2nd, ridden and outpaced after 2 out, stayed on under pressure run-in, finished fifth, beaten ten and a half lengths by Buveur D'Air in Champion Hurdle

Deservedly popular ten-year-old who will be making his debut at 3m at his seventh Cheltenham Festival having taken in a Champion Bumper, a Neptune (which he won) and four Champion Hurdles. Came closest to 2m glory when third to Jezki having almost been brought to a standstill by the fall of Our Conor in 2013, but otherwise looked to lack the natural speed to cope with the best over that trip, although has still been capable of high-class form, including when second to My Tent Or Yours conceding 6lb in the International in December. Trainer has finally bitten the bullet and confirmed him for this, but even if he does stay – many are convinced he will, although I'm not one – it may just be a year too late.

Going preference Has won on all types, better ground suits
Star rating ✪✪

Yanworth

8 ch g; Trainer Alan King
Hurdles form 11112111D1, best RPR 165
Left-handed 112D1, best RPR 160
Right-handed 11111, best RPR 165
Cheltenham form (all) 412D1, best RPR 160
At the festival 11 Mar 2015 Held up towards rear, progress over 3f out, not clear run over 2f out and lost place, driven and ran on from over 1f out, nearest finish, finished fourth, beaten three and a quarter lengths by Moon Racer in Champion Bumper
16 Mar 2016 Held up in rear, progress on wide outside after 7th, close up when mistake 3 out, challenged after 2 out, chased winner before last, stayed on but not pace to challenge, finished second, beaten one and three-quarter lengths by Yorkhill in Neptune Investment Management Novices' Hurdle
14 Mar 2017 In touch, hit 3rd, lost place and outpaced after 3 out, plugged on under pressure run-in when no danger, finished 7th, disqualified (banned substance in sample) from Champion Hurdle won by Buveur D'Air

Has two chase options but has not looked a total natural over fences despite showing high-quality form and trainer has given himself the option of running here instead. That makes sense given that Supasundae, the

Unowhatimeanharry: prolific winner is a big price

horse he beat when stepped up to 3m for the first time in the Liverpool Hurdle last April, is now favourite. Certainly has the ability to play a hand if he does take this route, but probably needs to step up on that Aintree effort to do so.

Going preference Acts on any, but 6-7 on soft or heavy and 6-11 on faster
Star rating ✪✪✪

Unowhatimeanharry

10 b g; Trainer Harry Fry
Hurdles form 3335334237P1111111131123, best RPR 166
Left-handed 33534111111312, best RPR 166
Right-handed 3237P1113, best RPR 166
Cheltenham form 11113, best RPR 165
At the festival 18 Mar 2016 Held up, hampered 8th, headway after 3 out, pushed along after 2 out, switched left before last where carried left, mistake and led, soon hung right, kept on well towards finish, won Albert Bartlett Hurdle by a length and a quarter from Fagan 16 Mar 2017 Midfield, headway 7th, ridden to take 2nd on long run before last where every chance and jumped left, edged right run-in, no extra final 100yds, finished third, beaten four and a quarter lengths by Nichols Canyon in Stayers' Hurdle

Fine servant to Harry Fry, winning ten of 13 starts since joining him from Helen Nelmes in 2015, including the 2016 Albert Bartlett. Was sent off a shade of odds-on for this last year having gone through the season unbeaten until then, but came up short when it mattered, finishing third to Nichols Canyon. He gained his revenge on that rival when winning the Punchestown version and started well enough this season with a win at Aintree, but was then surprisingly beaten by Beer Goggles at Newbury and thumped 11 lengths by Sam Spinner in the Long Walk. Easy to argue he's a bigger price than he should be now on his best form, but others are going forwards and he seems to be going the other way.

Going preference Probably needs it soft to be a factor
Star rating ✪✪✪✪✪

Wholestone

7 br g; Trainer Nigel Twiston-Davies
Hurdles form (all left-handed)
3F11211342612, best RPR 159
Cheltenham form 1211312, best RPR 159
At the festival 17 Mar 2017 Midfield, headway after 3 out, every chance and challenging between last 2, not quicken and switched left approaching last, kept on under pressure and edged right run-in but no impression, finished third, beaten seven and a half lengths by Penhill in Albert Bartlett Novices' Hurdle

Tough as a novice hurdler and fair effort to be third in the Albert Bartlett last year, although gave the impression 3m just stretched him a bit. You could argue the same this season as he's been beaten three times but beat Agrapart dropped to 2m4½f for the Relkeel Hurdle on New Year's Day. Runner-up reversed form in the 3m Cleeve on Trials Day but isn't entered and won't be supplemented unless the ground promises to be bottomless. Better ground will help with trip and he has run his two best races on his last two starts so there's always the possibility of more to come.

Going preference Handles all ground
Star rating ✪✪

La Bague Au Roi

7 b m; Trainer Warren Greatrex
Hurdles form 111761111, best RPR 153
Left-handed 111761, best RPR 143
Right-handed 111, best RPR 153
Cheltenham form 7, best RPR 131
At the festival 16 Mar 2017 Led, headed after 1st, remained with leader, hit 2nd, led, not fluent 2 out, headed between last 2, weakened before last, finished seventh, beaten 16 and a half lengths by Let's Dance in Trull House Stud Mares' Novices' Hurdle

Classy mare who is hard to weigh up as she has won seven of her eight hurdles starts against her own sex, but the defeats have come when well beaten in the mares' novice at the festival last season and when taking on the boys in the Mersey Novices' Hurdle at Aintree. She does look to be improving, though, and the step up to 3m could well be the making of her. Strolled home by 16 lengths in Grade 2 mares' event at Ascot in January, after which trainer said he was leaning towards the distance of this race rather than the Mares' Hurdle over half a mile shorter. With a best RPR of 153, she is going to need to improve, but not by much given she will be getting the 7lb sex allowance.

Going preference Handles any but trainer expects better ground to suit
Star rating ✪✪✪✪✪

Lil Rockerfeller

7 ch g; Trainer Neil King
Hurdles form 3324113312317322420316, best RPR 164
Left-handed 32432173423, best RPR 164
Right-handed 31131322016, best RPR 161
Cheltenham form 32742, best RPR 164
At the festival 15 Mar 2016 Midfield, ridden along from after 2nd, weakened before 2 out, finished seventh, beaten 20 lengths by Annie Power in Champion Hurdle
16 Mar 2017 Prominent, chased leader approaching 3 out, led on bend after 2 out, soon ridden, jumped left last, headed run-in, edged right final 100yds, held towards finish, finished second, beaten three-quarters of a length by Nichols Canyon in Stayers' Hurdle

Really game performer who ran his heart out last year to finish second to Nichols Canyon, but hasn't come close to reaching those heights in four starts since, three of them this term. He has won a race, battling well to beat L'Ami Serge in the Ascot Hurdle, but both looked to be well short of their best considering the 144-rated Wakea was only a head back in third. Trailed in 23 lengths behind Sam Spinner in the Long Walk at Ascot and needs the break to have freshened him up. Suspicion this might be a warmer contest than last year too.

Going preference The better the ground, the better his chance
Star rating ✪✪

The Worlds End

7 ch g; Trainer Tom George
Hurdles form 3111F1844, best RPR 154
Left-handed 3111F184, best RPR 150
Right-handed 4, best RPR 154
Cheltenham form F4, best RPR 147

At the festival 17 Mar 2017 Held up, rapid headway after 3 out, upsides when fell 2 out in Albert Bartlett Novices' Hurdle won by Penhill

Still looked to be going well when coming down two out in last season's Albert Bartlett and made amends at Liverpool by taking the Sefton Novices' Hurdle and many thought he was destined to take high rank among the staying hurdlers this season. It hasn't happened yet, though, as he was well thumped when sent off favourite for the old Fixed Brush Hurdle at Haydock and his subsequent 11-length fourth to Sam Spinner is his best hurdles effort so far with an RPR of just 154. Took a backward step when only fourth in the Cleeve but travelled well for a long way on the heavy ground there and could move it up a notch on better ground. Needs to, however.

Going preference Has won on soft but better ground suits
Star rating ✪✪

OTHERS TO CONSIDER

Apple's Jade is odds-on for the Mares' Hurdle and even longer odds-on to run in it, while it will be a massive surprise if **Faugheen** goes here. **Finian's Oscar** is probably going back chasing, but the likes of **Colin's Sister** and **Thomas Campbell** are likely runners. The latter has a bit to prove after a couple of below-par runs but he does like Cheltenham, is not rated much lower than some of those way ahead of him in the betting and will appreciate better ground.

VERDICT

There isn't much between a lot of these and it looks a wide-open renewal, but the one who interests me most at the prices is LA BAGUE AU ROI. Admittedly she has been beating up mares in softer races but she has been absolutely thumping them, particularly at Ascot last time, and it seems 3m is her trip. Her trainer has always thought of her as being a better performer on better ground and, while the evidence for that is shaky, she doesn't need to improve much to play a hand at a price.

	FORM	WINNER	AGE & WGT	Adj RPR	SP	TRAINER	BEST RPR LAST 12 MONTHS (RUNS SINCE)
17	-312F	**Nichols Canyon** CD	7 11-10	170-2	10-1	W Mullins (IRE)	won Punchestown Gd1 hurdle (2m) (2)
16	-2111	**Thistlecrack** CD	8 11-10	176T	Evensf	C Tizzard	won Gd2 Cleeve Hurdle (3m) (0)
15	-1234	**Cole Harden**	6 11-10	162-7	14-1	W Greatrex	2nd Newbury Gd2 hdl (3m½f) (2)
14	1-111	**More Of That** C	6 11-10	165-14	15-2	J O'Neill	won Gd2 Relkeel Hurdle (2m4½f) (0)
13	22/21	**Solwhit**	9 11-10	169-5	17-2	C Byrnes (IRE)	2nd Punchestown Hurdle (2m4f) (1)
12	1-111	**Big Buck's** CD	9 11-10	182T	5-6f	P Nicholls	won Gd1 Liverpool Hurdle (3m½f) (3)
11	11-11	**Big Buck's** CD	8 11-10	180T	10-11f	P Nicholls	won Gd1 World Hurdle (3m) (3)
10	11-11	**Big Buck's** CD	7 11-10	180T	5-6f	P Nicholls	won Gd1 Liverpool Hurdle (3m½f) (2)
09	1-U11	**Big Buck's** CD	6 11-10	170-7	6-1	P Nicholls	won Gd2 Cleeve Hurdle (3m) (0)
08	13-11	**Inglis Drever** C, D	9 11-10	174T	11-8f	H Johnson	won Newb Gd2 Long Distance Hurdle (3m½f) (1)

WINS-RUNS: 5yo 0-5, 6yo 3-30, 7yo 2-37, 8yo 2-28, 9yo 3-17, 10yo 0-8, 11yo 0-5, 13yo 0-2 **FAVOURITES:** -£0.05

TRAINERS IN THIS RACE (w-pl-r): Paul Nicholls 4-3-17, Colin Tizzard 1-0-3, Jonjo O'Neill 1-0-3, Willie Mullins 1-2-17, Warren Greatrex 1-0-3, Alan King 0-2-8, Gordon Elliott 0-0-1, Harry Fry 0-1-1, Nicky Henderson 0-2-12, Neil King 0-1-1, Jessica Harrington 0-0-2, Nigel Twiston-Davies 0-0-3

FATE OF FAVOURITES: 14111P2213 **POSITION OF WINNER IN MARKET:** 1311143614

Key trends

- Aged six to nine, 10/10
- Ran no more than four times since August, 10/10
- Top-two finish on last completed start, 9/10
- Adjusted RPR of at least 165, 9/10
- Previously ran at the festival, 8/10
- Not out of the first two in all completed hurdle starts that season, 8/10
- Won a Graded hurdle over at least 3m, 7/10
- Ran between nine and 20 times over hurdles, 7/10

Other factors

- A five-year-old has never won (one of the five to have run in the past ten seasons was placed)
- Four of the six Irish winners since the mid-1980s prepped in the Boyne Hurdle at Navan
- The record of Cleeve Hurdle winners is 117214213

Notes

4.10 Brown Advisory & Merriebelle Plate   ITV/RUK
2m5f handicap chase   Grade 3   £110,000

Overall this race (established in 1951 and traditionally known as the Mildmay of Flete) has been the biggest graveyard for favourites at the festival with just four winning.

The only two successful favourites in recent years both came from the Pipe stable – Majadou (trained by Martin) in 1999 and Salut Flo (trained by David) in 2012. The Pipe stable has won the race seven times in the past 20 runnings and is always to be respected. Apart from the Pipe favourites, no other winner since 1998 has gone off shorter than 12-1.

The last two runnings have gone to Ireland with Empire Of Dirt and Road To Respect, both in the colours of Gigginstown House Stud. Road To Respect became only the third winner in the last 14 years rated higher than 140 and was the third Irish winner in the race's long history.

Some of the bigger stables struggle to get runners at the lower end of the handicap and Paul Nicholls has not won in 29 attempts (second, third last year and fourth are his best showings).

Nicky Henderson has been more successful, with two winners, a third and a fourth from his last 16 runners. Venetia Williams is another trainer to note, having won three times in the last 11 runnings.

BROWN ADVISORY & MERRIEBELLE STABLE PLATE RESULTS AND TRENDS

	FORM WINNER	AGE & WGT	OR	SP	TRAINER	BEST RPR LAST 12 MONTHS (RUNS SINCE)
17	14322 **Road To Respect**	6 10-13	145-16	14-1	N Meade (IRE)	3rd Leopardstown Gd1 nov ch (2m1f) (2)
16	-F2P1 **Empire Of Dirt** D	9 10-11	142-13	16-1	C Murphy (IRE)	2nd Punchestown hcp ch (2m6f) (2)
15	7/157 **Darna** D	9 10-11	140-6	33-1	K Bailey	won Sedgefield class 3 hcp ch (2m3½f) (2)
14	P18-P **Ballynagour** D	8 10-9	140-1	12-1	D Pipe	8th Cheltenham Gd3 hcap ch (2m5f) (1)
13	4P61P **Carrickboy**	9 10-5	136-13	50-1	V Williams	won Chepstow class 2 hcap ch (2m3½f) (1)
12	112/0 **Salut Flo**	7 10-10	137-5	9-2f	D Pipe	12th Atlantic4 Gold Cup hcap ch (2m5f) (0)
11	152F1 **Holmwood Legend** (5x) D	10 10-6	130-5	25-1	P Rodford	won Sandown class 3 hcap ch (2m4½f) (0)
10	-3144 **Great Endeavour** D	6 10-1	135-11	18-1	D Pipe	4th Fontwell class 3 nov ch (2m6f) (1)
09	20272 **Something Wells**	8 10-7	139-1	33-1	V Williams	2nd Ascot class 2 hcap ch (2m5½f) (2)
08	547U5 **Mister McGoldrick** D	11 11-7	145-6	66-1	S Smith	4th Wetherby class 2 hcap ch (2m½f) (2)

WINS-RUNS: 5yo 0-3, 6yo 2-19, 7yo 1-39, 8yo 2-61, 9yo 3-48, 10yo 1-34, 11yo 1-15, 12yo 0-5, 13yo 0-1 **FAVOURITES:** -£4.50

FATE OF FAVOURITES: F2231022PP **POSITION OF WINNER IN MARKET:** 0000106087

Key trends

🏇 Won between 2m3f and 2m5f, 10/10

🏇 Won a Class 3 or higher, 9/10

🏇 Officially rated 135 to 145, 9/10

🏇 Carried no more than 10st 13lb, 9/10

🏇 No more than 12 runs over fences, 8/10

Other factors

🏇 None of the last ten winners had been placed in one of the big 2m4f-2m5f handicaps run at Cheltenham that season

🏇 Ireland has won the last two runnings (Empire Of Dirt and Road To Respect) but their last winner before them was Double-U-Again in 1982

🏇 Salut Flo in 2012 was the first winning favourite since Majadou (1999)

🏇 Four of the last six winners had been well beaten on their previous start (two pulled up, two unplaced)

🏇 Two winners were trained by David Pipe and had not run since the turn of the year

4.50 Trull House Stud Mares' Novices' Hurdle   RUK
2m1f Grade 2 £90,000

This newest addition to the festival line-up is in its third year and the first two runnings went to Willie Mullins, whose strength in the mares' division has long been evident in his dominance of the senior version of this race. Mullins cannot come back year after year with the same horse, as he did with six-time Mares' Hurdle winner Quevega, but the perennial renewal of his squad means he is always likely to have at least one strong candidate among the novices and that is the case again this year with ante-post favourite Laurina. The French recruit has won both starts over hurdles for Mullins by a combined total of 26 lengths, although there is an element of doubt over her ability to handle better ground as her wins in France were on very soft and the Irish victories on heavy. Mullins also has options with Salsaretta, Mystic Theatre and Stormy Ireland. The main British hope is the Stuart Edmunds-trained Maria's Benefit, while Nicky Henderson is set to send his best filly, Apple's Shakira, to the Triumph Hurdle but can still call on Countister for this contest.

Laurina: tops market to give Willie Mullins a third win in the race

TRULL HOUSE STUD MARES' NOVICES' HURDLE RESULTS

	FORM WINNER	AGE & WGT	Adj RPR	SP	TRAINER	BEST RPR LAST 12 MONTHS (RUNS SINCE)
17	21111 **Let's Dance** D	5 11-7	153ᵀ	11-8f	W Mullins (IRE)	won Leopardstown Gd2 nov hdl (2m4f) (0)
16	11 **Limini** D	5 11-7	148-4	8-11f	W Mullins (IRE)	won Fairyhouse Gd3 nov hdl (2m2f) (0)

WINS-RUNS: 4yo 0-3, 5yo 2-10, 6yo 0-13, 7yo 0-5, 8yo 0-1 **FAVOURITES:** £2.10

TRAINERS IN THIS RACE (w-pl-r): Willie Mullins 2-0-4, Henry de Bromhead 0-0-1, John Kiely 0-0-1, Jessica Harrington 0-0-1, Nicky Henderson 0-1-4, Paul Nicholls 0-0-1, Warren Greatrex 0-0-1

FATE OF FAVOURITES: 11 **POSITION OF WINNER IN MARKET:** 11

5.30 Fulke Walwyn Kim Muir Handicap Chase   RUK
3m2f   Amateur riders   £70,000

The best amateur jockeys are always in demand for this contest and Jamie Codd is the main man with four wins in the last nine runnings, most recently aboard Cause Of Causes in 2016. Non-claiming riders have the edge in quality and others to note include Patrick Mullins, Derek O'Connor and Sam Waley-Cohen (the last-named duo were second and third last year behind the Gina Andrews-ridden Domesday Book).

With little between most of the runners nowadays (9lb covered the field in 2016 and 12lb last year), the higher-rated runners have started to do well and eight of the last nine winners carried 11st 4lb or more (including topweights Character Building and Ballabriggs).

A number of the larger stables target this race and their runners always merit respect. Eight of the past 16 winners have come from the Pipe stable, Nicky Henderson and Donald McCain. David Pipe, whose father Martin won this race on three occasions, had the first two in 2011 and landed the spoils again in 2015, while Henderson has had three successes, including a couple of 1-2s, and McCain has had two winners and a runner-up.

Only three horses aged older than nine (eight- and nine-year-olds generally do best) have won the race in the last 25 runnings, and there is a trend of Kim Muir winners bouncing back from poor efforts (12 of the past 17 winners had been unplaced on their previous run).

KIM MUIR HANDICAP CHASE RESULTS AND TRENDS

	FORM WINNER	AGE & WGT	OR	SP	TRAINER	BEST RPR LAST 12 MONTHS (RUNS SINCE)
17	45683 **Domesday Book**	7 11-4	137-6	9-2	S Edmunds	3rd Leicester class 3 hcap ch (2m4f) **(0)**
16	8-005 **Cause Of Causes** C	8 11-9	142-6	9-2	G Elliott (IRE)	5th Naas Gd2 ch (2m) **(0)**
15	30-6P **The Package** CD	12 11-4	137^T	9-1	D Pipe	6th Cheltenham Gd3 hcap ch (3m3½f) **(1)**
14	13280 **Spring Heeled** (2ow)	7 11-8	140-5	12-1	J Culloty (IRE)	2nd Limerick hcap ch (3m) **(2)**
13	34136 **Same Difference**	7 11-0	137-2	16-1	N Twiston-Davies	3rd Newbury class 2 nov ch (3m) **(1)**
12	-37P9 **Sunnyhillboy** C	9 11-11	142-1	13-2f	J O'Neill	3rd Irish Grand National (3m5f) **(3)**
11	31-32 **Junior**	8 11-6	134-4	10-3f	D Pipe	3rd Cheltenham Gd3 hcap ch (3m3½f) **(1)**
10	0-311 **Ballabriggs** D	9 11-12	140^T	9-1	D McCain	won Ayr class 2 hcap ch (3m1f) **(0)**
09	14339 **Character Building** D	9 11-12	139-10	16-1	J Quinn	3rd Cheltenham class 2 hcap ch (3m2½f) **(1)**
08	1-43P **High Chimes**	9 10-10	127-7	14-1	E Williams	3rd Haydock class 2 hcap ch (3m) **(1)**

WINS-RUNS: 6yo 0-10, 7yo 3-48, 8yo 2-58, 9yo 4-58, 10yo 0-33, 11yo 0-16, 12yo 1-11, 13yo 0-2 **FAVOURITES:** £1.83

FATE OF FAVOURITES: U0311200UU **POSITION OF WINNER IN MARKET:** 8531106320

Key trends

- Rated within 7lb of RPR top-rated, 9/10
- Aged seven to nine, 9/10
- Officially rated 134 to 142, 9/10
- Ran over at least 3m last time out, 8/10
- Won over at least 3m, 8/10
- No more than 11 runs over fences, 8/10
- Finished in first three in either or both of last two starts, 6/10
- Won a handicap chase, 6/10

Other factors

- Ireland have won two of the last four runnings (Spring Heeled in 2014 and Cause Of Causes in 2016). The last Irish-trained winner before them was Greasepaint in 1983
- Seven winners had run at a previous festival
- Five winners had run within the past 33 days, the other five had been off for at least 58 days

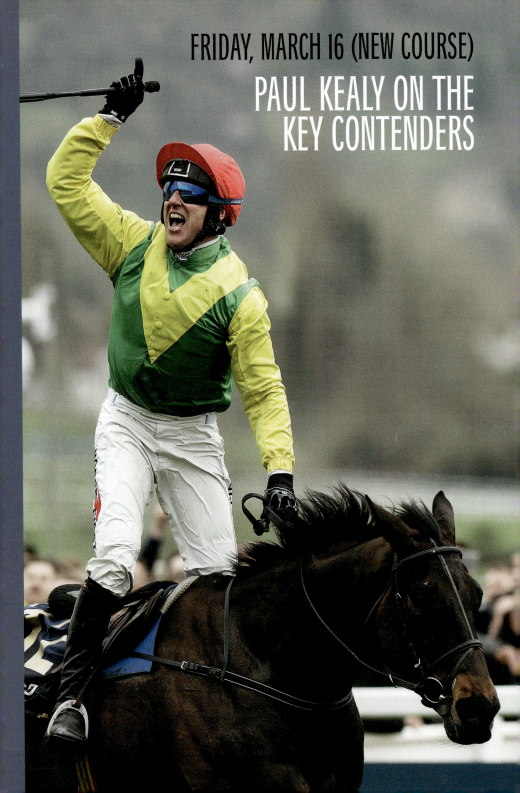

1.30 JCB Triumph Hurdle — ITV/RUK
🏇 2m1f   🏇 Grade 1   🏇 £125,000

JP McManus's famous green and gold colours have been carried to Triumph victory in the past two years by Ivanovich Gorbatov and Defi Du Seuil, and the festival's most successful owner has a first-rate chance of the hat-trick with long-time ante-post favourite Apple's Shakira. The three horses have come from different yards and this time it is the turn of Nicky Henderson with Apple's Shakira, who has won her three starts – all at Cheltenham – since arriving from France. Henderson is the most successful trainer in the Triumph with six wins and he has another leading candidate in We Have A Dream, who likewise has a 100 per cent record in Britain. He is owned by Simon Munir and Isaac Souede, whose Peace And Co in 2015 was Henderson's most recent winner of the race. Irish hopes could rest with Stormy Ireland and Mr Adjudicator (both trained by Willie Mullins) along with Gordon Elliott's Farclas, runner-up to Mr Adjudicator in the Grade 1 Spring Juvenile Hurdle, while another leading British challenger is Alan King's Redicean.

Apple's Shakira
4 b f; Trainer Nicky Henderson
Hurdles form 1111, best RPR 137
Left-handed 111, best RPR 137
Right-handed 1, best RPR 115
Cheltenham form 111, best RPR 137

Joined Nicky Henderson with a tall reputation from France, not least because she's a sister to odds-on Mares' Hurdle favourite Apple's Jade, and she has certainly looked the part in three unbeaten starts at Cheltenham. Strolled home by 17 lengths from Gumball, who looked out of sorts and has subsequently been beaten again at short odds, on her British debut in November, since when she has been a hot favourite for this even though she hasn't exactly had to do much in the interim. Was a 1-10 shot when winning unextended next time in November and 1-7 when scoring by eight lengths from Look My Way on Trials Day in January, though gave odds-on punters a few moments' worry when appearing to get outpaced at the top of the hill. Obviously has a nice enough profile but easy to argue her form doesn't really entitle her to be so far clear of the field in the betting. The average ten-year winning Racing Post Rating for this event is 151 and even with her 7lb sex allowance she falls a long way short of that – admittedly so does everything else this year, so it could be an average renewal. She needs to prove she can act on decent ground too. She is by the same sire as mudlark Bristol De Mai (Saddler Maker) and has so far raced only on soft ground and, while you could argue her sister does go on a decent surface, Apple's Jade got outpaced by Ivanovich Gorbatov in this race on good ground two years ago and subsequent events have shown her to be way superior to him. No filly has scored in this since Snow Drop in 2000 (only 20 have tried, three seconds), although it should be easier now as the sex allowance was just 5lb then.

Going preference Unproven on anything other than soft
Star rating ✪✪✪

Mr Adjudicator
4 b g; Trainer Willie Mullins
Hurdles form (left-handed) 11, best RPR 142

By a sprinter and didn't race beyond a mile for first seven starts on the Flat, but evidently stays a fair bit better than expected as final start before joining Willie Mullins resulted in a win over 1m3f. Finished Flat career with a rating of 81, which makes him a fair recruit, and he has certainly looked one in two starts for Ireland's top trainer. Won his maiden by an easy seven and a half lengths at Leopardstown over Christmas and then returned to land the Grade 1 Spring Juvenile Hurdle by just over a length from Farclas. Slight suspicion that the race developing into a sprint favoured him more than the more stoutly bred runner-up, but he was on top at the end and it's arguably the best piece of juvenile form on offer. The winning time was considerably faster than that of Samcro in the Deloitte on the same card and both winner and runner-up outsprinted the so-called Ballymore banker by around six lengths from two out to the line, so it could be very decent form.

Going preference Hurdles wins on soft, but won on good on the Flat
Star rating ✪✪✪✪

Stormy Ireland

4 b f; Trainer Willie Mullins
Hurdles form (left-handed) 221, best RPR 136

Four-race maiden in France, including in two hurdles when beaten a neck and a short neck, but the judge needed binoculars rather than a print to determine the second when she made her debut for Willie Mullins at Fairyhouse in December and strolled home by an incredible 58 lengths. Subsequent events have so far shown her rivals to be as useless as she made them look and she hasn't been seen since, while jockey Danny Mullins said she handled the heavy ground "with a fierce ease". Obviously has plenty of ability, but would like to get another look at her on a better surface and time is running out. Mares' novice is also an option.

Going preference Unproven on anything other than very soft ground
Star rating ✪✪✪

We Have A Dream

4 b g; Trainer Nicky Henderson
Hurdles form 5441111, best RPR 138
Left-handed 544111, best RPR 138
Right-handed 1, best RPR 138

Beaten on first three starts in France, but undefeated in four since joining Nicky Henderson. Cruised to success in first two, including the Grade 2 Summit at Doncaster, but then showed battling qualities to see off the persistent challenge of Sussex Ranger by a length and a half in the Grade 1 Finale Juvenile Hurdle at Chepstow in January (although the 12-length third was well thumped as favourite next time out). That race, usually run on heavy ground, as it was this year, is often seen as a bad guide to the Triumph in March, but last year Defi Du Seuil became the first to do the double since Mysilv in 1994 and We Have A Dream does have some good-ground form too. Made to work for a while by Act Of Valour in Scottish Triumph at Musselburgh in February, but second was one of the better Flat horses to go hurdling (rated 97) and the ability to travel and find means he's worthy of respect.

Going preference Seems to handle most ground
Star rating ✪✪✪✪

Farclas

4 gr g; Trainer Gordon Elliott
Hurdles form (left-handed) 22, best RPR 141

Maiden in two starts over hurdles but obviously considered decent by Gordon Ellliott from the outset as he started him in a Grade 2 at Leopardstown over Christmas. Had no answer to Espoir D'Allen that day

TRAINER'S VIEW

Nicky Henderson on We Have A Dream "It was probably my fault that he needed a little blow [at Musselburgh]. I probably hadn't over-prepared him and Daryl [Jacob] had to sit and wait for him to get his second wind. It's great to have two such strong horses for the race as him and Apple's Shakira and I'm glad I don't have to choose between them" *The last time Henderson had more than one Triumph runner under 10-1, in 2015, they finished first, second and third in price order*

but connections were reportedly confident he'd turn it around in the Spring Juvenile Hurdle at the Dublin festival and so he did. Unfortunately for him Espoir D'Allen, the hot favourite, was below form and already back-pedalling between the last two, when Farclas found himself in the lead. Jack Kennedy would ideally have liked a longer lead in the race and he ended up getting picked off by Mr Adjudicator after the last, but he certainly fought all the way to the line. Elliott's four-year-old was not as battle-hardened on the Flat as the winner and, being by Jukebox Jury, may well require a stiffer stamina test, which he ought to get at Cheltenham. He didn't win on the Flat in France until meeting good ground on his fourth and final start, so there is every reason for connections to think he can step up again when it matters. Elliott's Tiger Roll was second in the Spring in 2014 but reversed form to land the Triumph.

Going preference Handles soft but may improve for better ground
Star rating ✪✪✪✪

Redicean
4 b g; Trainer Alan King
Hurdles form (right-handed) 11, best RPR 128

Won a maiden on good to firm on the Flat, but best form undoubtedly on a soft surface when taking Redcar handicap off a mark of 80 on last start for David O'Meara before joining Alan King. Has won both hurdles starts for new yard, each by ten lengths on soft ground at Kempton, but fair to say jumping has left a lot to be desired. Clearly has an engine and impressed with the way he powered clear, but not entirely certain how much the form is worth as the fourth and fifth last time have been beaten further since, one in a handicap off just 110. Trainer never to be underestimated in this but peak RPR of 128 is more than 20lb below the ten-year average for a Triumph winner.

Going preference Handles good ground but best form on soft
Star rating ✪✪✪

We Have A Dream (left) beats Sussex Ranger at Chepstow

Sussex Ranger

4 b g; Trainer Gary Moore
Hurdles form 112, best RPR 135
Left-handed 12, best RPR 135
Right-handed 1, best RPR 133

Rated 76 on the Flat and progressive enough, but already looks better as a hurdler, winning his first two. Had some clock-watchers purring after second victory at Sandown, in which he powered 14 lengths clear of his rivals, and went some way to backing up that impression when running We Have A Dream to a length and a half in the Finale Juvenile Hurdle at Chepstow in January. Didn't seem to have much of a problem with the heavy ground that day, but he's by a Japanese sire whose form was all on rock-hard surfaces and he handled decent ground well enough on the Flat himself. Always a chance that's what he wants and boasts a good attitude.

Going preference No real evidence he wants it one way or the other
Star rating ✪✪✪

Saldier

4 b g; Trainer Willie Mullins
Hurdles form (right-handed) 1, RPR 125

Beaten just under three lengths in a Group 3 at Chantilly as a three-year-old last April, but latecomer to Triumph market having only made his debut over hurdles for the Willie Mullins/Rich Ricci team at Gowran Park in February. Did it very easily in maiden company there, sprinting clear for a ten-length win, but hard to rate the form highly given 40-1 runner-up and 50-1 third were also making their debuts, were 1-25 on the Flat between them and rated 53 and 48 in that sphere respectively. Obviously has lots of talent but could have hurdled a bit more fluently and would like to have seen him in better company first.

Going preference Flat win on heavy, but best RPR on good *Star rating* ✪✪

Esprit De Somoza

4 b g; Trainer Nick Williams
Hurdles form (right-handed) 51, best RPR 128

Beaten a long way by Sussex Ranger on his debut at Sandown in December, but that was his first sighting of a racecourse and showed the benefit when springing a 20-1 surprise in the Chatteris Fen at Huntingdon a month later, beating Gumball, a previous victim of Apple's Shakira, by five lengths. Slight suspicion the first and second favourites cut each other's throat by going too hard too soon, but described as "bloody gorgeous" by rider Lizzie Kelly, who also said he would be more precocious than a normal Nick Williams juvenile. Still needs to make a massive leap formwise but has run only twice.

Going preference Win on soft but too early to tell
Star rating ✪✪

Look My Way

4 b g; Trainer John Quinn
Hurdles form 212, best RPR 127
Left-handed 22, best RPR 127
Right-handed 1, best RPR 123
Cheltenham form 2, best RPR 127

Rated 90 on the Flat after sluicing up by 22 lengths in six-runner contest at Ffos Las on final start for Andrew Balding and has shown fair form in three hurdles starts, although he has won only one of them. Beaten by the slightly better quality Flat performer Act Of Valour on his debut and then an easy winner at Ludlow before looking to have Apple's Shakira in trouble for a brief spell in the Triumph trial at Cheltenham in January. Was beaten eight lengths in the end, though, so plenty to find and needs to prove he can be as good on better ground (did have reasonable form on good to firm on the Flat). Connections could be tempted by the Fred Winter off mark of 135.

Going preference Best form on soft/heavy
Star rating ✪✪

Act Of Valour

4 b g; Trainer Paul Nicholls
Hurdles form 152, best RPR 130
Left-handed 15, best RPR 130
Right-handed 2, best RPR 130

One of the best Flat performers, having left Ireland with a mark of 97, and really looked the part on hurdles debut when a smooth two-length winner from Look My Way. Sent off at only 7-4 in Grade 2 Summit against We Have A Dream next time, but beaten more than half a mile out when something was clearly amiss. Made the same horse work a bit harder when beaten only four and a half lengths in the Scottish Triumph at Musselburgh in February, but obviously needs more.

Going preference Best Flat form on good ground; other way round so far over hurdles

Star rating ✪✪

OTHERS TO CONSIDER

Mitchouka would be a second string for Gordon Elliott, but he has won three of his six starts over hurdles, boasts comparable form to some of those much shorter in the betting and would have joined Farclas in the Spring Juvenile Hurdle but for running a temperature. Willie Mullins has a few more entries but **Eoline Jolie** (same ownership as Stormy Ireland) has yet to run for him. **Birds Of Prey** was a progressive 90-rated Flat performer for John Oxx and may be the unraced one Paul Nicholls decides to chuck at the Adonis.

VERDICT

There has been no better guide for this in recent years than the Spring Juvenile Hurdle at Leopardstown – which provided the winner and fourth in 2013, the first and third in 2014, the first, third and fourth in 2016 and the second and third last year – and I'm fairly convinced one of the first two in that race will prevail this time. I should really back both and probably will save on Mr Adjudicator at some point, but I don't think things panned out as well for FARCLAS as they could have that day and I reckon he has a serious shot at reversing form. Better ground looks highly likely to suit and a stronger test and longer lead into the race will too.

Farclas (right): looks a serious player

	FORM	WINNER	AGE & WGT	Adj RPR	SP	TRAINER	BEST RPR LAST 12 MONTHS (RUNS SINCE)
17	11111	Defi Du Seuil CD	4 11-0	164ᵀ	5-2f	P Hobbs	won Gd1 Finale Hurdle (2m) (1)
16	14	Ivanovich Gorbatov D, BF	4 11-0	149⁻⁵	9-2f	A O'Brien (IRE)	won Leopardstown maiden hdl (2m) (1)
15	111	Peace And Co CD	4 11-0	159ᵀ	2-1f	N Henderson	2nd Doncaster Gd2 hdl (2m½f) (1)
14	12	Tiger Roll D	4 11-0	150⁻²	10-1	G Elliott (IRE)	2nd Gd1 Leopardstown nov hdl (2m) (0)
13	111	Our Conor	4 11-0	160⁻³	4-1	D Hughes (IRE)	won Gd1 Leopardstown nov hdl (2m) (0)
12	12123	Countrywide Flame D	4 11-0	151⁻⁶	33-1	J Quinn	2nd Gd1 Finale Hurdle (2m½f) (1)
11	1	Zarkandar	4 11-0	155⁻²	13-2	P Nicholls	won Gd2 Adonis Nov Hdl (2m) (0)
10	4211	Soldatino D	4 11-0	150⁻⁶	6-1	N Henderson	won Gd2 Adonis Nov Hdl (2m) (0)
09	11	Zaynar D	4 11-0	152⁻⁶	11-2	N Henderson	won Newb class 4 nov hdl (2m½f) (1)
08	12	Celestial Halo D, BF	4 11-0	145⁻¹¹	5-1	P Nicholls	won Newb class 3 nov hdl (2m½f) (1)

FAVOURITES: £2.00

TRAINERS IN THIS RACE (w-pl-r): Nicky Henderson 3-4-15, Paul Nicholls 2-2-18, Gordon Elliott 1-1-7, John Quinn 1-0-6, Philip Hobbs 1-0-2, Alan King 0-3-15, David Pipe 0-0-6, Nick Williams 0-0-2, Willie Mullins 0-4-16, Evan Williams 0-1-4, Venetia Williams 0-0-2, Warren Greatrex 0-0-1

FATE OF FAVOURITES: 2244364111 **POSITION OF WINNER IN MARKET:** 2333026111

Key trends

🏇Last ran between 19 and 55 days ago, 10/10

🏇Won at least 50 per cent of hurdle races, 10/10

🏇Top-three finish last time out, 9/10 (six won)

🏇Adjusted RPR of at least 150, 8/10

🏇By a Group 1-winning sire, 8/10

🏇Ran two or three times over hurdles, 7/10

Other factors

🏇Zarkandar is the only once-raced hurdler to win in the past 30 years

🏇Five of the last ten winners were undefeated over hurdles

🏇Five winners had landed Graded events (two had won the Adonis at Kempton in February)

🏇Four winners had raced on the Flat in Britain and Ireland and all had recorded an RPR of at least 83

🏇Since the introduction of the Fred Winter Hurdle in 2005, 12 of the 13 winners have had an SP of 10-1 or shorter

Notes

2.10 Randox Health County H'cap Hurdle   ITV/RUK
2m1f   Grade 3   £100,000

Ireland has accounted for eight of the last 11 winners, with six of them trained by a Mullins. Willie Mullins had his first festival handicap victory in this race with Thousand Stars in 2010, followed up in 2011 with Final Approach and confirmed his liking for the race with 25-1 winner Wicklow Brave in 2015 and Arctic Fire's 20-1 success off top weight in 2017 (he didn't have a runner in 2012 but had the runner-up in 2013 and 2014 and four of the first six in 2015). Melbourne Cup third Max Dynamite (fourth to stablemate Wicklow Brave in 2015) is an intriguing prospect for Mullins this year and has been heading the ante-post market.

The classy Arctic Fire defied a mark of 158, but the previous 11 winners were rated in the 130s. Since 1970 just eight winners have carried more than 11st.

Paul Nicholls has done best of the British trainers, winning four times in the last 14 runnings. Superb Story won in 2016 to give Dan Skelton (a former Nicholls assistant) his first festival success.

Second-season hurdlers have won 13 of the last 17 runnings. Only two horses older than six (Alderwood in 2012 and Arctic Fire) have won in the last ten runnings.

COUNTY HURDLE RESULTS AND TRENDS

	FORM	WINNER	AGE & WGT	OR	SP	TRAINER	BEST RPR LAST 12 MONTHS (RUNS SINCE)
17	1142-	**Arctic Fire** D	8 11-12	158-4	20-1	W Mullins (IRE)	Seasonal debutant (0)
16	44-12	**Superb Story** D	5 10-12	138T	8-1	D Skelton	2nd Cheltenham Gd3 hcap hdl (2m½f) (0)
15	F580P	**Wicklow Brave** D	6 11-4	138-1	25-1	W Mullins (IRE)	11th Newbury Gd3 hcap hdl (2m½f) (1)
14	8-141	**Lac Fontana** CD	5 10-11	139-3	11-1	P Nicholls	won Cheltenham class 2 hcap hdl (2m1f) (0)
13	31923	**Ted Veale**	6 10-6	134-2	10-1	A Martin (IRE)	3rd Boylesports Hcap Hurdle (2m) (0)
12	10120	**Alderwood** D	8 11-1	139-3	20-1	T Mullins (IRE)	won Killarney hcap hdl (2m6f) (2)
11	13-51	**Final Approach**	5 10-12	139-8	10-1	W Mullins (IRE)	won MCR Hcap Hurdle (2m) (0)
10	40110	**Thousand Stars** D	6 10-5	134-5	20-1	W Mullins (IRE)	14th MCR Hcap Hurdle (2m) (0)
09	1349	**American Trilogy** D	5 11-0	135-7	20-1	P Nicholls	3rd Cheltenham Gd2 nov hdl (2m½f) (2)
08	22233	**Silver Jaro** BF	5 10-13	132-11	50-1	T Hogan (IRE)	3rd Pierse Hcap Hurdle (2m) (1)

WINS-RUNS: 5yo 5-66, 6yo 3-77, 7yo 0-62, 8yo 2-29, 9yo 0-16, 10yo 0-9, 11yo 0-1 **FAVOURITES:** -£10.00

FATE OF FAVOURITES: 260000P046 **POSITION OF WINNER IN MARKET:** 0704035030

Key trends

- Achieved career-best RPR of at least 129 on a left-handed track, 10/10
- Officially rated between 132 and 139, 9/10
- Carried no more than 11st 1lb, 8/10 (both exceptions trained by Willie Mullins)
- Ran no more than 12 times over hurdles, 8/10 (both exceptions trained by Willie Mullins)
- Aged five or six, 8/10
- No previous festival form, 7/10

Other factors

- There have been five winning novices since 1996
- Four winners ran in the (now) Coral Hurdle, finishing 3013, but only one ran in Newbury's Betfair Hurdle (finished unplaced)
- Paul Nicholls has had four winners, two seconds and a fourth since 2004
- Ireland has won seven of the last ten, including four for Willie Mullins

2.50 Albert Bartlett Novices' Hurdle — ITV/RUK
3m — *Grade 1* — *£125,000*

The favourite for this staying novice hurdle often comes from one of the big Irish stables but Willie Mullins had three beaten favourites in five runnings before winning for the first time with 16-1 shot Penhill last year, while Gordon Elliott has yet to land the race and last year saddled beaten 13-8 favourite Death Duty. That may sound a note of caution with some punters but Ireland's big two still dominate the ante-post market with Next Destination (Mullins) and Cracking Smart (Elliott), who were separated by a length in a Grade 1 over 2m4f at Naas in early January. Elliott would have the short-priced favourite if Samcro ran here, but the Ballymore seems the more likely target. Nicky Henderson – successful once, with favourite Bobs Worth in 2011 – houses several of the main British hopes with Santini, Chef Des Obeaux and Mr Whipped.

Cracking Smart
6 b g; Trainer Gordon Elliott
Hurdles form F21122, best RPR 153
Left-handed 222, best RPR 150
Right-handed F11, best RPR 153

Has won only two of six hurdling starts but has still shown very smart form and staying is evidently his game. Found Next Destination too good for him over 2m4f at Navan in December and again over the same trip at Naas on latest start, but reduced the deficit from five and a half lengths to a length last time in first-time cheekpieces. Earlier Cork Listed win over 3m is arguably his best piece of form, although he did plod round in a time almost a minute outside the RP standard on the soft ground and would have to cover same trip at Cheltenham around 40 seconds faster if it's good. Called a big chaser for the future by his trainer, but that's no bad thing as three of the last ten winners went on to score over fences at the festival.

Going preference Has raced on soft/heavy over hurdles, did win bumper on good to yielding
Star rating ✪✪✪✪

Next Destination
6 b g; Trainer Willie Mullins
Hurdles form (left-handed) 111, best RPR 152
Cheltenham form (bumper) 4, best RPR 127
At the festival 15 Mar 2017 Chased leaders, pushed along over 2f out, ridden and not quicken over 1f out, stayed on final 100yds, not pace of leaders, finished fourth, beaten three lengths by Fayonagh in Champion Bumper

Dealt with in more detail in Wednesday's Ballymore section as he has yet to run over 3m and trainer said that was his most likely target after his latest win at Naas in January. Renowned for changing his mind, though, and bookmakers offering shorter price for this than any of the novices. That could just be because there's no standout market leader in this event, but he does boast back-to-back wins over the current favourite.

Going preference Handles soft/heavy fine but Champion Bumper fourth, on only second start after winning a five-runner bumper, shows he's versatile
Star rating ✪✪✪✪

Santini
6 b g; Trainer Nicky Henderson
Hurdles form (left-handed) 11, best RPR 144
Cheltenham form 1, RPR 144

Point winner in March and only made hurdles debut in December when showing good form to beat better-fancied stablemate Chef Des Obeaux by four and a half lengths at Newbury. Improved on that on Trials Day at Cheltenham, getting up close home to beat Black Op in the Ballymore trial. Looked held for much of the last three furlongs (runner-up traded at 1-25) but kept staying on and when Black Op made a mistake at the last he was able to pounce. Yet to try 3m but trainer did not bother putting him in anything other than this, although did not seem that keen on committing him, suggesting it might be a year too soon. Seems to hold him in serious regard, saying after Cheltenham win: "If he improves as much as he did from last year to this year then he'll be an absolute machine – he's a proper horse." Sire (Milan) has had two winners and two seconds from 14 runners in 3m Cheltenham Festival hurdles.

Going preference Has run only on soft/heavy
Star rating ✪✪✪✪

Chef Des Obeaux
6 b g; Trainer Nicky Henderson
Hurdles form 2111, best RPR 152
Left-handed 211, best RPR 152
Right-handed 1, best RPR 144

Very promising horse who gives Nicky Henderson a strong hand. No match for stablemate Santini on hurdles debut in December, but increasingly impressive in each of three subsequent starts and bolted up by 15 lengths in Grade 2 trial for this at Haydock in February. That is arguably some of the best form, but it came on heavy ground, which he seemed to handle better than everything. That ought not to be a surprise as he is by Saddler Maker, whose best progeny tend to love it deep (he is the sire of Bristol De Mai). Looks all about stamina and sure to be a staying chaser in time.

Going preference Has raced only on soft/heavy, which sire's progeny tend to love
Star rating ✪✪✪

Mr Whipped
5 br g; Trainer Nicky Henderson
Hurdles form 1112, best RPR 148
Left-handed 11, best RPR 148
Right-handed 12, best RPR 148

Third potential contender for Nicky Henderson and biggest price of the three, but on Racing

Post Ratings has achieved the most. Won first three starts at 2m-2m5f, the last in the Grade 2 Leamington Novices' Hurdle at Warwick won by last season's Neptune winner Willoughby Court. Had to battle a bit there as jumping wasn't the most fluent but was always in control. Step up to 3m resulted in first defeat in Musselburgh's Albert Bartlett trial, in which he came under pressure some way out and couldn't get to Red River. Was conceding 3lb to the highly regarded winner, however.

Going preference Has won on good to soft and soft
Star rating ✪✪✪

Red River
5 ch g; Trainer Kim Bailey
Hurdles form (right-handed) 131, best RPR 148

Ran out a 13-length winner on his debut at Wincanton over 2m5½f and didn't go unbacked in Grade 2 Winter Novices' Hurdle at Sandown but, after closing up on the run to the second-last, he was left behind by the winner and second, finishing a 20-length third to On The Blind Side. Trainer put that down to a breathing issue and gave him a wind operation in December and it seemed to work as he returned in February to win the Musselburgh trial for this, taking it up at halfway and finding plenty in front to see off Mr Whipped by just over two lengths. Considered an exciting prospect by trainer.

Going preference Has won on good and soft
Star rating ✪✪✪

Black Op
7 br g; Trainer Tom George
Hurdles form (left-handed) 412, best RPR 144
Cheltenham form 2, best RPR 144

Was running all over Santini until mistake at last in Ballymore trial on heavy ground in January. Shorter for this than that race, but the way he travels suggests he should stay at 2m5f and dealt with in more detail in Wednesday's section.

Going preference Seems to handle anything
Star rating ✪✪

Poetic Rhythm

7 ch g; Trainer Fergal O'Brien
Hurdles form (all left-handed) 5330131, best RPR 152
Cheltenham form (all) 153303, best RPR 152
At the festival 15 Mar 2017 Held up in rear, badly hampered 5th, no danger and behind after, finished 11th, beaten 50 lengths by Willoughby Court in Neptune Investment Management Novices' Hurdle

Second-season novice who was fairly highly tried in first season and was beaten a whopping 50 lengths as a 66-1 chance in last season's Neptune. Has looked more the finished article this season and has won two of three starts, all in Graded company. Saved best for latest when landing Grade 1 Challow Hurdle at Newbury in December, winning a protracted battle with Mulcahys Hill by a short head. That was on heavy ground but plenty of form on good and this race the aim despite never having tried the trip. More battle-hardened than most in this field, which might stand him in good stead.

Going preference Seems to act on any
Star rating ✪✪✪

Dortmund Park

5 b g; Trainer Gordon Elliott
Hurdles form 6114, best RPR 145
Left-handed 64, best RPR 135
Right-handed 11, best RPR 145

Has won two of four starts since joining Gordon Elliott after going 2-2 in bumpers in France and looked useful staying prospect when streaking clear by 16 lengths over 2m6½f at Thurles in January. Couldn't back that up in Grade 1 company over a similar trip at Leopardstown's Dublin Festival when only fourth to 25-1 rag Tower Bridge (winner only has Ballymore entry) but that was only a couple of weeks after his Thurles effort. Another viewed as a chaser for the future by Elliott and he also expects him to be better on decent ground.

Going preference Only raced on soft/heavy over hurdles, won bumper on good
Star rating ✪✪✪✪

Ballyward

6 b g; Trainer Willie Mullins
Hurdles form (left-handed) 41, best RPR 139

Bumper winner in December 2016, but almost exactly a year until he returned over hurdles and went down by five lengths on debut at Leopardstown. Showed benefit of that run when scoring by a length in maiden hurdle at Naas over 2m3f, with trainer calling it a "dour staying performance". Also said he's looked at both the Ballymore and this race for him, but you'd have to think it comes too soon.

Going preference Acts on heavy and yielding
Star rating ✪

Enniscoffey Oscar

6 b g; Trainer Emma Lavelle
Hurdles form 47311, best RPR 145
Left-handed 711, best RPR 145
Right-handed 43, best RPR 129

Always quite highly regarded by trainer and after winning Polytrack bumper last February he was pitched straight into the Aintree Grade 2 bumper at the Grand National meeting, where he was a highly encouraging second for a horse expected to stay well and finished ahead of the likes of Western Ryder, If The Cap Fits, Claimantakinforgan and Black Op. First three starts over hurdles suggested he'd have his limitations, but improved as he went up in trip and bolted by up 15 lengths on second attempt at 2m5f at Doncaster in December. That led to a crack at the same course's Grade 2 River Don over 3m½f, in which he was a well-backed second favourite and battled all the way to the line for a short-head win (28-length fourth won Pertemps qualifier next time out). That was on soft ground, but trainer says he hates it and big bumper run was on good. Looks tough and just the sort to go well.

Going preference Acts on soft and good, trainer convinced he wants better ground
Star rating ✪✪✪✪

Real Steel

5 b g; Trainer Willie Mullins
Hurdles form 21F5, best RPR 145
Left-handed 2F5, best RPR 145
Right-handed 1, best RPR 128

Another Mullins horse the bookmakers have no idea what to do with. He's actually half the price for this than either of the other two novice hurdles, although he has yet to run over further than 2m for his current trainer (ran once at 2m2f in France). Was vying for lead (although likely to come off second best) when falling at last in the Future Champions Novice Hurdle at Leopardstown in December, but below that form when well behind Samcro in the Deloitte. Lack of form over at least 2m4f gives him an unlikely profile.

Going preference Has raced only on soft over hurdles
Star rating ✪

Gowiththeflow

5 b g; Trainer Ben Pauling
Hurdles form (left-handed) 221, best RPR 129

Point winner on fast ground in May last year and fair form in three hurdles, finishing second to Chooseyourweapon at Chepstow in November and going down by three lengths to Mr Whipped at Newbury a month later. Earned ticket to Cheltenham with novice hurdle win over 2m5f at Doncaster in February, seeing off Paisley Park (beaten only a length by Mr Whipped in Graded company the time before) by a length and a quarter. Trainer leaning towards Ballymore at the time, but would be shorter for this, although still has plenty to find.

Going preference Seems to act on any
Star rating ✪✪✪

Calett Mad

6 bb g; Trainer Nigel Twiston-Davies
Hurdles form 34311541, best RPR 145
Left-handed 343154, best RPR 143
Right-handed 11, best RPR 145
Cheltenham form (all) 915, best RPR 143
At the festival 14 Mar 2017 Midfield, headway when mistake 9th, every chance 3 out, weakened before 2 out, finished ninth, beaten 33 and a half lengths by Tiger Roll in National Hunt Chase

Unusual profile in that he started chasing in Britain before hurdling – as did 2008 winner Nenuphar Collonges – and reached a fair level. Started well over hurdles this term when winning at Perth and Cheltenham but then ran two shockers at Cheltenham and Doncaster either side of a wind operation. Benefit of that op seemed to show when he won a Pertemps qualifier at Musselburgh in February, but might have done it a bit too easily as he went up 7lb to a mark of 145 for that effort.

Going preference Seems to act on any
Star rating ✪✪✪

OTHERS TO CONSIDER

I've mentioned plenty here purely because this has been the hardest novice hurdle in which to find the winner, which is probably because horses who want 3m in their novice hurdle careers tend to be big, backward future staying chasers and have no idea what has hit them when asked to run hard and fast for 3m on quick ground so young.

VERDICT

A pattern has started to emerge for this race because if you include point and bumper/Flat runs the 13 previous winners had the following number of starts before lining up at Cheltenham: 26-17-9-7-8-6-5-15-6-11-8-5-15. Of those who had fewer than seven runs, two went on to win the RSA Chase the following season (one of those a Gold Cup a year later too), so they probably had a serious class edge. Otherwise being battle-hardened looks an advantage. The last four winners went off at 33-1, 14-1, 11-1 and 16-1 and, as none of the main market contenders is that heavily raced, I wouldn't be surprised if we had another shock. I'll be throwing a few arrows, with CALETT MAD (15 runs in all disciplines) and ENNISCOFFEY OSCAR (eight runs) top of the list and Poetic Rhythm (16 runs) not far behind.

	FORM	WINNER	AGE & WGT	Adj RPR	SP	TRAINER	BEST RPR LAST 12 MONTHS (RUNS SINCE)
17	11141	Penhill D	6 11-5	157-2	16-1	W Mullins (IRE)	won Limerick Gd2 nov hdl (3m) (0)
16	-1111	Unowhatimeanharry CD	8 11-5	154-9	11-1	H Fry	won Exeter class 2 hcap hdl (2m7f) (0)
15	11F12	Martello Tower D	7 11-7	151-6	14-1	M Mullins (IRE)	2nd Leopardstown Gd2 nov hdl (2m4f) (0)
14	-1253	Very Wood	5 11-7	143-18	33-1	N Meade (IRE)	3rd Naas Gd2 nov hdl (2m4f) (0)
13	-1111	At Fishers Cross CD	6 11-7	161T	11-8f	R Curtis	won Cheltenham Gd2 nov hdl (2m5f) (0)
12	2111	Brindisi Breeze D	6 11-7	157-6	7-1	L Russell	won Haydock Gd2 nov hdl (3m) (0)
11	1-111	Bobs Worth C	6 11-7	160T	15-8f	N Henderson	won Cheltenham Gd2 nov hdl (2m4½f) (0)
10	12F34	Berties Dream	7 11-7	155-3	33-1	P Gilligan (IRE)	3rd Cheltenham Gd2 nov hdl (2m5f) (1)
09	-5112	Weapon's Amnesty D, BF	6 11-7	150-12	8-1	C Byrnes (IRE)	2nd Leopardstown Gd2 nov hdl (2m4f) (0)
08	1-212	Nenuphar Collonges CD	7 11-7	146-12	9-1	A King	2nd Warwick Gd2 nov hdl (2m5f) (0)

WINS-RUNS: 5yo 1-37, 6yo 5-87, 7yo 3-38, 8yo 1-13, 9yo 0-1 **FAVOURITES:** -£4.75

TRAINERS IN THIS RACE (w-pl-r): Willie Mullins 1-4-28, Alan King 1-0-6, Harry Fry 1-0-3, Nicky Henderson 1-1-8, Lucinda Russell 1-0-1, Noel Meade 1-0-4, Rebecca Curtis 1-0-8, Margaret Mullins 1-0-1, Ben Pauling 0-0-1, Brian Ellison 0-0-1, Emma Lavelle 0-1-5, Colin Tizzard 0-1-6, David Pipe 0-1-5, Dan Skelton 0-0-2, Mouse Morris 0-0-2, Jessica Harrington 0-0-1, Nigel Twiston-Davies 0-2-8, Paul Nicholls 0-3-8, Philip Hobbs 0-0-4, Tom George 0-0-3, Gordon Elliott 0-2-4

FATE OF FAVOURITES: 32P121F0PU **POSITION OF WINNER IN MARKET:** 5401219767

Key trends

🐎 At least three runs over hurdles, 10/10

🐎 Won over at least 2m5f, 9/10

🐎 Adjusted RPR of at least 150, 8/10

🐎 Top-three finish in a Graded hurdle last time out, 8/10 (four won)

🐎 Aged six or seven, 8/10

🐎 Rated within 9lb of RPR top-rated, 7/10

Other factors

🐎 Seven winners had won a Graded hurdle

🐎 Four winners had raced at least twice at Cheltenham (all had won at the course)

Notes

3.30 Timico Cheltenham Gold Cup ITV/RUK
*3m2½f   *Grade 1   *£625,000*

Might Bite produced an extraordinary finish in last year's RSA Chase – almost throwing the race away before grabbing it back in the final strides – and he returns as Gold Cup favourite, having moved into the top rank of the senior division with his King George VI Chase victory at Christmas, although not everyone was convinced by his one-length margin over 50-1 shot Double Shuffle. Sizing John, who won last year at the relatively young age of seven, looked set for a period of dominance after his reappearance victory in the John Durkan but gave up favouritism after he was a well-beaten seventh in the Leopardstown Christmas Chase. Native River, third last year, was off for 11 months after that run but returned impressively to win the Denman Chase at Newbury. Among the fancied Gold Cup first-timers from Ireland are Our Duke, Killultagh Vic and Road To Respect, while the north has a live hope in Definitly Red.

Might Bite

9 b g; Trainer Nicky Henderson
Chase form 521F11111, best RPR 173
Left-handed 521111, best RPR 173
Right-handed F1, best RPR 173
Cheltenham form (all) 1571, best RPR 173
At the festival 15 Mar 2017 Led 2nd, pushed clear after 4 out, 12 lengths up 2 out, soon ridden, mistake last, idling when veered right 1f out, headed final 130yds, ran on again final 90yds, led final stride, won RSA Novices' Chase by a nose from Whisper

Quirky if hugely talented horse who had one failed attempt at chasing in November 2015 but returned to the game a year later to prove much the best of the novice stayers. Gave first hint that he might be a bit special when well on his way to destroying his field by around 20 lengths in the Kauto Star Novices' Chase in December 2016 only to be asked for a big one by Daryl Jacob at the last and plough through it, falling heavily. Has been ridden by Nico de Boinville ever since and the pair have gone on a five-race winning streak, including three Grade 1s. After winning a modest novice at odds of 1-7 to get his confidence back at Doncaster, he rocked up at Cheltenham as 7-2 favourite for the RSA Chase and looked to be in the process of thrashing the field as he should have done at Kempton but then decided to veer right towards the exit and got

caught and headed by stablemate Whisper before finally consenting to put his head down and get back up on the line. That was one of the most dramatic finishes in Cheltenham Festival history, but there was little doubt Might Bite was much the best and he proved it with a more straightforward victory, albeit by only two lengths, from Whisper at Aintree on his final start of the season. He is 2-2 this campaign, starting with what looked and was a straightforward assignment at Sandown, although the horse he toyed with, Frodon, has since soared up the ratings to a mark of 164. Then came the King George at Kempton, where he duly won at 6-4, although the race was unsatisfactory for a couple of reasons. For a start, several of his main rivals failed to produce their form, with Bristol De Mai not as good anywhere else as he is at Haydock,

TRAINER'S VIEW

Nicky Henderson on Might Bite "We can't guarantee he'll stay the Gold Cup trip as he has never tried three miles two and a half furlongs. That said, he does stay. The biggest concern is not the stamina but whether he jumps the final fence and keeps straight. That has to be the crucial thing" *Has won all five completed starts at 3m-plus but yet to go beyond 3m1f*

Fox Norton well beaten long before stamina should have been an issue and Whisper also a spent force by the first fence down the back straight on the final circuit. Of course, you can only beat what's left and Might Bite did that, but he won by only a length from Double Shuffle, who carried a rating of 151 into the race and made a good half-dozen minor jumping errors on the way round.

If someone had told you at the start of the season a length win from that Tom George-trained seven-year-old would have resulted in 3-1 Gold Cup favouritism you'd have called for the men in white coats – but that's what he is and, on balance, he probably deserves to be. He did also try to run to the exit when winning at Cheltenham over hurdles and also hung right on the final bend for one of his

hurdles defeats there, and even his trainer said he can't be sure what's going to happen when he jumps the last.

Going preference Act on soft, prefers it quicker

Star rating ✪✪✪✪✪

Native River

8 ch g; Trainer Colin Tizzard
Chase form 311332111131, best RPR 174
Left-handed 3132111131, best RPR 174
Right-handed 13, best RPR 153
Cheltenham form (all) F923, best RPR 168
At the festival 13 Mar 2015 Prominent, blundered 6th and lost place, weakened after 3 out, finished ninth, beaten 53 lengths by Martello Tower in Albert Bartlett Novices' Hurdle

15 Mar 2016 In touch, blundered 13th, chased winner 19th (water), lost 2nd and ridden after 4 out, outpaced after 3 out, rallied run-in and hung left, went 2nd final 120yds, stayed on to close on winner near finish, finished second, beaten one and a quarter lengths by Minella Rocco in National Hunt Chase

17 Mar 2017 Disputed lead 2nd until 9th, led 15th, ridden after 3 out, narrowly headed 2 out, stayed on very gamely in held 3rd from last to regain 2nd final 50yds, lost 2nd final stride, finished third, beaten two and three-quarter lengths by Sizing John in Gold Cup

Ultra-tough and game competitor who finished second in the National Hunt Chase as a novice before winning Grade 1 at Aintree and then put up some high-quality weight-

Might Bite: King George winner deservedly heads the Gold Cup market

carrying performances in handicaps last season. After a warm-up for the Hennessy at Newbury in a Grade 2 hurdle at Wetherby (second) he lined up as 7-2 favourite for the big one under 11st 1lb and, having raced prominently and led at halfway, powered clear from four out and was never in danger even though runner-up Carole's Destrier had closed to half a length at the line. Just a month later he was out under 11st 12lb in the Welsh National and again he never looked in much danger as he beat Raz De Maree (winner of the race this season) just under two lengths with the rest a long way away. Trainer Colin Tizzard believes he might have won the Gold Cup had he not taken in both big handicaps, but he also ran him in (and won) the Denman Chase at Newbury after Chepstow and it's hard to argue that his Gold Cup third was a massively below-par effort. He certainly ran much better than a lot of the yard's horses that week. Even so, Native River has deliberately been given a much lighter campaign this season, reappearing only for a 12-length win from the non-staying Cloudy Dream in the Denman Chase in February. That was his first run since the Gold Cup and he has to avoid the dreaded bounce factor, but trainer reports there were no serious problems bar some minor ligament damage and a below-par run would be very much against the grain for him.

Going preference Goes on any but could probably do with some ease in a Gold Cup
Star rating ✪✪✪

Sizing John

7 b g; Trainer Jessica Harrington
Chase form 1122332111117, best RPR 173
Left-handed 2232117, best RPR 171
Right-handed 113111, best RPR 173
Cheltenham form (all) 321, best RPR 171
At the festival 10 Mar 2015 Tracked leader, led 2 out, soon ridden, headed before last, kept on but no extra when lost 2nd run-in, finished third, beaten seven lengths by Douvan in Supreme Novices' Hurdle
15 Mar 2016 Led, headed 3rd, remained in close 2nd place until before 3 out, outpaced on bend before hampered and left 2nd 2 out, stayed on run-in but no chance with winner, finished second, beaten seven lengths by Douvan in Racing Post Arkle
17 Mar 2017 Travelled well most of way, mid-division, headway after 4 out, led soon after 2 out, 3 lengths up last, stayed on well, ridden out, won Gold Cup by two and three-quarter lengths from Minella Rocco

Spent early part of his career running into the backside of Douvan, but decision to step him up in trip last season proved a stroke of genius and he didn't look back after his opening second to his old rival, winning the Kinloch Brae over 2m4f at Thurles and then the Irish Gold Cup on his first start at 3m by three-quarters of a length from Empire Of Dirt. That gave him pretty much the perfect profile for a second-season chaser heading for gold and he proved what a potent weapon 2m speed is allied to 3m stamina when always travelling well at Cheltenham and doing the stayers for pace after the second-last. He closed the campaign by just holding off Gold Cup fourth Djakadam and Coneygree in a terrific finish to the Punchestown Gold Cup and looked set for just as good a season this time around when slamming Djakadam by seven lengths in the 2m4f John Durkan Memorial at Punchestown on his return in December. In hindsight, however, he and the runner-up did get racing a long way out on very heavy ground and they both ran miles below form in the Leopardstown Christmas Chase just 18 days later, Sizing John finishing a 32-length seventh to new kid on the block Road To Respect and Djakadam being pulled up. The latter has also run poorly since, so it has to be hoped the John Durkan hasn't had a lasting effect on both of them, and Jessica Harrington has almost certainly done the right thing in freshening up her Gold Cup winner for his defence. He will certainly appreciate better ground at Cheltenham and has yet to run a bad race at the festival in three previous visits. That said, we may have been spoiled by the likes of Best Mate and Kauto Star this century but they are the only two multiple Gold Cup winners since L'Escargot in 1970-71 and staying at the top is just as hard as getting there in the first place.

Going preference Goes on any but likes good ground
Star rating ✪✪✪✪

Killultagh Vic

9 b g; Trainer Willie Mullins
Chase form 11F, best RPR 168
Left-handed 1F, best RPR 168
Right-handed 1, best RPR 151
Cheltenham form (all) 61, best RPR 147
At the festival 12 Mar 2014 Well in touch, not much room 5f out, ridden well over 2f out, not quicken and kept on same pace after, finished sixth, beaten five lengths in Champion Bumper by Silver Concorde
13 Mar 2015 Mid-division, lost place 5th, smooth headway after 3 out, strong challenge and going well after 2 out, led before last where went left, soon ridden, narrowly headed final 100yds, rallied well, led on nod final stride, won Martin Pipe Conditional Jockeys' Handicap Hurdle by a head from Noble Endeavor

Hugely talented horse who won the Martin Pipe Conditional Jockeys' Handicap Hurdle in 2015 and then beat Thistlecrack over 3m at Punchestown before turning his sights to chasing the following season. Stamped himself as a high-class recruit when scooting up by 15 lengths on debut at Fairyhouse and was in the process of another easy win until nearly falling after overjumping at the last in a Grade 2 at Leopardstown the following month and coming to a virtual standstill. Somehow Ruby Walsh managed to galvanise him to get back up, but the damage might have been done as he was off the track for 23 months until reappearing in a 2m4f hurdle at Punchestown on New Year's Eve. He made slightly hard work of that, which can be forgiven, and he then proved he is well up to his entry in the Gold Cup when travelling like much the best in the Irish Gold Cup. Unfortunately he fell at the last having just taken up the running (jumped slightly sideways) and now needs to

Sizing John: last season's Gold Cup winner now has plenty to prove

prove he's over that. Player if he's suffered no ill effect as he has a huge engine.

Going preference Most of best form on soft but beat Thistlecrack on good to yielding

Star rating ✪✪✪

Our Duke

8 b g; Trainer Jessica Harrington
Chase form 1121741, best RPR 170
Left-handed 1124, best RPR 166
Right-handed 171, best RPR 170

Was one of the best staying novices around last year, winning the Grade 1 Neville Hotels Novice Chase over 3m at Leopardstown by half a length from Coney Island and then running Disko to just under two lengths dropped in trip for the Flogas back at the same course in February. Deliberately missed Cheltenham last season as connections were worried about how this big horse would handle quick ground, but then they tried on good to yielding in the Irish National at Fairyhouse and he seemed to relish it, running out one of the easiest winners you'll see by 14 lengths. On the strength of that he was made favourite for the Gold Cup by some, but his opening two efforts this season were underwhelming, most obviously the first when he was a 51-length seventh of eight in the JNwine.com Champion Chase at Down Royal. A back issue was diagnosed then and he did a lot better in the Irish Gold Cup in February, although a 16-length fourth was still some way off his novice efforts and he made a couple of jolting errors. However, he put himself back in the picture in a big way a fortnight later when giving 7lb and a length beating to top novice Presenting Percy in the Grade 2 Red Mills Chase at Gowran Park. The runner-up would have wanted further but the same could be said of the winner and it was a good performance to pull 17 lengths clear of third-placed Ballycasey, rated 155, especially after the almighty clout he gave the third-last. Jumping is going to be the issue for many and, while he can jump very well, he is always prone to the odd howler and getting away with one in the hustle and bustle of a Gold Cup won't be easy. That said, he was near faultless in the Irish National on the quickest ground he has encountered and there's always a chance better ground will help. Big player now.

Going preference Handles any

Star rating ✪✪✪✪

Road To Respect

7 ch g; Trainer Noel Meade
Chase form 1432211121, best RPR 169
Left-handed 132211, best RPR 169
Right-handed 4112, best RPR 167
Cheltenham form 1, best RPR 162
At the festival
16 Mar 2017 Jumped left at times, prominent when hit 1st, settled midfield after 3rd, headway from 8th, led approaching 2 out, drew clear between last 2, not fluent last, kept on well, pushed out, won Brown Advisory & Merriebelle Stable Plate Handicap Chase by six lengths from Baron Alco

Second-season chaser who improved rapidly last spring, giving Noel Meade his first chase winner at the Cheltenham Festival after years of trying when turning the Brown Advisory & Merriebelle Stable Plate into a procession (although would probably have landed on his side at the first had he not had a wall of horses

TRAINER'S VIEW

Jessica Harrington on Our Duke "He wouldn't have liked the ground [in the Red Mills Chase] but it was a good performance to beat Presenting Percy giving him 7lb, plus he's not really a two-and-a-half-mile horse. When they go a good gallop it makes the difference [to his jumping]. He has a very high cruising speed, but when he's going just below that he's not concentrating" *Has won three out of four in double-figure fields over fences*

on his left) and then beating the wayward-jumping JLT winner Yorkhill in the Ryanair Gold Cup Novice Chase at Fairyhouse. Still had a rating of only 157 after that, so there was work to do, but Road To Respect has risen to the challenge so far, winning a fair Grade 3 at Punchestown on his return, just being run out of the JNwine.com Champion Chase at Down Royal by Outlander on soft ground, but then turning around that form in the Leopardstown Christmas Chase with a length-and-a-quarter victory over Balko Des Flos with Outlander a couple of lengths further away in third. That form is going to need improving on again at Cheltenham but, as with Sizing John last year, it gives Road To Respect the near-perfect profile for a second-season chaser tackling the race and we know he handles the course, having hacked up on the Thursday last year.

Going preference Handles soft but prefers better ground
Star rating ✪✪✪✪

Definitly Red

9 ch g; Trainer Brian Ellison
Chase form (left-handed) 122F131U1P311, best RPR 172
Cheltenham form (all) 71PF1, best RPR 172
At the festival 12 Mar 2014 Chased leader to over 2f out, steadily faded, finished seventh, beaten eight and three-quarter lengths by Silver Concorde in Champion Bumper
13 Mar 2015 Close up, ridden briefly after 5th, weakened after 3 out, tailed off when pulled up before last in Albert Bartlett Novices' Hurdle won by Martello Tower
15 Mar 2016 Midfield, not fluent 9th, lost place when hit 17th, in rear when blundered 3 out, fell 2 out in National Hunt Chase won by Minella Rocco

Really tough northern-trained chaser whose best last season was a Grimthorpe Chase win at Doncaster off a mark of 149, but has got himself on the fringes of Gold Cup contention with two excellent recent efforts. Tailed off when pulled up in the Grand National in April, he didn't exactly promise that much when beaten 24 lengths by Bristol De Mai

on his return in the Charlie Hall at Wetherby, but then beat the talented Cloudy Dream by seven lengths at Aintree and followed up with an excellent win in the Cotswold Chase at Cheltenham on Trials Day. His trainer had specifically targeted that race as he wanted to find out once and for all if Definitly Red had a problem with the course following heavy defeats in the National Hunt Chase and the Albert Barlett (he had won a bumper at the track) and he gave him all the right answers with a dour staying performance to pull eight lengths clear of the promising mudlover American. A Racing Post Rating there of 172 hasn't been beaten in recent seasons by many of his rivals and it's arguable that 16-1 underplays his form chance, but it did come on heavy ground, which he handles well, and he is probably going to need it on the soft side to be a factor.

Going preference Would much prefer soft ground or worse
Star rating ✪✪

Minella Rocco

8 b g; Trainer Jonjo O'Neill
Chase form 3P6213FU24P4F, best RPR 168
Left-handed 3P613FU2P4F, best RPR 168
Right-handed 24, best RPR 151
Cheltenham form P6132P, best RPR 168
At the festival 15 Mar 2016 Held up, reminder after 8th, headway 4 out, upsides 2 out, led just before last, stayed on well and edged right run-in, kept up to work towards finish, won National Hunt Chase by a length and a quarter from Native River
17 Mar 2017 Held up, outpaced after 3 out, headway between last 2, went 4th soon after last, finished strongly, snatched 2nd final stride, without threatening to reach winner, finished second, beaten two and three-quarter lengths by Sizing John in Gold Cup

Just one look at those chase form figures and you'd be forgiven for asking what on earth this horse is doing in the Gold Cup preview, but there is something that brings out the best in him here – although not all the time as there have been some pretty heavy defeats. However, his sole chase win came in the

National Hunt Chase in 2016 when he beat Native River and he again finished ahead of that rival when the pair were second and third to Sizing John in the Gold Cup. It looks very much like Cheltenham in the spring is what brings him to life, but it's going to need to as he has managed to finish just two of his chase starts this term, being well beaten by Road To Respect each time, and was well beaten when falling at the last in the Irish Gold Cup on his latest outing. Obviously has the talent when putting it altogether but jumping is dodgy at the best of times and he's hard to fancy now.

Going preference Prefers decent ground
Star rating ✪

Edwulf

9 b g; Trainer Joseph O'Brien
Chase form F3U21F1PP1, best RPR 169
Left-handed F3UF1PP1, best RPR 169
Right-handed 21, best RPR 138
Cheltenham form P
At the festival 14 Mar 2017 Held up, headway approaching 4 out, went 2nd before 2 out and every chance briefly, landed awkwardly 2 out, about 5 lengths down and held when blundered last, went wrong and pulled up inside final furlong on run-in in National Hunt Chase won by Tiger Roll

Remarkable horse who almost died at the Cheltenham Festival last season but recovered to become a Grade 1 winner when landing the Irish Gold Cup just 11 months later. Having been pulled up after the last in the National Hunt Chase, Edwulf suffered a fit and collapsed as a result of oxygen starvation to the brain and was on the ground for a good 40 minutes. It was even longer before he could finally be taken away to an equine hospital and just to get back on to the racecourse was some achievement. However, Edwulf did not look like a horse about to make a fairytale return to the big time when pulled up three out in the Leopardstown Christmas Chase and just as surprising as his neck victory over Outlander in February was his starting odds of just 33-1. There are certainly stronger contenders for the Gold Cup than this one, but he has already defied the odds to win one of Ireland's premier staying chases and surely few would begrudge him an even more unlikely success.

Going preference Best form on soft/heavy
Star rating ✪✪

Djakadam

9 b g; Trainer Willie Mullins
Chase form 11F81221F23213422P3, best RPR 177
Left-handed 11F82F2334P3, best RPR 177
Right-handed 1212122, best RPR 175
Cheltenham form F2F24, best RPR 177
At the festival 13 Mar 2014 Chased leaders, not fluent 3rd, hit 9th, disputing 3 lengths 2nd and going okay when fell 4 out in JLT Novices' Chase won by Taquin Du Seuil
13 Mar 2015 Mid-division, smooth headway 16th, tracked leaders travelling well 18th, ridden in close 3rd approaching 2 out, hit last, stayed on to go 2nd run-in, held when drifted right final 70yd, finished second, beaten one and a half lengths by Coneygree in Gold Cup
16 Mar 2016 In touch, tracked leaders 10th, upsides after 16th, narrow lead after next, ridden and headed after 3 out, not fluent next, stayed on from last but no impression on winner, finished second, beaten four and a half lengths by Don Cossack in Gold Cup
17 Mar 2017 Travelled well most of way, tracked leaders, challenged after 4 out, narrow advantage when mistake 2 out, soon ridden and headed, kept pressing but held from last, no extra close home, finished fourth, beaten three and a quarter lengths by Sizing John in Gold Cup

Plenty have called for this one to run in the Ryanair over the last couple of years and he may well go there, but he has compiled Gold Cup form figures of 224 and is entitled to take his place again should his owner so wish. The only problem is he has looked a shadow of himself since running second to Sizing John when trying to win a third straight John Durkan at Punchestown in December. Pulled up in the Leopardstown Christmas Chase, he improved on that to be third to Edwulf in the Irish Gold Cup but was readily left behind approaching the last and would have been no better than fourth had Killultagh Vic not fallen. May be too late for him to win any race at the festival.

Going preference Acts on any
Star rating ✪

OTHERS TO CONSIDER

Blaklion and **Total Recall** are heading to the Grand National, while **Outlander** is a shorter price for the Ryanair. That said, he was only 10-1 when disappointing in this last year, has won a Grade 1 this season and was only beaten a neck in the Irish Gold Cup. Talking of horses not beaten far in top trials, **Double Shuffle** was a 40-1 shot at the time of writing with 14 ahead of him in the betting despite going down by only a length to the 3-1 Gold Cup favourite Might Bite in the King George. It's easy enough to argue that is a bit odd and, while Tom George's eight-year-old likes Kempton, his Cheltenham form includes a third in the Close Brothers Novices' Handicap Chase a couple of years ago. **Bachasson**, **Balko Des Flos**, **Cue Card** and **Sub Lieutenant** will surely go for the Ryanair, but **Anibale Fly**, not entirely done with when coming down in the Irish Gold Cup, is another possible contender at big odds.

VERDICT

A wide-open race and it wouldn't really surprise me if any of the top ten in the betting were to win, but my preference is for ROAD TO RESPECT, who keeps improving, is still only seven and loves the track. He didn't have the classy form at shorter trips boasted by Sizing John last year, but he showed loads of pace when winning the Plate 12 months ago and that will stand him in good stead on decent ground. The one who really worries me now is Our Duke, who bounced back in great style at Gowran and might jump a lot better given some decent ground. A look back at that Irish Grand National win tells you he's a serious talent.

Djakadam: form in the book but may have missed his chance

	FORM WINNER	AGE & WGT	Adj RPR	SP	TRAINER	BEST RPR LAST 12 MONTHS (RUNS SINCE)
17	3211 **Sizing John**	7 11-10	172-12	7-1	J Harrington (IRE)	won Gd1 Irish Gold Cup (3m½f) **(0)**
16	111F1 **Don Cossack**	9 11-10	185T	9-4f	G Elliott (IRE)	won Gd1 Punchestown Gold Cup (3m1f) **(4)**
15	3/111 **Coneygree** C	8 11-10	173-9	7-1	M Bradstock	won Newbury Gd2 chase (2m7½f) **(0)**
14	1-876 **Lord Windermere** C	8 11-10	161-24	20-1	J Culloty (IRE)	7th Gd1 Lexus Chase (3m) **(1)**
13	321-1 **Bobs Worth** C, D	8 11-10	178-6	11-4f	N Henderson	won Gd3 Hennessy Gold Cup (3m2½f) **(0)**
12	-P731 **Synchronised**	9 11-10	175-12	8-1	J O'Neill	won Gd1 Lexus Chase (3m) **(0)**
11	13-31 **Long Run**	6 11-10	184-2	7-2f	N Henderson	won Gd1 King George VI Chase (3m) **(0)**
10	1-P25 **Imperial Commander** C	9 11-10	181-15	7-1	N Twiston-Davies	2nd Gd1 Betfair Chase (3m) **(1)**
09	2-1U1 **Kauto Star** CD	9 11-10	188-1	7-4f	P Nicholls	won Gd1 King George VI Chase (3m) **(0)**
08	1-111 **Denman** C, D	8 11-10	184-5	9-4	P Nicholls	won Gd3 Hennessy Gold Cup (3m2½f) **(2)**

WINS-RUNS: 6yo 1-3, 7yo 1-20, 8yo 4-38, 9yo 4-32, 10yo 0-21, 11yo 0-9, 12yo 0-3 **FAVOURITES:** £4.25

TRAINERS IN THIS RACE (w-pl-r): Paul Nicholls 2-6-23, Nicky Henderson 2-2-9, Gordon Elliott 1-0-2, Jessica Harrington 1-0-1, Jonjo O'Neill 1-2-7, Nigel Twiston-Davies 1-0-5, Mark Bradstock 1-0-4, Alan King 0-0-5, Colin Tizzard 0-1-3, Noel Meade 0-1-3, Philip Hobbs 0-0-1, Venetia Williams 0-1-4, Willie Mullins 0-5-12, Henry de Bromhead 0-0-2, Nick Williams 0-0-2

FATE OF FAVOURITES: 21F1315014 **POSITION OF WINNER IN MARKET:** 2131317214

Key trends

- Grade 1 chase winner, 10/10
- Aged between seven and nine, 9/10
- Two to five runs that season, 9/10
- Adjusted RPR of at least 172, 9/10
- Won over at least 3m, 9/10
- Won a Graded chase that season, 8/10
- No more than ten starts over fences, 8/10
- Won or placed previously at the festival, 8/10
- Within 12lb of RPR top-rated, 8/10

Other factors

- In 2015, Coneygree became the first winner not to have run at a previous festival since Imperial Call in 1996. He was also the first novice to win since Captain Christy in 1974
- The most popular reappearance race among the last ten winners was the Hennessy, with three victors making their seasonal debut in the Newbury handicap. Two won (Denman and Bobs Worth) and the other finished eighth (Lord Windermere)
- Bobs Worth, Coneygree and Sizing John were the only three of the last ten winners not to have run in the King George or Lexus that season

Notes

4.10 St James's Place Foxhunter Chase ITV/RUK
3m2½f · Amateur riders · £45,000

Rising star Bryony Frost announced herself on the big stage by winning last year on Pacha Du Polder and her Paul Nicholls-trained mount now has a shot at back-to-back victories, a feat achieved recently by Salsify (2012-13) and On The Fringe (2015-16) but by only two others since the second world war, with a total of eight dual winners in that time.

Nicholls, who also won the race in 2004 and 2005 with Earthmover and Sleeping Night, has another leading contender in Wonderful Charm, who was a closing neck second last year.

Since the first Irish-trained victory in 1983 there have been ten subsequent wins, including for six consecutive years between 2011 and 2016.

The punchestown.com Hunters Chase (formerly known as the Raymond Smith Memorial and run at Leopardstown) in early February is the best Irish trial. Three of the last six winners have gone on to victory here, although On The Fringe was only second and seventh in that race before winning here. This year's winner, Gilgamboa, is not qualified to run here, but Burning Ambition ran a good trial in second place.

Seventeen of the last 26 winners have been aged nine or younger, but the last three were ten or 11.

FOXHUNTER CHASE RESULTS AND TRENDS

	FORM	WINNER	AGE & WGT	Adj RPR	SP	TRAINER	BEST RPR LAST 12 MONTHS (RUNS SINCE)
17	-3341	Pacha Du Polder CD, BF	10 12-0	143-8	16-1	P Nicholls	3rd Uttoxeter Listed hcap ch (3m2f) (2)
16	11-17	On The Fringe CD, BF	11 12-0	148T	13-8f	E Bolger (IRE)	won Aintree Fox Hunters (2m5f) (2)
15	-1122	On The Fringe	10 12-0	144T	6-1	E Bolger (IRE)	1st Punchestown hunt ch (2m7f) (4)
14	-6213	Tammys Hill BF	9 12-0	139-9	15-2	L Lennon (IRE)	2nd Down Royal hunt ch (2m7f) (2)
13	-1221	Salsify CD	8 12-0	143-6	2-1f	R Sweeney (IRE)	won Foxhunter Chase (3m2½f) (5)
12	-11P1	Salsify	7 12-0	132-14	7-1	R Sweeney (IRE)	won Leopardstown hunt ch (3m) (0)
11	44-21	Zemsky	8 12-0	125-23	33-1	I Ferguson (IRE)	won Musselburgh cl 6 hunt ch (3m½f) (0)
10	2-121	Baby Run	10 12-0	144-7	9-2jf	N Twiston-Davies	won Warwick class 6 hunt ch (3m½) (0)
09	11	Cappa Bleu	7 12-0	130-14	11-2	S Crow	won Chaddesley Corbett open (3m) (0)
08	-P211	Amicelli	9 12-0	128-6	33-1	C Coward	won Brocklesby Park open (3m) (1)

WINS-RUNS: 6yo 0-3, 7yo 2-16, 8yo 2-35, 9yo 2-43, 10yo 3-50, 11yo 1-47, 12yo 0-31, 13yo 0-6, 14yo 0-4 **FAVOURITES:** £-1.63

TRAINERS IN THIS RACE (w-pl-r): Enda Bolger 2-1-5, Paul Nicholls 1-1-11, Fergal O'Brien 0-0-3, Colin McBratney 0-2-3, Gordon Elliott 0-0-3, James Joseph Mangan 0-2-4, Warren Greatrex 0-2-4, Willie Mullins 0-0-1

FATE OF FAVOURITES: P014215314 **POSITION OF WINNER IN MARKET:** 0210314216

Key trends
- Ran between 20 and 41 days ago, 10/10
- Won over at least 3m, 9/10
- Top-three finish last time out, 9/10
- Aged seven to ten, 9/10
- Adjusted RPR of at least 130, 8/10

Other factors
- The record of the previous year's winner is 04U114
- Salsify (2012-13) and On The Fringe (2015-16) were back-to-back winners. The last one before them was Double Silk in 1993-94
- Four winners had competed at the festival and all finished in the first five
- Those aged 12 or older are winless in the last ten years. The 13-year-old Earthmover (2004) is the only winner from this category since 1990

4.50 Martin Pipe Conditional Jockeys' Hcap Hdl RUK
2m4½f ~ £70,000

Willie Mullins and Paul Nicholls have dominated this handicap hurdle, winning five times between them in the last seven years. Gordon Elliott became the second Irish trainer to win the race with Champagne Classic last year, with stablemate Runfordave finishing third. Notably, Ireland had the first four home in 2015.

Champagne Classic was the third winner in the Gigginstown colours after Sir Des Champs and Don Poli and, with this race earning a reputation as a proving ground for future top chasers, their runners are worth a close look. Dortmund Park might be one to represent the Elliott/Gigginstown team this year.

The Mullins and Elliott winners have had the shortest SPs (9-2 favourite, 7-1 and 12-1 twice) with the others sent off at 14-1 or bigger.

Although the race is open to four-year-olds and upwards, only five- and six-year-olds have been successful. They have also been placed 17 times. The lowest-rated runner in 2016 and 2017 ran off a mark of 135, while eight of the nine winners were within 7lb of the top-rated. Runners rated between 133 and 139 have won seven of the nine runnings.

David Pipe has yet to win the race named in honour of his father, having had the beaten favourite three times and two unplaced second favourites.

Charles Byrnes's Off You Go would be a fascinating contender if he gets a run and isn't diverted to one of the other handicap hurdles. The five-year-old won the competitive Coral Hurdle at Leopardstown and, as a son of Presenting, can be expected to improve again on spring going.

MARTIN PIPE HANDICAP HURDLE RESULTS AND TRENDS

	FORM	WINNER	AGE & WGT	OR	SP	TRAINER	BEST RPR LAST 12 MONTHS (RUNS SINCE)
17	23213	Champagne Classic D	6 11-3	138·9	12-1	G Elliott (IRE)	won Thurles mdn hdl (2m6½f) (1)
16	4-235	Ibis Du Rheu	5 11-7	139·4	14-1	P Nicholls	3rd Lanzarote hcap hdl (2m5f) (1)
15	-5123	Killultagh Vic D	6 11-1	135·5	7-1	W Mullins (IRE)	3rd Leopardstown Gd2 nov hdl (2m4f) (0)
14	2-211	Don Poli	5 11-5	143·4	12-1	W Mullins (IRE)	won Clonmel Gd3 nov hdl (3m) (0)
13	-4251	Salubrious D	6 11-5	141·9	16-1	P Nicholls	won Musselburgh cl 3 hcap hdl (2m4f) (0)
12	135P1	Attaglance	6 11-3	139T	20-1	M Jefferson	won M Rasen class 3 hcap hdl (2m3f) (0)
11	1-1	Sir Des Champs	5 11-3	134T	9-2f	W Mullins (IRE)	won Navan hdl (2m) (0)
10	-445U	Pause And Clause D	6 11-10	137·3	14-1	E Lavelle	4th Haydock Listed hcap hdl (3m1f) (2)
09	-4134	Andytown C, D	6 11-2	133·6	25-1	N Henderson	won Chelt class 3 cond hcap hdl (2m5f) (1)

WINS-RUNS: 4yo 0-1, 5yo 3-56, 6yo 6-70, 7yo 0-42, 8yo 0-25, 9yo 0-8, 10yo 0-6, 12yo 0-1 **FAVOURITES:** -£3.50

FATE OF FAVOURITES: 3010P0300 **POSITION OF WINNER IN MARKET:** 061086267

Key trends

~ Officially rated 133-143, 9/9

~ Aged five or six, 9/9

~ Top-three finish in at least one of last two starts, 8/9

~ No more than eight hurdle runs, 8/9

~ Rated within 6lb of RPR top-rated, 7/9

~ Had won that season, 7/9

Other factors

~ Willie Mullins (three) and Gordon Elliott (one) account for the four Irish-trained winners, three of whom were owned by Gigginstown

~ All 82 runners aged seven or older have been beaten

~ Seven of the nine winners carried between 11st 1lb and 11st 5lb

5.30 Grand Annual Handicap Chase RUK
2m½f · Grade 3 · £110,000

Victory went to runners rated 129-134 in nine out of ten runnings up to 2010 but, as with the other festival handicaps, the threshold is moving upwards and six of the last seven winners have been in the 140s. The last four winners, Savello (11st 5lb), Next Sensation (11st 2lb), Solar Impulse (11st) and Rock The World (11st 5lb), have ended a 14-year run where no winner carried more than 10st 13lb.

Alderwood in 2013 is the only successful favourite since 2004 and eight of the last 12 winners were sent off 12-1 or bigger, emphasising that this is a difficult 'getting out stakes' for punters.

Four of the last nine winners were officially novices. This has been a good race for novices with 12 winners, rated from 129 to 140, since 1983.

The 2008 winner Tiger Cry is the only winner aged older than nine in the past 15 years, while Palarshan (2003) is the only five-year-old to win in the past 50 years.

The race's title has commemorated Nicky Henderson's father Johnny since 2005 and the trainer won the following year with Greenhope and again in 2012 with Bellvano (both 20-1 shots). He has also had four runner-ups and three thirds from a total of 36 runners.

Solar Impulse in 2016 was a third winner in the past 14 runnings for Paul Nicholls (the previous two carried 10st 1lb and 10st 11lb), although he has also had five beaten favourites.

Ireland has won seven of the last 18 runnings, including three times in the past five years, and three of them prepped over hurdles – two of the exceptions were the novices Fota Island and Alderwood.

Seven of the last ten British-trained winners had won at Cheltenham before.

Any Second Now: near the top of the market for trainer Ted Walsh

	FORM	WINNER	AGE & WGT	OR	SP	TRAINER	BEST RPR LAST 12 MONTHS (RUNS SINCE)
17	63-3P	**Rock The World** C, D	9 11-5	147-2	10-1	J Harrington (IRE)	2nd Punchestown hcap ch (2m) **(2)**
16	63-3P	**Solar Impulse** D	6 11-0	140-8	28-1	P Nicholls	3rd Haydock class 2 ch (2m½f) **(1)**
15	5-604	**Next Sensation** D	8 11-2	143-5	16-1	M Scudamore	4th Newbury class 2 hcap ch (2m½f) **(0)**
14	-3439	**Savello** D	8 11-5	147-2	16-1	A Martin (IRE)	3rd Leopardstown hcap ch (2m1f) **(1)**
13	-S312	**Alderwood** C, D	9 10-11	140T	3-1f	T Mullins (IRE)	2nd Punchestown hcap ch (2m) **(0)**
12	-1621	**Bellvano** D	8 10-2	138T	20-1	N Henderson	won Kelso class 2 nov ch (2m1f) **(0)**
11	U6483	**Oiseau De Nuit** CD	9 10-13	145-3	40-1	C Tizzard	3rd Newbury Gd2 ch (2m1f) **(0)**
10	222F5	**Pigeon Island** C, D	7 10-1	129T	16-1	N Twiston-Davies	2nd Cheltenham Gd2 nov ch (2m5f) **(2)**
09	423F2	**Oh Crick** (1oh) C, D	6 10-0	130-13	7-1	A King	2nd Hereford class 3 nov ch (2m3f) **(0)**
08	4P-36	**Tiger Cry** D	10 10-6	134-1	15-2	A Moore (IRE)	3rd Ascot class 2 hcap ch (2m1f) **(0)**

WINS-RUNS: 5yo 0-5, 6yo 2-23, 7yo 1-44, 8yo 3-56, 9yo 3-43, 10yo 1-28, 11yo 0-12, 12yo 0-1 **FAVOURITES:** -£6.00

FATE OF FAVOURITES: 20P0012430 **POSITION OF WINNER IN MARKET:** 2280019706

Key trends

🐎 Distance winner, 10/10

🐎 No more than 12 runs over fences, 9/10

🐎 Aged nine or under, 9/10

🐎 Top-three finish on at least one of last two starts, 8/10

🐎 Carried no more than 11st 2lb, 8/10

🐎 Officially rated 134 to 147, 8/10

🐎 Yet to win that season, 8/10

🐎 Had run at a previous festival, 7/10

🐎 No more than four runs since August, 6/10

Other factors

🐎 Five winners had won at the course – three of the exceptions had been placed in this race previously

🐎 There have been four winning novices

🐎 Since 2005, when the race was renamed in honour of his father, Nicky Henderson's runners have finished 346, 180P, 800, 20, 3P, 20P, 60, 1240PF, 2589PF, 590, 0, 3 (no runner in 2015 when the race was named after AP McCoy)

🐎 The record of the previous year's winner is 45B00

Notes